200 SMALL HOUSE PLANS

SECOND EDITION

Design 9252, page 132

Innovative Plans for Sensible Lifestyles
Designs Under 2,500 Square Feet

HOME PLANNERS, LLC
Wholly owned by Hanley-Wood, LLC

D1206195

Published by Home Planners, LLC
Wholly owned by Hanley-Wood, LLC
Editorial and Corporate Offices:
3275 West Ina Road, Suite 110
Tucson, Arizona 85741

Distribution Center:
29333 Lorie Lane
Wixom, Michigan 48393

Patricia Joseph, President
Jan Prideaux, Editor in Chief
Paulette Mulvin, Senior Editor
Laura Hurst Brown, Associate Editor
Nick Nieskes, Plans Editor
Paul D. Fitzgerald, Senior Graphic Designer
Karen L. Leanio, Graphic Designer
Matthew Kauffman, Graphic Designer
Peter Zullo, Graphic Production Artist

Photo Credits
Front Cover: © Courtesy of Design Basics, Inc.
Back Cover: © Jon Riley, Jon Riley Photography, Inc.

First Printing, March 2001

10   9   8   7   6   5   4   3   2   1

Printed in the United States of America.

Library of Congress Catalog Card Number: 00-108662

ISBN: 1-881955-80-X

72937

On the front cover: Design 9252, a chic blend of old and new, with a Victorian flavor.
To view floor plans, see page 132.

On the back cover: Design 9645, a charming country-style bestseller with natural
character. See page 75 for a closer look.

Design 3652, page 45

TABLE OF CONTENTS

EDITOR'S NOTE

Home is a personal thing—it has to do with our needs and values. Building a home is an investment in lifestyle as well as in land and materials, and the *best* homes breathe with a relaxed spirit and natural character.

These designs, all less than 2,500 square feet, are big on style and comfort and—despite their modest size—luxury. I've selected exterior styles that are strong and distinctive enough to make a statement, and interior plans that are bold and forthright but never showy.

You'll find acres of variety here, from Southwesterns to Cape Cods. But let me take a moment to point out a few of the bestsellers: our prairie-style farmhouse on page 147 (Design 2774), our Rocky Mountain Victorian on page 67 (Design 2974), and a cozy starter home on page 12 (Design 2947). If yours is a growing family, check out our stunning move-up homes starting on page 126.

This selection of homes offers the height of quality and tradition that's been Home Planners' hallmark for 50 years, and introduces a thought: How you feel in a home is as important as how the house looks. Our plans create real homes—homes you can live in and love for years.

ABOUT THE DESIGNERS

The Blue Ribbon Designer Series™ is a collection of books featuring the home plans of a diverse group of outstanding home designers and architects known as the Blue Ribbon Network of Designers. This group of companies is dedicated to creating and marketing the finest possible plans for home construction on a regional and national basis. Each of the companies exhibits superior work and integrity in all phases of the stock-plan business including modern, trendsetting floor planning, a professionally executed blueprint package and a strong sense of service and commitment to the consumer.

Alan Mascord Design Associates, Inc.
Alan Mascord Design Associates of Portland, Oregon began to successfully publish plans nationally in 1985. They quickly received a reputation for homes that are easy to build yet meet the rigorous demands of the buyers' market.

Breland & Farmer
Designer Edsel Breland is owner and president of Breland & Farmer Designers, Inc., which he founded in 1973. The homes designed by Breland have a definite Southern signature, but fit perfectly in any region.

Design Basics, Inc.
For nearly a decade, Design Basics has been developing plans for custom home builders. Since 1987, the firm has consistently appeared in *Builder* magazine, the official magazine of the National Association of Home Builders, as the top-selling designer.

Donald A. Gardner Architects, Inc.
The firm of Donald A. Gardner Architects, Inc. was established in response to a growing demand for residential designs that reflect constantly changing lifestyles. The company's specialty is providing homes with refined, custom-style details and unique features such as passive-solar designs and open floor plans.

Frank Betz Associates, Inc.
Frank Betz Associates, Inc. located in Smyrna, Georgia, is one of the nation's leaders in the design of stock plans. FBA, Inc. has provided builders and developers with home plans since 1977.

Home Design Services, Inc.
Home Design Services of Longwood, Florida, has been formulating plans for the Sun Country lifestyle. They are consistently praised for their highly detailed, free-flowing floor plans, imaginative and exciting interior architecture and elevations, which have gained international appeal.

Home Planners
All of Home Planners' designs are created with the care and professional expertise that fifty years of experience in the home-planning business affords. Their homes are designed to be built, lived in and enjoyed for years to come.

Larry E. Belk Designs
Larry E. Belk's design philosophy combines traditional exteriors with upscale interiors designed for contemporary lifestyles. Dynamic exteriors reflect Larry's extensive home construction experience, painstaking research and talent as a fine artist.

Larry James & Associates
The Larry James goal is to create a collection of timeless designs. He likes to design new homes that trigger pleasant memories of times-gone-by. "Twenty-first Century living wrapped in a turn-of-the-century package."

Living Concepts Home Planning
Innovative and versatile, the diversified staff of Living Concepts shows unlimited wealth in both the architectural styles of its designs and its talent. The company's plans range from classical to European.

Nelson Design Group
Michael N. Nelson is a certified member of the American Institute of Building Designers, providing both custom and stock residential home plans. He designs homes that families enjoy now and which also bring maximum appraisal value at resale.

Select Home Designs
Select Home Designs has 50 years of experience delivering top-quality and affordable residential designs to the North American housing market. Since 1948, more than 350,000 homes throughout North America and overseas have been built from Select's plans.

Stephen Fuller, Inc.
Stephen S. Fuller's designs mix a sense of balance and restraint with the tenets of innovation, quality, originality and uncompromising architectural techniques in traditional and European homes. Stephen Fuller, Inc. plans are known for their extensive detail and thoughtful design.

The Sater Design Collection
The Sater Design Collection provides South Florida with extraordinary custom designed homes. Their goal is to fulfill each client's particular need for an exciting approach to design by merging creative vision with elements that satisfy a desire for a distinctive lifestyle.

United Designers & Architects
Starting as a designer of homes for Houston-area residents, United Designers & Associates has been marketing designs nationally for the past ten years. Numerous accolades have been awarded to the company for excellence in architecture.

BRILLIANT BEGINNINGS

Beautiful Homes For First-Time Builders

Few experiences measure up to the joy of building a new home. It's exciting to lay out fresh plans for the first time. Starter homes may be the humble beginnings of a grander scheme, but they may well offer the vigorous spirit of the design of our dreams.

First-time builders generally appreciate amenities such as a clustered bedroom plan—with a nearby nursery or study— a kitchen with breakfast nook, and a spacious family or gathering room. Naturally cozy spaces are important. Recently, a Home Planners customer mentioned he enjoyed stretching out on the living room floor with his golden retriever—in front of a warming fireplace, of course. No problem. (Check out Design 2878 on page 8.)

Economy is an attractive element of these plans. But perhaps the most appealing feature is their flexibility: there's room for change and growth. A study could become a nursery or a third bedroom; a den becomes a media room or home office.

Selecting a design for the first time invites imagination and a bit of instinct, and we pledge to help you find just the right plan. This section offers a sampling of 31 plans for starter homes, but we have many more—thousands more—to choose from. Each promises a happy marriage of style and comfort, and a place you'll simply love for years to come.

Design 3655

Square Footage: 1,418

L

If you need a guest or mother-in-law suite, you'll love this compact design. The suite—which could also be used as a home office—enjoys its own courtyard, a cozy fireplace and a private bath. The efficient floor plan also features a spacious living area, which offers patio access and a three-sided fireplace that shares its warmth with a formal dining area with built-in shelves for curiosa. A thoughtfully planned kitchen offers a corner sink with window, as well as easy access from the garage. Clustered bedrooms include a spacious master suite with a whirlpool tub, a double-bowl vanity and twin closets. Two nearby family bedrooms share a full bath.

DESIGN BY
Home Planners

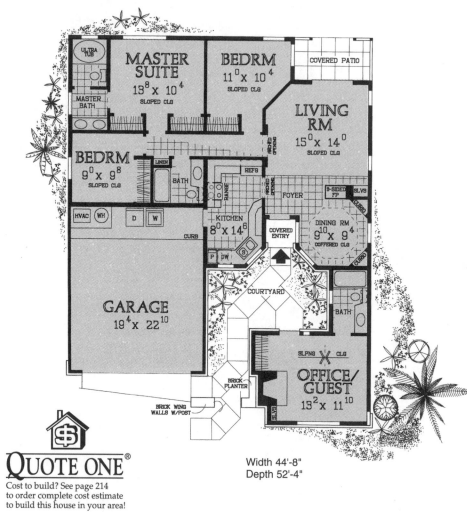

Width 44'-8"
Depth 52'-4"

Design 3659

Square Footage: 1,118

L

Compact yet comfortable, this home offers many appealing amenities. From the covered front porch, the entrance foyer opens onto the sunlit, octagonal dining room and to the gracious living room which offers a sloped ceiling and access to a rear covered patio. To the left of the foyer is the efficient kitchen that has the added bonus of no cross-room traffic. The luxurious master suite includes a lavish bath complete with a corner tub, a separate shower, a walk-in closet and twin vanities. A secondary bedroom has access to a full hall bath.

DESIGN BY
Home Planners

QUOTE ONE®

Cost to build? See page 214 to order complete cost estimate to build this house in your area!

Width 44'-4"
Depth 47'-4"

Floor Plan Labels

- WALK-IN CLOSET
- SHOWER
- LIN
- MASTER BATH
- ULTRA TUB
- MASTER SUITE 15¹⁰ x 12⁸ SLOPED CLG
- COVERED PATIO
- LIVING RM 15⁰ x 14⁰ SLOPED CLG
- BEDRM 9⁰ x 9⁸ SLOPED CLG
- LINEN
- BATH
- REF.
- RANGE
- FOYER
- 3-SIDED FP
- SLVS
- CURB'D
- HVAC
- WH
- D
- W
- KITCHEN 8⁰ x 14⁶
- P
- DW
- S
- DINING RM 9⁰ x 9⁴ COFFERED CLG
- CURB
- COVERED PORCH
- GARAGE 19⁴ x 22¹⁰
- RAILING
- RAILING

Photo by Andrew D. Lautman

This home, as shown in the photograph, may differ from the actual blueprints. For more detailed information, please check the floor plans carefully.

Design 2878

Square Footage: 1,530

L D

This charming, compact design combines traditional styling with sensational commodities and modern livability. Thoughtful zoning places sleeping areas to one side, apart from household activity. The plan includes a spacious gathering room with sloped ceiling and centered fireplace, and a formal dining room overlooking a rear terrace. A handy pass-through connects the breakfast room with the efficient kitchen. The laundry is conveniently positioned nearby. An impressive master suite enjoys access to a private rear terrace and offers a separate dressing area with walk-in closet. Two family bedrooms, or one and a study, are nearby and share a full bath.

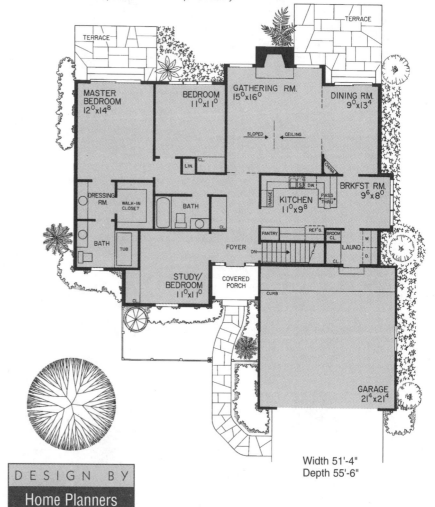

TERRACE

TERRACE

MASTER BEDROOM
12^0x14^8

BEDROOM
11^0x11^0

GATHERING RM.
15^0x16^0

DINING RM.
9^0x13^4

SLOPED CEILING

DRESSING RM.

WALK-IN CLOSET

LIN.

CL.

BATH

KITCHEN
11^0x9^8

BRKFST RM.
9^6x8^0

RANGE

PASS THRU

PANTRY

REF'G.

BROOM CL.

BATH

TUB

FOYER

DN

LAUND.

W.

D.

STUDY/ BEDROOM
11^0x11^0

COVERED PORCH

CURB

GARAGE
21^4x21^4

Width 51'-4"
Depth 55'-6"

QUOTE ONE®

Cost to build? See page 214
to order complete cost estimate
to build this house in your area!

DESIGN BY

Home Planners

TERRACE

TERRACE

FORMAL DINING

GATHERING RM. 23⁶ x 11⁰ - 14⁸

SLOPED CEILING

SLOPED CEILING

SLOPED CEILING

STUDY/ BEDROOM 9² x 11⁰

MASTER BEDROOM 13⁸ x 11⁰

SLOPED CEILING

BRKFST. RM. 8⁸ x 10⁴

SNACK BAR

SHLVS

PANTRY

ETAGERE

BAR

LIN.

OPEN OVER CLOSET

CL.

CL.

DESK

KITCHEN 12⁰ x 9⁰

S.

DW.

DRESSING RM.

BRM CL.

RANGE

REF'G.

VANITY

SLOPED CEILING

W. D.

LAUNDRY DN

FOYER

BATH

CL.

BATH

LEDGE

P.

CURB

SKY. LIGHT

TUB

SKY. LIGHT

TUB

COVERED PORCH

BEDROOM 10⁰ x 10⁰

ENTRANCE COURT

GARAGE 19⁴ x 21⁸

Width 49'-8"
Depth 52'

Design 2864

Square Footage: 1,387

L D

Projecting the garage to the front of a house is economical in two ways: by reducing the required lot size and by protecting the interior from street noise. Many other features deserve mention as well. A formal dining area opens to a spacious gathering room with a large, centered fireplace; both areas offer a sloped ceiling. The well-appointed kitchen services an adjacent breakfast room as well as a counter snack bar. Clustered bedrooms offer convenience for families just starting out. Use a third bedroom with wet bar area as a study. Sliding glass doors in three rooms open to the rear terrace.

DESIGN BY
Home Planners

Quote One®

Cost to build? See page 214 to order complete cost estimate to build this house in your area!

Design 2871

Living Area: 1,824 square feet
Greenhouse Area: 81 square feet
Total: 1,905 square feet

D

A greenhouse area off the dining room and living room provides a cheerful focal point for this comfortable three-bedroom Trend home. The spacious living room features a cozy fireplace and a sloped ceiling. In addition to the dining room, there's a less formal breakfast room just off the modern kitchen. Both kitchen and breakfast areas look out onto a front terrace. Stairs just off the foyer lead down to a recreation room. The master bedroom suite opens to a terrace. A mud room and a wash room off the garage allow rear entry to the house during inclement weather.

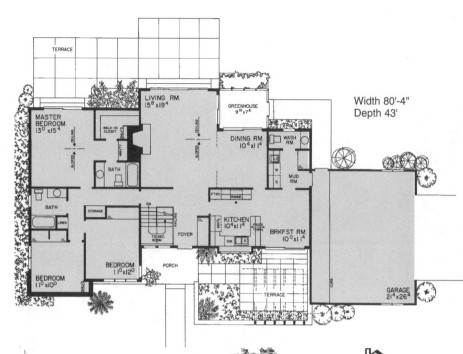

Width 80'-4"
Depth 43'

Quote One®

Cost to build? See page 214 to order complete cost estimate to build this house in your area!

DESIGN BY
Home Planners

T his smart design features multi-gabled ends, varied rooflines and vertical windows. Inside, effective zoning offers privacy for sleeping quarters and convenience for living areas. The grand foyer opens to a large, central gathering room with a fireplace, a sloped ceiling, and its own special view of the rear terrace. The modern kitchen features a snack bar and a pass-through to a sunny breakfast room with rear terrace access. The adjacent formal dining room enjoys terrace access and opens to the gathering room. A secluded media room offers built-ins designed to accomodate a sophisticated entertainment center—or start a library! Amenities abound in the master suite, complete with a whirlpool bath, a walk-in closet and knee-space vanity. A two-car garage with sloped ceiling has an additional storage area.

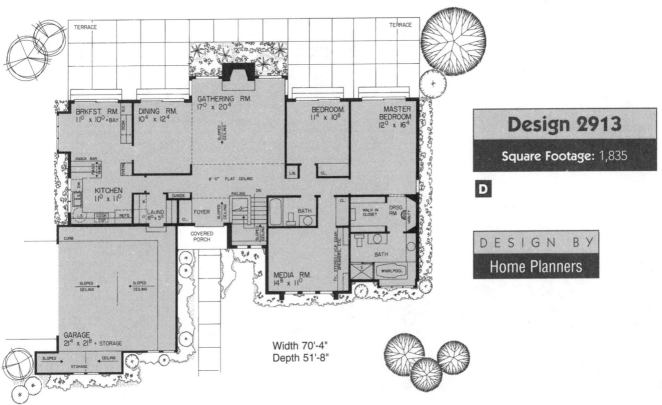

Design 2913

Square Footage: 1,835

D

DESIGN BY
Home Planners

Width 70'-4"
Depth 51'-8"

Photos by Andrew D. Lautman

This home, as shown in the photographs, may differ from the actual blueprints. For more detailed information, please check the floor plans carefully.

Design 2947

Square Footage: 1,830

L **D**

This charming, one-story traditional home greets visitors with a covered porch. A galley-style kitchen shares a snack bar with the spacious gathering room, where a fireplace is the focal point. An ample master suite offers a luxury bath with a whirlpool tub and a separate dressing room. Two additional bedrooms—one could double as a study—are located at the front of the home.

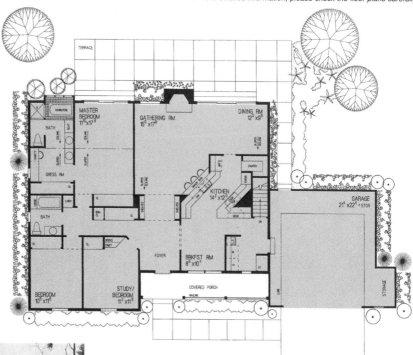

Width 75'
Depth 43'-5"

DESIGN BY
Home Planners

QUOTE ONE®
Cost to build? See page 214
to order complete cost estimate
to build this house in your area!

Design 3332

Square Footage: 2,203

L

QUOTE ONE®

Cost to build? See page 214
to order complete cost estimate
to build this house in your area!

Nothing warms a traditional-style home quite as wonderfully as a country kitchen with a fireplace. Additional features include a second fireplace (with raised hearth) and a sloped ceiling in the living room, a nearby dining room with an attached porch, and a snack bar pass-through in the kitchen. A clustered bedroom plan offers two family bedrooms, which share a full bath and a grand master suite with rear terrace access, a walk-in closet, a whirlpool tub and a double-bowl vanity. A handy washroom is near the laundry, just off the two-car garage. A second terrace is located to the rear of this area.

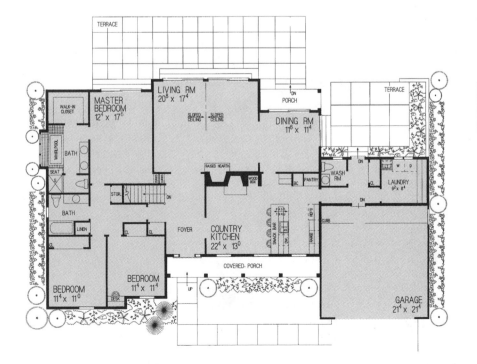

DESIGN BY
Home Planners

Width 76'-4"
Depth 46'

This home, as shown in the photograph, may differ from the actual blueprints. For more detailed information, please check the floor plans carefully.

Photo by Riley & Riley Photography, Inc.

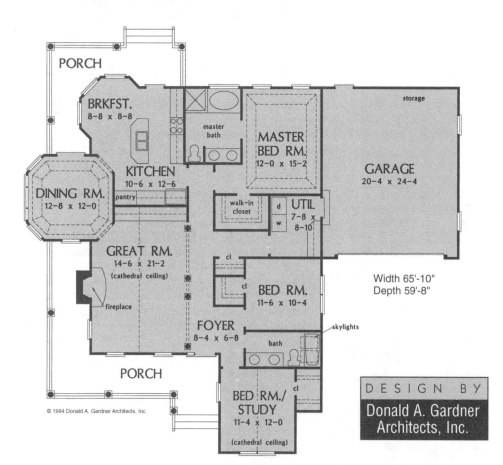

PORCH

BRKFST.
8-8 x 8-8

master bath

MASTER BED RM.
12-0 x 15-2

storage

GARAGE
20-4 x 24-4

KITCHEN
10-6 x 12-6

pantry

DINING RM.
12-8 x 12-0

walk-in closet

UTIL
7-8 x 8-10

d

w

GREAT RM.
14-6 x 21-2
(cathedral ceiling)

cl

cl

fireplace

cl

BED RM.
11-6 x 10-4

Width 65'-10"
Depth 59'-8"

FOYER
8-4 x 6-8

skylights

PORCH

bath

© 1994 Donald A. Gardner Architects, Inc.

BED RM./
STUDY
11-4 x 12-0

cl

(cathedral ceiling)

Design HPT440001

Square Footage: 1,737

Inviting porches are just the beginning of this lovely country home. To the left of the foyer, a columned entry supplies a classic touch to the spacious great room, which features a cathedral ceiling, built-in bookshelves and a fireplace that invites you to share its warmth. An octagonal dining room with a tray ceiling provides a perfect setting for formal occasions. The adjacent kitchen is designed to easily serve both formal and informal areas. The sunny breakfast area is just a step away. The owners suite, separated from two family bedrooms by the walk-in closet and utility room, offers privacy and comfort.

DESIGN BY
Donald A. Gardner Architects, Inc.

Design 3460

Square Footage: 1,389

L

Width 44'-8"
Depth 54'-6"

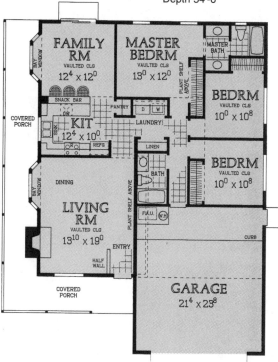

FAMILY RM
VAULTED CLG
12⁴ x 12⁰

MASTER BEDRM
VAULTED CLG
13⁰ x 12⁰

MASTER BATH

BEDRM
VAULTED CLG
10⁰ x 10⁸

SNACK BAR

PANTRY

D | W

LAUNDRY

KIT
12⁴ x 10⁰

SINK

DW

REFG

LINEN

BEDRM
VAULTED CLG
10⁰ x 10⁸

BATH

COVERED PORCH

DINING

PLANT SHELF ABOVE

F.A.U. | W.H.

LIVING RM
VAULTED CLG
13¹⁰ x 19⁰

ENTRY

HALF WALL

CURB

COVERED PORCH

GARAGE
21⁴ x 23⁸

DESIGN BY
Home Planners

QUOTE ONE®
Cost to build? See page 214
to order complete cost estimate
to build this house in your area!

A double dose of charm, this special farmhouse plan offers two elevations in its blueprint package—one showcases a delightful wraparound porch. The formal living room has a warming fireplace and a sunny bay window. The kitchen separates this area from the more casual family room. In the kitchen, you'll find an efficient snack bar as well as a pantry for additional storage space. Three bedrooms include two family bedrooms which share a full bath, and a lovely master suite with a private bath. Notice the location of the washer and dryer—convenient to all of the bedrooms.

© 1994 Donald A. Gardner Architects, Inc.

Design 7601

Square Footage: 1,787
Bonus Room: 326 square feet

Aneighborly porch as friendly as a handshake wraps around this charming country home. Inside, cathedral ceilings promote an aura of spaciousness. To the left of the foyer, the great room offers a fireplace and built-in bookshelves. A unique formal dining room separates the kitchen and breakfast area. Enjoy outdoor pursuits—rain or shine—from the screen porch. The private master suite features a walk-in closet and a luxurious bath—two additional bedrooms, one with a walk-in closet, share a skylit bath. A second-floor bonus room is available to develop later as a study, home office or play area. Please specify basement or crawlspace foundation when ordering.

D E S I G N   B Y

Donald A. Gardner,
Architects, Inc.

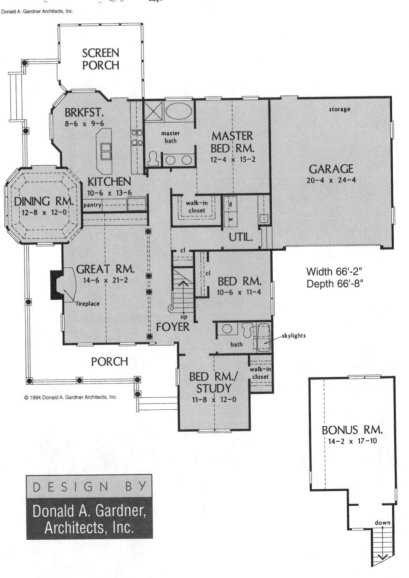

SCREEN PORCH

BRKFST.
8-6 x 9-6

master bath

MASTER BED RM.
12-4 x 15-2

storage

GARAGE
20-4 x 24-4

KITCHEN
10-6 x 13-6

pantry

DINING RM.
12-8 x 12-0

walk-in closet

d

w

UTIL.

GREAT RM.
14-6 x 21-2

fireplace

cl

cl

BED RM.
10-6 x 11-4

Width 66'-2"
Depth 66'-8"

FOYER

up

bath

skylights

PORCH

BED RM./STUDY
11-8 x 12-0

walk-in closet

© 1994 Donald A. Gardner Architects, Inc.

BONUS RM.
14-2 x 17-10

down

©1994 Donald A. Gardner Architects, Inc.

B. NATHAN

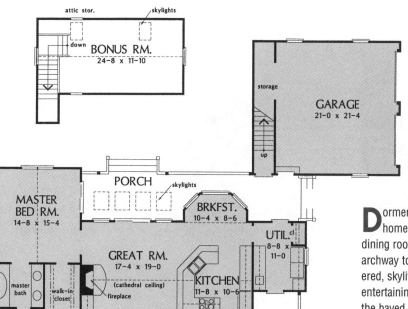

attic stor.   skylights

down

BONUS RM.
24-8 x 11-10

storage

GARAGE
21-0 x 21-4

up

PORCH   skylights

MASTER BED RM.
14-8 x 15-4

BRKFST.
10-4 x 8-6

UTIL. cl
8-8 x 11-0

GREAT RM.
17-4 x 19-0

(cathedral ceiling)

fireplace

KITCHEN
11-8 x 10-6

master bath

walk-in closet

linen

bath

cl

sto.   cl

DINING
11-4 x 12-8

FOYER
8-8 x 8-0

BED RM.
12-2 x 12-4

BED RM.
10-10 x 12-4

cl

PORCH

© 1994 Donald A. Gardner Architects, Inc.

Width 70'-8"
Depth 70'-2"

Quote One®

Cost to build? See page 214
to order complete cost estimate
to build this house in your area!

D E S I G N   B Y

Donald A. Gardner, Architects, Inc.

Dormers, arched windows and covered porches lend this home a country appeal. Inside, the foyer opens to the dining room on the right and leads through a columned archway to the great room, warmed by a fireplace. The covered, skylit rear porch provides opportunities for outdoor entertaining. The open kitchen easily serves the great room, the bayed breakfast area and the dining room. A cathedral ceiling graces the master bedroom, which offers a walk-in closet and a private bath with dual vanity and whirlpool tub. Two additional bedrooms share a full bath. A detached garage with a skylit bonus room is connected to the rear covered porch.

Design 9764

Square Footage: 1,815

This house not only accommodates a narrow lot, but it also fits a sloping site. Notice how the two-car garage is tucked away under the first level of the house. The angled corner entry gives way to a two-story living room with a tiled hearth. The dining room shares an interesting angled space with this area and enjoys service from the efficient kitchen. A large pantry and an angled corner sink add character to this area. The family room offers double doors to a refreshing balcony. A powder room and a laundry room complete the main level. Upstairs, three bedrooms include a vaulted master suite with a private bath. Bedrooms 2 and 3 each take advantage of direct access to a full bath.

Design 9509

First Floor: 1,022 square feet
Second Floor: 813 square feet
Total: 1,835 square feet

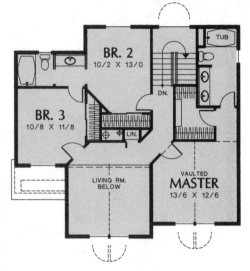

BR. 2
10/2 X 13/0

BR. 3
10/8 X 11/8

TUB

DN.

LIN.

LIVING RM. BELOW

VAULTED
MASTER
13/6 X 12/6

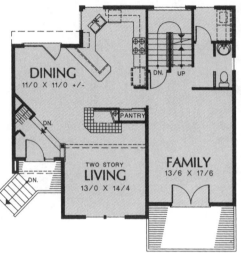

DINING
11/0 X 11/0 +/-

DN.

DN. UP

PANTRY

TWO STORY
LIVING
13/0 X 14/4

FAMILY
13/6 X 17/6

DN.

DESIGN BY

Alan Mascord
Design Associates, Inc.

Width 36'
Depth 33'

Design 9235

First Floor: 919 square feet
Second Floor: 927 square feet
Total: 1,846 square feet

QUOTE ONE®

Cost to build? See page 214
to order complete cost estimate
to build this house in your area!

This wonderful design begins with a quintessential wraparound porch. Explore further and find a two-story entry with a roomy coat closet and a plant shelf above. The island kitchen with a boxed window over the sink is adjacent to a large bay-windowed breakfast room. The great room includes triple windows and a warming fireplace. A powder bath and laundry room are conveniently placed on the first floor. Upstairs, the large master suite contains His and Hers walk-in closets, corner windows and a bath area featuring a double vanity and a whirlpool tub. Two pleasant secondary bedrooms offer interesting angles. A third bedroom in the front features a volume ceiling and an arched window.

DESIGN BY
Design Basics, Inc.

Width 44'
Depth 40'

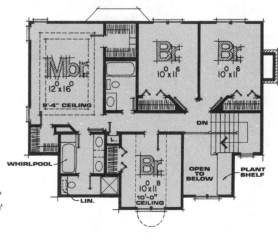

Design HPT440002

First Floor: 1,039 square feet
Second Floor: 915 square feet
Total: 1,954 square feet
Bonus Room: 488 square feet

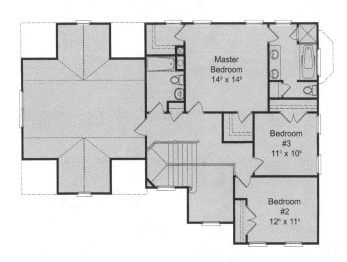

Master Bedroom
14⁹ x 14⁹

Bedroom #3
11⁰ x 10⁶

Bedroom #2
12⁰ x 11⁰

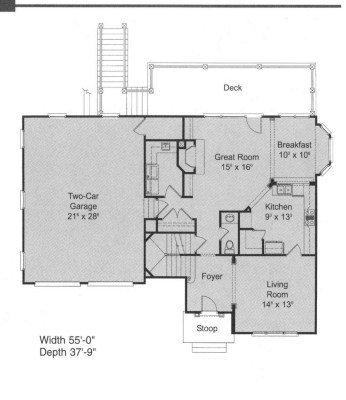

Deck

Great Room
15⁶ x 16⁰

Breakfast
10⁰ x 10⁶

Two-Car Garage
21⁶ x 28⁶

Kitchen
9³ x 13³

Foyer

Living Room
14⁶ x 13³

Stoop

Width 55'-0"
Depth 37'-9"

DESIGN BY
Stephen Fuller, Inc.

Double-hung windows and a paneled door framed by pilasters and a pediment announce the Colonial Revival influences of this stately home. The enticing floor plan, however, is designed for modern lifestyles. Multi-pane windows brighten the living room to the right of the foyer, which opens to a gourmet kitchen with a walk-in pantry. A breakfast room with a bay window allows family and friends to enjoy the view while sharing meals. The great room provides a fireplace flanked by built-in bookshelves and has access to a rear deck. A railed staircase off the foyer leads to the second-floor sleeping zone, where two family bedrooms share a full bath and a luxurious owners suite is equipped with two walk-in closets and double vanities. This home is designed with a basement foundation.

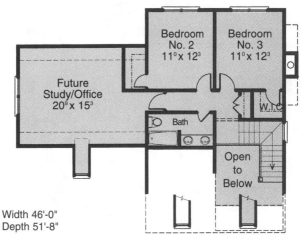

Design HPT440003

First Floor: 1,355 square feet
Second Floor: 490 square feet
Total: 1,845 square feet
Bonus Room: 300 square feet

Bedroom No. 2
11^0 x 12^3

Bedroom No. 3
11^0 x 12^3

Future Study/Office
20^9 x 15^3

Bath

W.i.c.

Open to Below

Width 46'-0"
Depth 51'-8"

Master Bedroom
11^9 x 16^0

Deck

Master Bath

Breakfast
11^0 x 10^0

Laundry

Great Room
14^0 x 17^0

Two Car Garage
20^9 x 20^9

Kitchen
9^0 x 12^0

Powder

Dining Room
10^9 x 12^0

Foyer
12^6 x 11^0

Porch

DESIGN BY
Stephen Fuller, Inc.

A pair of rocking chairs will add a charming touch to the porch on this traditional home. Inside, a fireplace dresses up the great room, which opens to the rear deck. The breakfast room and owners bedroom also access the deck. An efficient kitchen easily serves the breakfast room as well as the formal dining room. Upstairs, two secondary bedrooms—each with a walk-in closet—share a bath, and there's plenty of room for a future study or office. This home is designed with a basement foundation.

Design 8229

Square Footage: 1,955

DESIGN BY
Larry E. Belk Designs

A finely detailed covered porch and arch-topped windows announce a scrupulously designed interior, replete with amenities. A grand foyer with 10-foot ceiling and columned archways set the pace for the entire floor plan. Clustered sleeping quarters to the left feature a luxurious master suite with a sloped ceiling, corner whirlpool bath and walk-in closet, and two family bedrooms which share a bath. Picture windows flanking a centered fireplace lend plenty of natural light to the great room, which is open through grand, columned archways to the formal dining area and the bay-windowed breakfast room. The kitchen, conveniently positioned between the dining and breakfast rooms, shares an informal eating counter with the great room. A utility room and walk-in pantry are tucked neatly to the side of the plan. Please specify crawlspace or slab foundation when ordering.

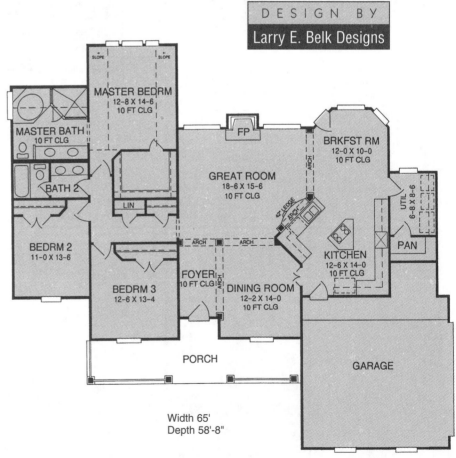

MASTER BEDRM
12-8 X 14-6
10 FT CLG

MASTER BATH
10 FT CLG

BATH 2

LIN

BEDRM 2
11-0 X 13-6

BEDRM 3
12-6 X 13-4

FOYER
10 FT CLG

FP

GREAT ROOM
18-6 X 15-6
10 FT CLG

BRKFST RM
12-0 X 10-0
10 FT CLG

ARCH   ARCH

DINING ROOM
12-2 X 14-0
10 FT CLG

KITCHEN
12-6 X 14-0
10 FT CLG

UTIL
6-8 X 8-6

PAN

PORCH

GARAGE

Width 65'
Depth 58'-8"

Design 8180

Square footage: 1,862

DESIGN BY
Larry E. Belk Designs

This charming traditional has all the amenities of a larger plan in a compact layout. Ten-foot ceilings give this home an expansive feel. An angled eating bar separates the kitchen and great room while leaving these areas open to one another for family gatherings and entertaining. The master bedroom includes a huge walk-in closet and a superior master bath with a whirlpool tub and separate shower. A large utility room and an oversized storage area are located near the secondary entrance to the home. Two additional bedrooms and a bath finish the plan. Please specify crawlspace or slab foundation when ordering.

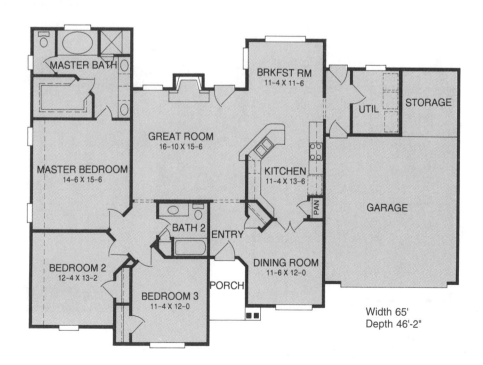

MASTER BATH

BRKFST RM
11-4 X 11-6

UTIL

STORAGE

GREAT ROOM
16-10 X 15-6

KITCHEN
11-4 X 13-6

MASTER BEDROOM
14-6 X 15-6

PAN

GARAGE

BATH 2

ENTRY

BEDROOM 2
12-4 X 13-2

DINING ROOM
11-6 X 12-0

BEDROOM 3
11-4 X 12-0

PORCH

Width 65'
Depth 46'-2"

Design 8181

Square Footage: 1,500

This bestselling traditional home is compact in size but packed with all of the amenities you'd expect in a larger home. The foyer opens to a formal dining room with a classic bay window. The adjacent kitchen opens to a breakfast nook and shares an angled eating bar with the living room, which offers a cozy fireplace flanked by picture windows. The master suite features His and Hers vanities, a whirlpool tub/shower combination and a walk-in closet. Ten-foot ceilings in the major living areas as well as in two of the bedrooms contribute an aura of spaciousness to this plan. Please specify crawlspace or slab foundation when ordering.

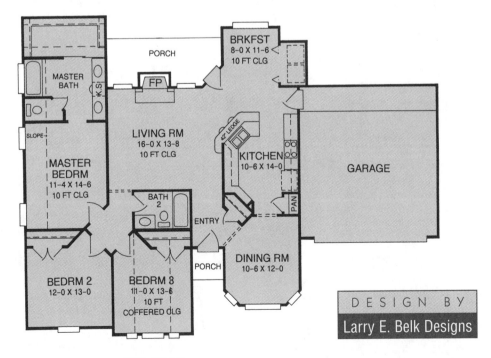

PORCH

BRKFST
8-0 X 11-6
10 FT CLG

MASTER
BATH

LIVING RM
16-0 X 13-8
10 FT CLG

FP

KITCHEN
10-6 X 14-0

GARAGE

MASTER
BEDRM
11-4 X 14-6
10 FT CLG

SLOPE

BATH
2

ENTRY

PAN

BEDRM 2
12-0 X 13-0

BEDRM 8
11-0 X 13-6
10 FT
COFFERED CLG

PORCH

DINING RM
10-6 X 12-0

DESIGN BY
Larry E. Belk Designs

Width 59'-10"
Depth 44'-4"

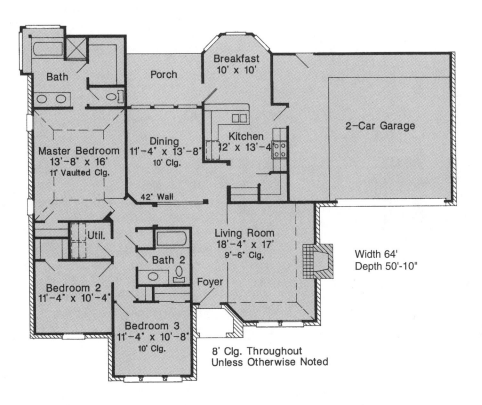

Bath

Porch

Breakfast
10' x 10'

2-Car Garage

Master Bedroom
13'-8" x 16'
11' Vaulted Clg.

Dining
11'-4" x 13'-8"
10' Clg.

Kitchen
12' x 13'-4"

42' Wall

Util.

Bath 2

Living Room
18'-4" x 17'
9'-6" Clg.

Foyer

Width 64'
Depth 50'-10"

Bedroom 2
11'-4" x 10'-4"

Bedroom 3
11'-4" x 10'-8"
10' Clg.

8' Clg. Throughout
Unless Otherwise Noted

No slouch on amenities, this plan is a popular choice with those just starting out. High ceilings in the dining room and the master suite add a sense of space. A decorative front wall separates the formal dining area from the foyer while preserving the openness of the area. A bay-windowed breakfast room adjoins the kitchen area and opens to a rear porch for outdoor dining. Sleeping quarters include a master suite with vaulted ceiling, walk-in closet, glass-surrounded tub and separate shower, as well as two family bedrooms which share a full bath. The laundry area is conveniently located near the bedrooms.

DESIGN BY
Larry W. Garnett & Associates, Inc.

Design 9028

Square Footage: 1,707

QUOTE ONE®
Cost to build? See page 214
to order complete cost estimate
to build this house in your area!

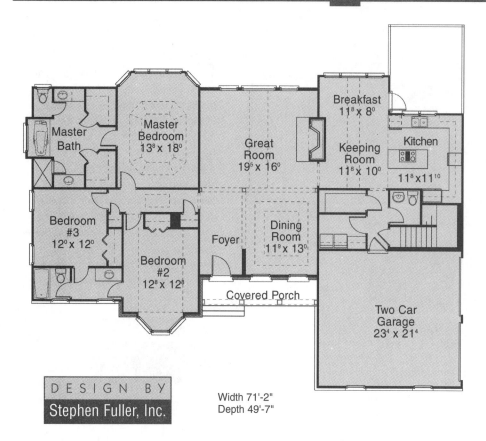

Design HPT440004

Square Footage: 2,204

Master Bath

Master Bedroom
13⁸ x 18⁰

Breakfast
11⁸ x 8⁰

Kitchen
11⁸ x 11¹⁰

Great Room
19⁶ x 16⁰

Keeping Room
11⁸ x 10⁰

Bedroom #3
12⁰ x 12⁰

Foyer

Dining Room
11⁹ x 13⁰

Bedroom #2
12⁸ x 12⁸

Covered Porch

Two Car Garage
23⁴ x 21⁴

DESIGN BY
Stephen Fuller, Inc.

Width 71'-2"
Depth 49'-7"

A bay window is accented by a gracefully covered porch on this three-bedroom home. If entertaining is your forte, note how the great room and the formal dining room are separated by elegant columns, providing ease for any gathering. The large U-shaped kitchen is sure to please, with a work island, plenty of counter and cabinet space and an adjacent breakfast room. Two secondary bedrooms—one with a bay window—share a full bath, while the master suite is full of amenities. This home is designed with a walkout basement foundation.

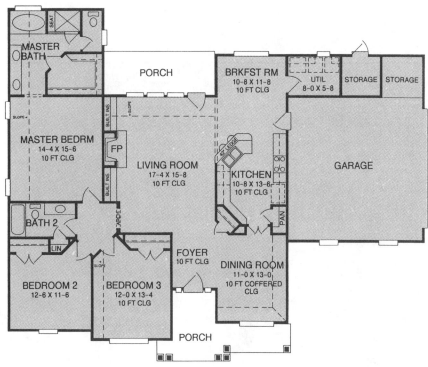

MASTER BATH

PORCH

BRKFST RM
10-8 X 11-8
10 FT CLG

UTIL
8-0 X 5-8

STORAGE

STORAGE

MASTER BEDRM
14-4 X 15-6
10 FT CLG

FP

LIVING ROOM
17-4 X 15-8
10 FT CLG

KITCHEN
10-8 X 13-6
10 FT CLG

GARAGE

PAN

BATH 2

LIN

FOYER
10 FT CLG

DINING ROOM
11-0 X 13-0
10 FT COFFERED CLG

BEDROOM 2
12-6 X 11-6

BEDROOM 3
12-0 X 13-4
10 FT CLG

PORCH

Width 65'-10"
Depth 53'-5"

Design 8183

Square footage: 1,890

This classic home exudes elegance and style and offers sophisticated amenities in a compact size. Ten-foot ceilings throughout the plan lend an aura of spacious hospitality. A generous living room with a sloped ceiling, built-in bookcases and a centerpiece fireplace, offers views as well as access to the rear yard. The nearby breakfast room shares an informal eating counter with the ample kitchen, which serves the coffered-ceiling dining room through French doors. Three bedrooms include a sumptuous master suite with windowed whirlpool tub and walk-in closet, and two family bedrooms which share a full bath. Please specify slab or crawlspace foundation when ordering.

DESIGN BY
Larry E. Belk Designs

The lines of this traditional home are very clean, with classical detailing that defines elegance. Columns, brickwork and shuttered windows remind us of the best homes of turn-of-the-century America. Inside, contemporary amenities prevail. A columned foyer opens to the right to a formal dining room with French doors to a thoroughly modern kitchen. To the left of the foyer, a convenient powder room accomodates guests. Directly ahead, the foyer leads to a wide open living area that shares the warmth of a hearth, centered in the great room, framed by glass and light. This area is particularly well-suited to entertaining—both formally and informally—with an open kitchen and bay-windowed breakfast nook as well as access to the rear deck. Upstairs, the master suite features a tray ceiling, whirlpool tub, twin lavatories and compartmented toilet. Bedrooms 2 and 3 each have separate access to a full bath. The laundry room is found on this level, convenient to any of the bedrooms. This home is designed with a basement foundation.

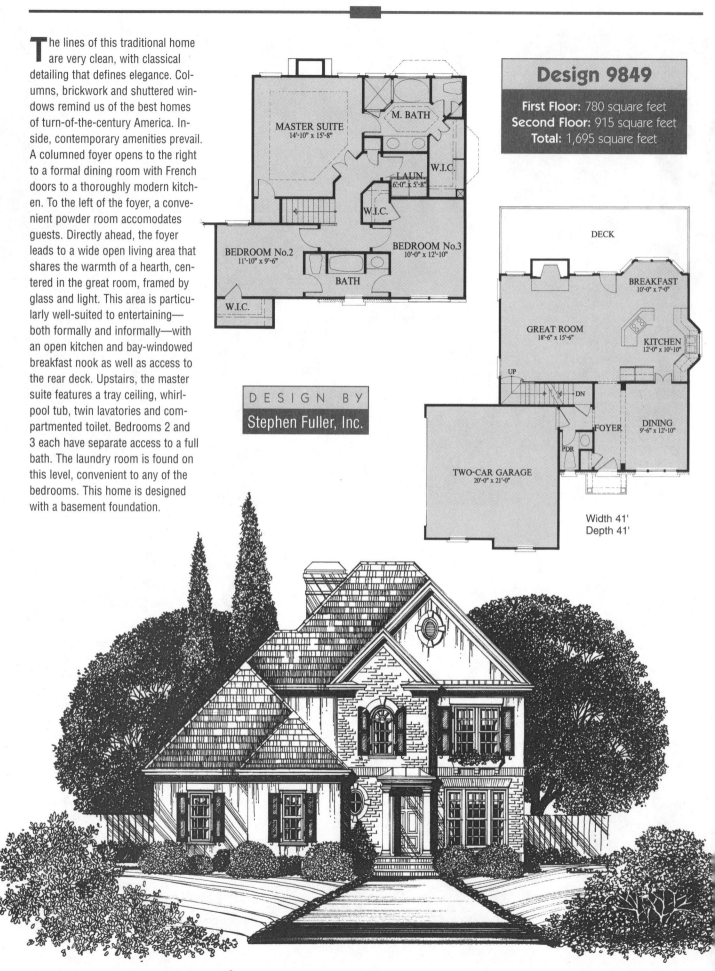

DESIGN BY
Stephen Fuller, Inc.

Design 9849

First Floor: 780 square feet
Second Floor: 915 square feet
Total: 1,695 square feet

MASTER SUITE
14'-10" x 15'-8"

M. BATH

W.I.C.

LAUN.
6'-0" x 5'-8"

W.I.C.

BEDROOM No.2
11'-10" x 9'-6"

BEDROOM No.3
10'-0" x 12'-10"

BATH

W.I.C.

DECK

BREAKFAST
10'-0" x 7'-0"

GREAT ROOM
18'-6" x 15'-6"

KITCHEN
12'-0" x 10'-10"

UP

DN

FOYER

DINING
9'-6" x 12'-10"

PDR

TWO-CAR GARAGE
20'-0" x 21'-0"

Width 41'
Depth 41'

Design 9902

First Floor: 830 square feet
Second Floor: 1,060 square feet
Total: 1,890 square feet

MASTER SUITE
14'-10" x 15'-8"

M. BATH

W.I.C.

LAUN
6'-0" x 5'-8"

BEDROOM NO. 2
12'-0" X 14'-0"

BEDROOM No.3
10'-0" x 12'-10"

BATH

Width 41'
Depth 40'-6"

DECK

BREAKFAST
10'-0" x 7'-0"

GREAT ROOM
18'-6" x 15'-6"

KITCHEN
12'-0" x 10'-10"

UP

DN

FOYER

DINING
9'-6" x 12'-10"

POWDER

TWO-CAR GARAGE
20'-0" x 21'-0"

PORCH

DESIGN BY
Stephen Fuller, Inc.

The pleasing character of this house does not stop with its charming facade. The foyer opens into a large formal dining room on the right and, directly ahead, into the great room. Open planning in the living areas invites formal as well as informal gatherings. The well-equipped kitchen shares natural light from the bay-windowed breakfast nook and opens to the great room, sharing its view of the rear yard. Stairs lead from the great room to the second floor—and here's where you'll find the laundry! The master suite spares none of the popular amenities: full bath with double vanity, shower and tub, walk-in closet. Bedrooms 2 and 3 share a full bath. This home is designed with a basement foundation.

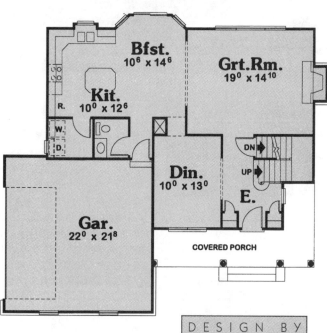

Bfst.
10⁶ x 14⁶

Grt.Rm.
19⁰ x 14¹⁰

Kit.
10⁰ x 12⁶

R.

W.
D.

Din.
10⁰ x 13⁰

DN

UP

E.

Gar.
22⁰ x 21⁸

COVERED PORCH

DESIGN BY
Design Basics, Inc.

This siding and brick traditional home puts its focus on the family. A charming covered porch welcomes guests; inside, a formal dining area and great room with a fireplace are perfect for entertaining. A large efficient kitchen with an easy-access island and bayed breakfast area is handy for easy meals. Three family bedrooms and a comfortable master suite with a whirlpool bath and separate shower are located on the second floor. A loft area can be a popular family retreat.

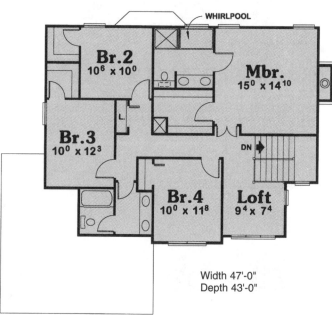

WHIRLPOOL

Br.2
10⁶ x 10⁰

Mbr.
15⁰ x 14¹⁰

L.

Br.3
10⁰ x 12³

DN

Br.4
10⁰ x 11⁸

Loft
9⁴ x 7⁴

Width 47'-0"
Depth 43'-0"

Design HPT440005

First Floor: 1,006 square feet
Second Floor: 1,099 square feet
Total: 2,105 square feet

Design 9282

First Floor: 1,042 square feet
Second Floor: 803 square feet
Total: 1,845 square feet

At 1,845 square feet, this classic two-story home is perfect for a variety of lifestyles. Upon entry from the covered front porch, the thoughtful floor plan is immediately evident. To the right of the entry is a formal volume living room with ten-foot ceiling. Nearby is the formal dining room with a bright window. Serving the dining room and bright bayed dinette, the kitchen features a pantry, Lazy Susan and window sink. Off the breakfast area, step down into the family room with a handsome fireplace and wall of windows. Upstairs, two secondary bedrooms share a hall bath. The private master bedroom has a boxed ceiling, walk-in closet and a pampering dressing area with double vanity and whirlpool.

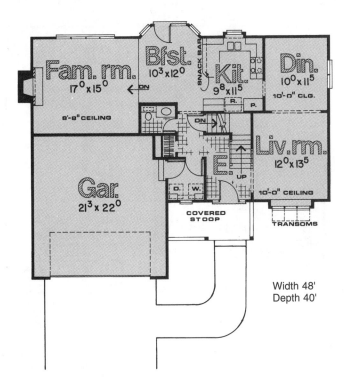

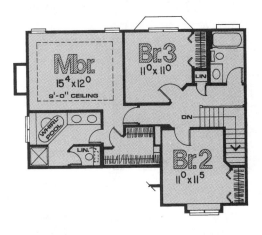

Width 48'
Depth 40'

DESIGN BY
Design Basics, Inc.

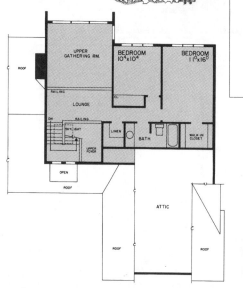

Width 49'-8"
Depth 55'-8"

Design 2905

First Floor: 1,342 square feet
Second Floor: 619 square feet
Total: 1,961 square feet

L **D**

All of the livability in this plan is in the back! With this sort of configuration, this home makes a perfect lakefront or beachfront home. The first-floor living areas, except the kitchen, maintain access to the rear terrace via sliding glass doors. However, the kitchen is open to the breakfast room and thus takes advantage of the view. The master bedroom delights with its private bath and walk-in closet. Two secondary bedrooms comprise the second floor. One utilizes a walk-in closet while both make use of a full hall bath. A lounge overlooks the foyer as well as the gathering room below.

QUOTE ONE®
Cost to build? See page 214 to order complete cost estimate to build this house in your area!

DESIGN BY
Home Planners

Design 2622

First Floor: 624 square feet
Second Floor: 624 square feet
Total: 1,248 square feet
Bonus Room: 247 square feet

L **D**

This Colonial adaptation provides a functional design that allows for expansion in the future. A cozy fireplace in the living room adds warmth to this space as well as the adjacent dining area. The roomy L-shaped kitchen features a breakfast nook and an over-the-sink window. Upstairs, two secondary bedrooms share a full bath with a double vanity. The master bedroom is on this floor as well. Its private bath contains access to attic storage. An additional storage area over the garage furnishes options for future development that may include a bedroom, an office, a study or an exercise room.

DINING RM.
11⁶ x 10⁰

KITCHEN
11⁶ x 13⁶

NOOK

PDR. RM.

LIVING RM.
11⁶ x 15⁰

GARAGE
21⁸ x 23⁴

ENTRY

PORCH

Width 46'
Depth 26'

DESIGN BY
Home Planners

QUOTE ONE®
Cost to build? See page 214 to order complete cost estimate to build this house in your area!

BED RM.
9⁰ x 10⁰

BED RM.
11⁶ x 10⁰

HALL

LIN.

BATH

STORAGE AREA OVER GARAGE -
FUTURE BED RM, OFFICE, ETC.

UP TO ATTIC   BATH

MASTER BED RM.
11⁶ x 12⁸

ROOF

Design 2682

First Floor (Basic Plan): 1,016 square feet
First Floor (Expanded Plan): 1,272 square feet
Second Floor (Both Plans): 766 square feet
Total (Basic Plan): 1,782 square feet
Total (Expanded Plan): 2,038 square feet

L **D**

Here is an expandable Colonial with a full measure of Cape Cod Charm. For those who wish to build the basic house, there is an abundance of low budget livability. Twin fireplaces serve the formal living room and the informal country kitchen. Note the spaciousness of both areas. A dining room and a powder room are also on the first floor of this basic plan. Upstairs are three bedrooms and two full baths.

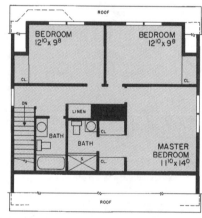

DESIGN BY
Home Planners

Cost to build? See page 214 to order complete cost estimate to build this house in your area!

Width 32'
Depth 32'

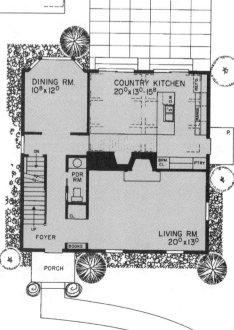

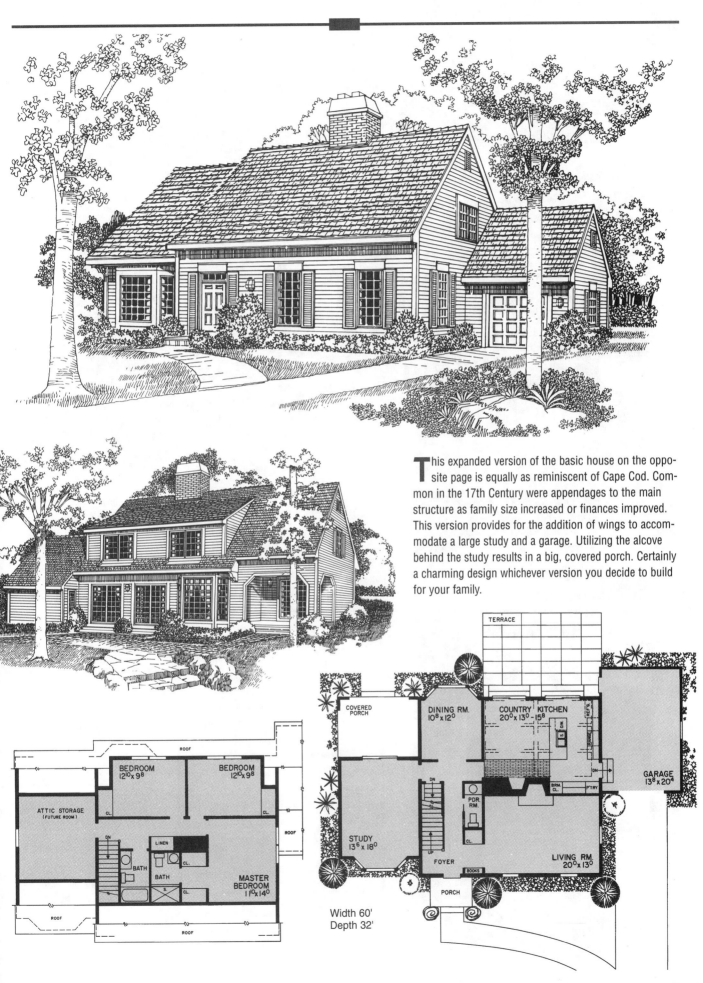

This expanded version of the basic house on the opposite page is equally as reminiscent of Cape Cod. Common in the 17th Century were appendages to the main structure as family size increased or finances improved. This version provides for the addition of wings to accommodate a large study and a garage. Utilizing the alcove behind the study results in a big, covered porch. Certainly a charming design whichever version you decide to build for your family.

TERRACE

COVERED PORCH

DINING RM.
10⁸ x 12⁰

COUNTRY KITCHEN
20⁰ x 13⁰ - 15⁸

REF'G

RANGE

DW

GARAGE
13⁸ x 20⁴

DN

PDR. RM.

BRM. CL.

P'TRY

DN

CL.

STUDY
13⁶ x 18⁰

UP

FOYER

BOOKS

LIVING RM.
20⁰ x 13⁰

PORCH

Width 60'
Depth 32'

ROOF

BEDROOM
12¹⁰ x 9⁸

BEDROOM
12¹⁰ x 9⁸

ATTIC STORAGE
(FUTURE ROOM)

ROOF

CL.

CL.

DN

LINEN

CL.

BATH

BATH

CL.

MASTER BEDROOM
11¹⁰ x 14⁰

ROOF

ROOF

Design 2661

First Floor: 1,100 square feet
Second Floor: 808 square feet
Total: 1,908 square feet

L D

It would be difficult to find a starter or retirement home with more charm than this. Inside, it contains a very livable floor plan. An outstanding first floor centers around the huge country kitchen which includes a beam ceiling, a raised-hearth fireplace, a window seat and rear-yard access. The living room with its warming corner fireplace and private study is to the front of the plan. Upstairs are three bedrooms and two full baths. Built-in shelves and a linen closet in the upstairs hallway provide excellent storage.

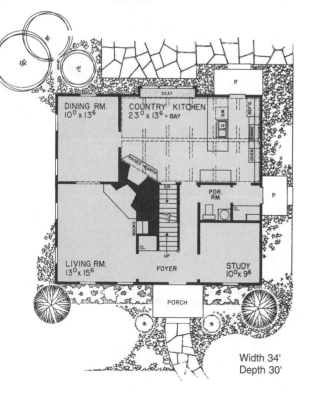

DINING RM. 10⁰ x 13⁶

COUNTRY KITCHEN 23⁰ x 13⁶ + BAY

SEAT

RAISED HEARTH

LIVING RM. 13⁰ x 15⁶

PDR. RM.

STUDY 10⁰ x 9⁶

FOYER

UP

PORCH

Width 34'
Depth 30'

ROOF

BATH

BATH

BEDROOM 12⁴ x 11⁰

LINEN

MASTER BEDROOM 13⁰ x 15⁸

WALK-IN CLOSET

BEDROOM 11⁰ x 12⁰

CEILING CLIP

ROOF

QUOTE ONE®

Cost to build? See page 214 to order complete cost estimate to build this house in your area!

DESIGN BY
Home Planners

EMPTY-NEST ESPRIT

Super "Sunny-Side" Homes

Here's a vibrant collection of plans, carefully selected for people who are ready to relax and enjoy life! There's no scrimping on style or luxury here. Although the square footages are conveniently modest, sumptuous master suites, split bedroom plans, handy U-shaped kitchens and sunny outdoor areas abound.

Some of our best traditional designs are here; traditional, but with a twist. With classic features such as gables, dormers, wraparound porches and verandas, they don't just look traditional, they look authentic—as if they had been family homes for generations. Some wear a country charm; some sport a spicier, more cosmopolitan appearance.

Our classic Cape Cod, Design 2563 (on the next page), delivers a contemporary floor plan, complete with a farm kitchen and a secluded master suite— all with a timeless appeal. And our sweet ranch-style retreat on page 39 captures a healthy splash of prairie flavor with its slightly rustic exterior.

So go ahead, dream! We'd love to help create your new home and, since we've been doing this for 50 years now, we're able to help you define your vision pretty accurately. Visual appeal and design integrity are proven ingredients in all of our plans, but the most impressive quality is the way you feel when you live in them. Have you ever thought of falling in love with a home?

Photo by Laszlo Regos

This home, as shown in the photograph, may differ from the actual blueprints.
For more detailed information, please check the floor plans carefully.

This charming Cape Cod will capture your heart with its warm appeal. From the large living room with fireplace and the adjacent dining room to the farm kitchen with an additional fireplace, the plan works toward livability. The first-floor laundry and walk-in pantry further aid in the efficiency of this plan. The master bedroom is located on this level for privacy and is highlighted by a luxurious bath and sliding glass doors to the rear terrace. A front study might be used as a guest bedroom or a library. Upstairs there are two bedrooms and a sitting room plus a full bath to accommodate the needs of family members. Both bedrooms have access to the attic. A three-car garage allows plenty of room for vehicles and storage space.

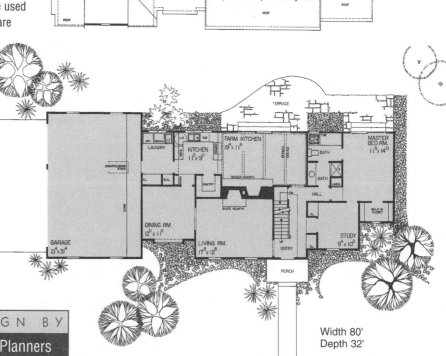

Design 2563

First Floor: 1,500 square feet
Second Floor: 690 square feet
Total: 2,190 square feet

L D

Cost to build? See page 214
to order complete cost estimate
to build this house in your area!

DESIGN BY
Home Planners

Width 80'
Depth 32'

Columns, transom windows and an eyebrow dormer lend this house a stylish country charm. Inside, a built-in media center, fireplace, skylights and columns add to the wonderful livability of this home. The modified-galley kitchen features a serving bar and an island workstation. Escape to the relaxing owners suite, which features a private sitting room and a luxurious bath set between His and Hers walk-in closets. Three bedrooms share a bath on the other side of the plan, ensuring privacy. Please specify basement, crawlspace or slab foundation when ordering.

Design HPT440055

Square Footage: 2,360

DESIGN BY

Larry James & Associates, Inc.

Basement Stair Location

Width 75'-2"
Depth 68'-0"

Retreat
15-3x8-6

Bath
12-0x11-9

Owner's
Bedroom
15-3x15-8

Laundry
12-0x7-6

Porch
28-4x11-0

Bedroom
11-9x13-6

Greatroom
14-6x17-5

Dining
11-0x17-5

Garage
23-6x21-6

Bedroom
11-6x13-6

Bedroom
11-8x13-6

Foyer

Kitchen
12-6x13-9

Storage
13-4x5-8

Porch
32-0x8-0

Design HPT440056

Square Footage: 1,434

With this grand, elegant facade, who would believe this home contains a compact but spacious 1,434 square feet? The super-efficient design of this three-bedroom home creates a fabulous impression, but the interior plan is not at all imposing. The spacious owners suite possesses a grand bath and a walk-in closet. Both of the liberal-size secondary bedrooms also contain walk-in closets. The living room is open to porches via French doors on the front and back. The open living areas feature ten-foot ceilings. Please specify crawlspace or slab foundation when ordering.

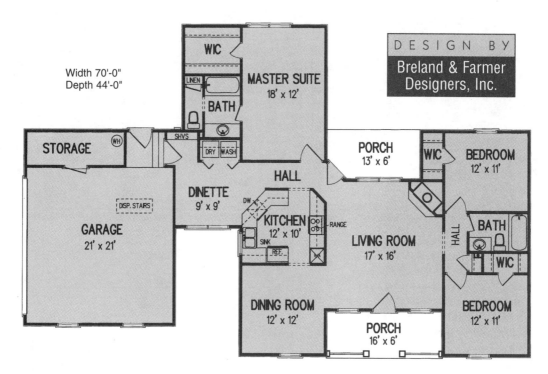

Width 70'-0"
Depth 44'-0"

DESIGN BY
Breland & Farmer
Designers, Inc.

DESIGN BY
Home Planners

Quote One®

Cost to build? See page 214
to order complete cost estimate
to build this house in your area!

Country living is the focus of this charming design. A cozy covered porch invites you into the foyer with the sleeping area on the right and the living area straight ahead. From the windowed front-facing breakfast room, enter the efficient kitchen with its corner laundry room, large pantry, snack-bar pass-through to the gathering room, and passage to the dining room. The massive gathering room and dining room feature sloped ceilings, an impressive fireplace and access to the rear terrace. Terrace access is also available from the master bedroom with its sloped ceiling and a master bath that includes a whirlpool tub, a separate shower and a separate vanity area. A study at the front of the house can also be converted into a third bedroom.

Design 3487

Square Footage: 1,835

Width 71'
Depth 43'-5"

DESIGN BY
Breland & Farmer
Designers, Inc.

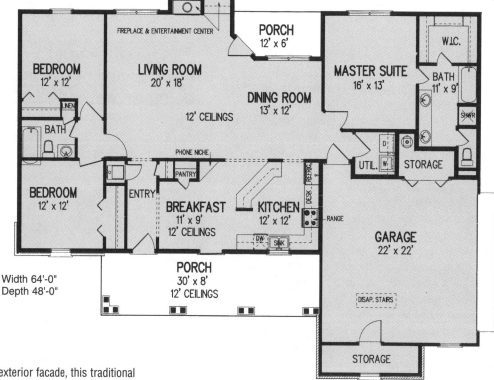

FIREPLACE & ENTERTAINMENT CENTER

PORCH
12' x 6'

BEDROOM
12' x 12'

LIVING ROOM
20' x 18'

DINING ROOM
13' x 12'

MASTER SUITE
16' x 13'

W.T.C.

BATH
11' x 9'

12' CEILINGS

LINEN

BATH

SHWR

PHONE NICHE

PANTRY

STORAGE

UTIL.

BEDROOM
12' x 12'

ENTRY

BREAKFAST
11' x 9'
12' CEILINGS

KITCHEN
12' x 12'

DESK

REFRIG.

RANGE

GARAGE
22' x 22'

DW

SINK

Width 64'-0"
Depth 48'-0"

PORCH
30' x 8'
12' CEILINGS

DISAP. STAIRS

STORAGE

Using wood and stone for the exterior facade, this traditional Prairie-style home boasts a large receiving porch and free-flowing interior spaces. The living room is open to the dining room and has a fireplace and built-in entertainment center. The breakfast area, kitchen, and dining and living area have twelve-foot ceilings. The owners suite is secluded for privacy and features a bath with a tub, separate shower and walk-in closet. Please specify crawlspace or slab foundation when ordering.

Design HPT440057

Square Footage: 1,770

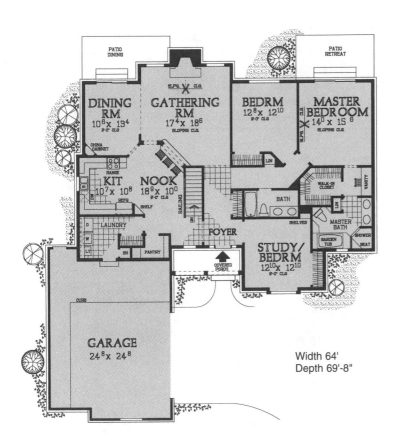

PATIO DINING

PATIO RETREAT

DINING RM
10⁸ x 13⁴
8'-0" CLG

GATHERING RM
17⁴ x 18⁶
SLOPING CLG

BEDRM
12⁸ x 12¹⁰
9'-0" CLG

MASTER BEDROOM
14⁰ x 15⁶
SLOPING CLG

CHINA CABINET

RANGE

KIT
10⁷ x 10⁸

NOOK
18⁹ x 10⁰
8'-0" CLG

REFG

SHELF

WALK-IN CLOSET

LIN

VANITY

BATH

RAILING

DN

LAUNDRY

SHELVES

MASTER BATH

GARDEN TUB

SHOWER SEAT

PANTRY

FOYER

COVERED PORCH

STUDY/ BEDRM
12¹⁰ x 12¹⁰
8'-0" CLG

CURB

GARAGE
24⁸ x 24⁸

Width 64'
Depth 69'-8"

Design 3491

Square Footage: 2,098

L D

T his is a fine home for a young family or for empty-nesters. The versatile bedroom/study offers room for growth or a quiet haven for reading. The U-shaped kitchen includes a handy nook with a snack bar and easy accessibility to the dining room or the gathering room—perfect for entertaining. The master bedroom includes its own private outdoor retreat, a walk-in closet and an amenity-filled bathroom. An additional bedroom and a large laundry room with an adjacent, walk-in pantry complete the plan.

DESIGN BY
Home Planners

Small but inviting, this one-story ranch-style farmhouse is the perfect choice for empty-nesters—and it's loaded with amenities to please the most particular homeowner. Step into a spectacular foyer, bathed in sunlight streaming through dual clerestories, front and rear. The foyer opens to formal living areas on the left and right and leads to split sleeping quarters toward the rear of the plan. Guests and family alike will enjoy the spacious living room, complete with sloped ceiling, warming fireplace, entertainment center and decorative plant shelves. The formal dining room offers a wet bar, sloped ceiling, built-in shelves and natural light from windows to the front and rear of the plan. A sumptuous master suite boasts a warming fireplace, sloped ceiling, whirlpool bath and separate shower. A family bedroom or guest suite offers a full bath on the opposite side of the plan. The kitchen is replete with popular amenities and shares light with a sunny breakfast nook with access to the entertainment terrace.

DESIGN BY

Home Planners

Width 89'
Depth 46'-2"

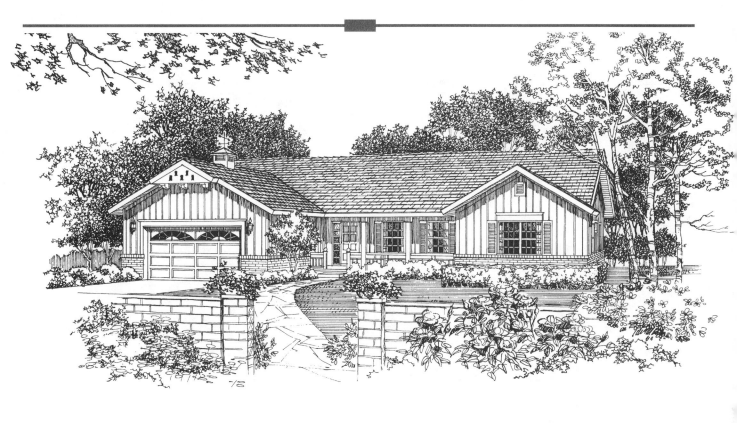

MASTER
BEDRM
17⁴ x 14⁰

LIVING
RM
17⁰ x 15⁴

DINING
RM
10⁰ x 12⁶

BEDRM
14⁴ x 12⁰

PATIO

WALK-IN
CLOSET

LINEN

LINEN

BATH

MASTER
BATH

SNACK BAR

FOYER

KIT
19⁰ x 11²

SHOWER

GARDEN
TUB

LAUNDRY

BEDRM
14⁴ x 14⁴

COVERED
PORCH

RAILING

GARAGE
21⁴ x 20⁴

Width 64'-8"
Depth 54'-7"

Quote One®

Cost to build? See page 214
to order complete cost estimate
to build this house in your area!

Design 3652

Square Footage: 2,076

L **D**

Small, but so livable, this charming ranch home is great for starters or empty-nesters. The cozy covered porch opens to a tiled foyer and then into the huge kitchen on the right. The kitchen connects to the living room/dining room area via a snack bar. Look for a warming fireplace in the living room and a sunny patio through sliding glass doors in the dining room. Bedrooms are split with two family bedrooms and a full bath on the right and the master suite on the left. A handy laundry room connects the home to a two-car garage.

DESIGN BY

Home Planners

Design 9238

First Floor: 1,421 square feet
Second Floor: 448 square feet
Total: 1,869 square feet

Always a welcome site, the covered front porch of this home invites investigation of its delightful floor plan. Living areas to the back of the house include the great room with see-through fireplace to the bay-windowed breakfast area and hearth kitchen. A clever snack bar, a planning desk and a large corner walk-in pantry highlight this area. The formal dining room offers a built-in hutch for precious china or curiosa as well as a view to the front property through triple windows. A split bedroom plan offers privacy for the luxurious first-floor master suite, which includes a corner whirlpool bath, while two additional bedrooms and a full bath reside upstairs —a perfect plan for empty-nesters.

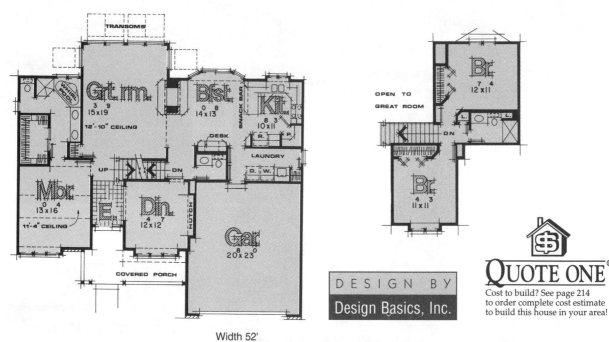

Width 52'
Depth 47'-4"

DESIGN BY
Design Basics, Inc.

QUOTE ONE®
Cost to build? See page 214 to order complete cost estimate to build this house in your area!

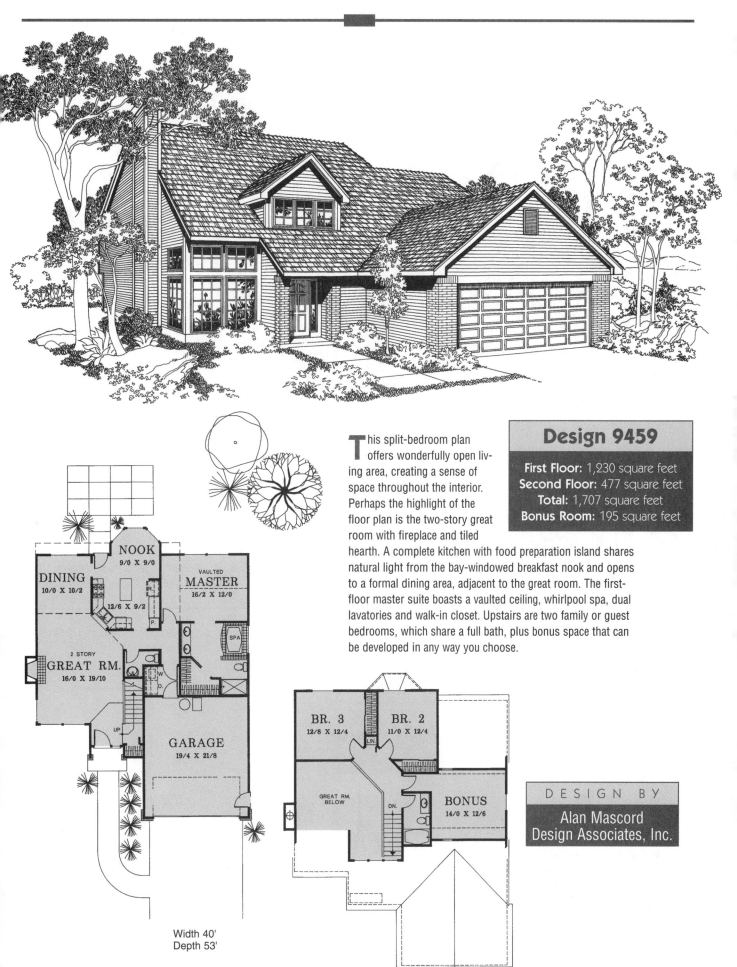

Design 9459

First Floor: 1,230 square feet
Second Floor: 477 square feet
Total: 1,707 square feet
Bonus Room: 195 square feet

This split-bedroom plan offers wonderfully open living area, creating a sense of space throughout the interior. Perhaps the highlight of the floor plan is the two-story great room with fireplace and tiled hearth. A complete kitchen with food preparation island shares natural light from the bay-windowed breakfast nook and opens to a formal dining area, adjacent to the great room. The first-floor master suite boasts a vaulted ceiling, whirlpool spa, dual lavatories and walk-in closet. Upstairs are two family or guest bedrooms, which share a full bath, plus bonus space that can be developed in any way you choose.

NOOK
9/0 X 9/0

DINING
10/0 X 10/2

VAULTED
MASTER
16/2 X 12/0

12/6 X 9/2

2 STORY
GREAT RM.
16/0 X 19/10

SPA

UP

GARAGE
19/4 X 21/8

BR. 3
12/8 X 12/4

BR. 2
11/0 X 12/4

GREAT RM.
BELOW

DN.

BONUS
14/0 X 12/6

DESIGN BY

Alan Mascord
Design Associates, Inc.

Width 40'
Depth 53'

© 1995 Donald A. Gardner Architects, Inc.

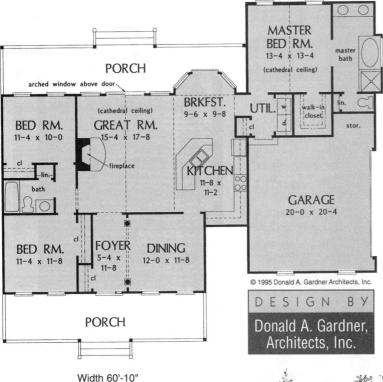

PORCH

arched window above door

BED RM.
11-4 x 10-0

cl

lin.

bath

BED RM.
11-4 x 11-8

GREAT RM.
15-4 x 17-8
(cathedral ceiling)

fireplace

cl

FOYER
5-4 x
11-8

cl

DINING
12-0 x 11-8

BRKFST.
9-6 x 9-8

KITCHEN
11-8 x
11-2

UTIL.
w
d
cl

MASTER
BED RM.
13-4 x 13-4
(cathedral ceiling)

master
bath

walk-in
closet

lin.

stor.

GARAGE
20-0 x 20-4

PORCH

© 1995 Donald A. Gardner Architects, Inc.

DESIGN BY
Donald A. Gardner,
Architects, Inc.

Width 60'-10"
Depth 51'-6"

Design 9780

Square Footage: 1,561

Special touches such as interior columns, a bay window and dormers add their own special brand of charm to this wonderful country home. Inside, the centrally located great room features a cathedral ceiling, a welcoming fireplace and a clerestory window that fills the room with natural light. Whether entertaining guests or gathering with the family, you'll find that the adjoining kitchen and sun-filled breakfast area combine with the great room to create an open, comfortable space. Split for privacy, the master bedroom provides a quiet getaway. For ultimate relaxation, indulge yourself in a pampering master bath that offers a double-bowl vanity, a separate shower and a whirlpool tub. Two additional bedrooms share a full bath.

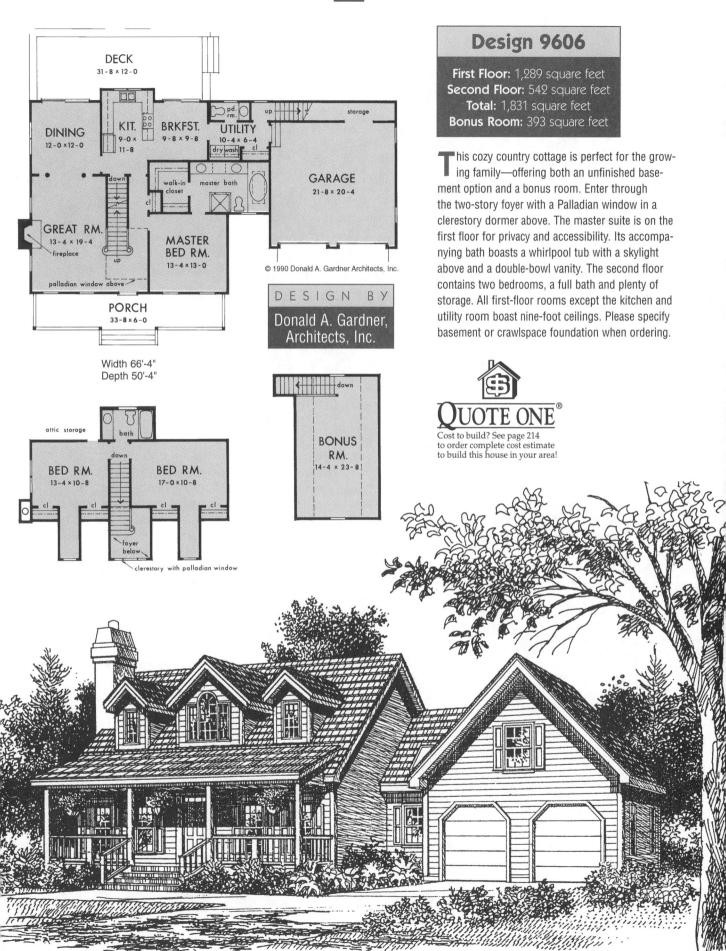

DECK
31-8 × 12-0

DINING
12-0 × 12-0

KIT.
9-0 × 11-8

BRKFST.
9-8 × 9-8

UTILITY
10-4 × 6-4

pd. rm.

up

storage

dry wash

cl

GREAT RM.
13-4 × 19-4

fireplace

down

walk-in closet

master bath

cl

GARAGE
21-8 × 20-4

up

MASTER BED RM.
13-4 × 13-0

palladian window above

PORCH
33-8 × 6-0

© 1990 Donald A. Gardner Architects, Inc.

Width 66'-4"
Depth 50'-4"

DESIGN BY
Donald A. Gardner, Architects, Inc.

attic storage

bath

down

BED RM.
13-4 × 10-8

BED RM.
17-0 × 10-8

cl

cl

cl

cl

foyer below

clerestory with palladian window

down

BONUS RM.
14-4 × 23-8

This cozy country cottage is perfect for the growing family—offering both an unfinished basement option and a bonus room. Enter through the two-story foyer with a Palladian window in a clerestory dormer above. The master suite is on the first floor for privacy and accessibility. Its accompanying bath boasts a whirlpool tub with a skylight above and a double-bowl vanity. The second floor contains two bedrooms, a full bath and plenty of storage. All first-floor rooms except the kitchen and utility room boast nine-foot ceilings. Please specify basement or crawlspace foundation when ordering.

QUOTE ONE®

Cost to build? See page 214
to order complete cost estimate
to build this house in your area!

Design 3682

First Floor: 1,093 square feet
Second Floor: 603 square feet
Total: 1,696 square feet

L D

A rustic country style combined with contemporary livability set this plan apart from the rest. Arch-topped dormer windows and a wraparound porch with a balustrade create a welcoming exterior, but the real charm begins within. A tiled foyer opens to a two-story great room with sloped ceiling, raised-hearth fireplace and views of the front property through triple windows. The tiled kitchen and windowed eating nook offer a snack bar, open to the great room, and access to the rear covered porch. An impressive master suite with a walk-in closet, garden tub and separate shower, is snugly tucked away to the side of the first-floor plan. Upstairs, two additional bedrooms and a loft/study with dormer window seat share a full bath as well as the view below to the great room.

Width 46'
Depth 52'

COVERED PORCH

RAILING

RANGE REFG

KIT/ NOOK
18⁸ x 10¹⁰

FURN
WH SHWR

MASTER BATH

SNACK BAR

UTILITY
D
W

LINE OF FLOOR ABOVE

UP

PWDR

GREAT RM
12¹⁰ x 16¹⁰
SLOPING CLG

RAISED HEARTH

RAILING

LIN

FOYER

MASTER BEDRM
12⁴ x 12¹⁰

RAILING

RAILING

COVERED PORCH

RAILING

ATTIC ACCESS

BEDRM
10⁰ x 11⁴

BATH

BEDRM
10⁶ x 11⁴

WALK-IN CLOSET

SHELVES & CLB

OPEN TO BELOW

DN

RAILING

LOFT/ STUDY
14⁸ x 9⁰

LIN BC STOR

ATTIC ACCESS

SEAT

DESIGN BY
Home Planners

DESIGN BY
Breland & Farmer Designers, Inc.

Width 64'-0"
Depth 48'-0"

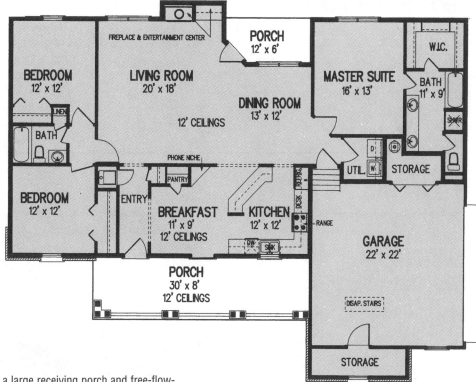

This traditional-style home boasts a large receiving porch and free-flowing interior spaces. The spacious living room is open to the adjacent dining room and has a built-in fireplace and entertainment center. The entry, breakfast area, kitchen, and the dining and living area have twelve foot ceilings, while other rooms have traditional eight-foot ceilings. The private owners suite is conveniently located only steps away from the kitchen. Please specify crawlspace or slab foundation when ordering.

Design HPT440058

Square Footage: 1,770

© 1995 Donald A. Gardner Architects, Inc.

B. NATHAN

Design 9779

Square Footage: 1,632

PORCH

BED RM.
11-4 x 11-0

(cathedral ceiling)
GREAT RM.
15-4 x 18-6

fireplace

cl

lin.

bath

walk-in
closet

BED RM./
STUDY
11-0 x 11-8

FOYER
6-0 x 8-4

cl

DINING
11-0 x 11-8

PORCH

BRKFST.
10-4 x 8-8

cl

KIT.
11-4 x
12-10

MASTER
BED RM.
13-4 x 16-4

master
bath

skylight

walk-in
closet

lin.

w
d

storage

UTIL.

GARAGE
21-0 x 21-8

storage

(optional door location)

© 1995 Donald A. Gardner Architects, Inc.

Width 62'-4"
Depth 55'-2"

DESIGN BY
**Donald A. Gardner,
Architects, Inc.**

This country home has a big heart in a cozy package. Inside, interior columns, a bay window and dormers add elegance. The central great room features a cathedral ceiling and a fireplace. A clerestory window splashes the room with natural light. The open kitchen easily services the breakfast area and the nearby dining room. The private master suite, with a tray ceiling and a walk-in closet, boasts amenities found in much larger homes. The bath features skylights over the whirlpool tub. Two additional bedrooms share a bath. The front bedroom features a walk-in closet and also doubles as a study.

©1995 Donald A. Gardner, Architects, Inc.

B. NATHAN

© 1994 Donald A. Gardner Architects, Inc.

Design 9747

First Floor: 1,335 square feet
Second Floor: 488 square feet
Total: 1,823 square feet

Elegant dormers and arch-topped windows offer a charming facade for this traditional design, with plenty of fabulous amenities to be found within. Lead guests leisurely through the foyer and central hall to a magnificent great room with vaulted ceiling and skylight, centered fireplace, decorative plant shelf and access to the rear deck. Attached to the nearby kitchen, a breakfast nook opens to a screened porch, perfect for informal dining alfresco. The well-appointed kitchen also serves the adjacent dining room for more formal occasions. A secluded main-floor master suite introduces high elegance with a cathedral ceiling and a Palladian-style window. A spacious walk-in closet, a whirlpool tub and a separate shower complete the comforts of this suite. Upstairs, a balcony hall connects two additional bedrooms which share a full bath.

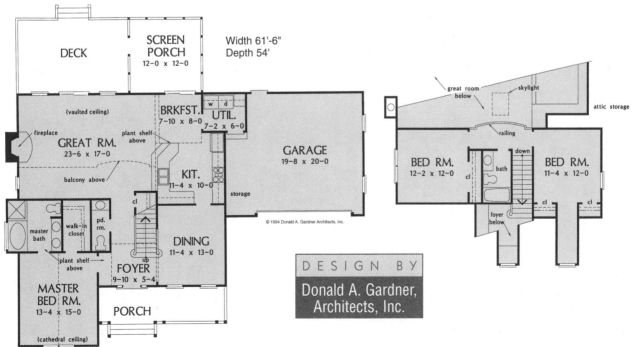

Width 61'-6"
Depth 54'

© 1994 Donald A. Gardner Architects, Inc.

DESIGN BY

Donald A. Gardner, Architects, Inc.

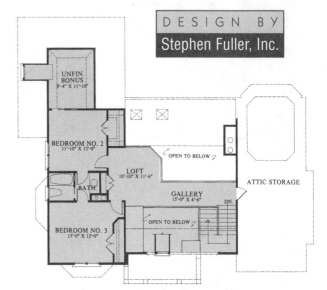

Design HPT440060

First Floor: 1,725 square feet
Second Floor: 650 square feet
Total: 2,375 square feet
Bonus Room: 140 square feet

Width 60'-6"
Depth 50'-6"

TWO CAR GARAGE 21'-4" X 21'-4"

PATIO

BREAKFAST 9'-8" X 9'-0"

LAUNDRY 6'-0" X 6'-0"

KITCHEN 12'-0" X 12'-0"

GREAT ROOM 15'-0" X 16'-2"

MASTER BEDROOM 13'-10" X 16'-10"

DINING ROOM 11'-4" X 11'-4"

UP   DN

POWDER

FOYER 11'-0" X 8'-10"

MASTER BATH

LIVING ROOM 15'-4" X 12'-0"

W.I.C.

PORCH

DESIGN BY
Stephen Fuller, Inc.

UNFIN. BONUS 9'-4" X 11'-10"

BEDROOM NO. 2 11'-10" X 12'-0"

BATH

LOFT 10'-10" X 11'-6"

OPEN TO BELOW

ATTIC STORAGE

GALLERY 15'-0" X 4'-6"

DN.

BEDROOM NO. 3 13'-0" X 12'-0"

OPEN TO BELOW

This example of Classic American architecture features a columned front porch and wood framing. Straight ahead from the foyer, the great room is largely glass and opens to the vaulted breakfast area. The octagonal kitchen is designed to promote the flow of family traffic. The dining room and living room share a hearth. The owners bedroom at the right rear of the home features a large bay window and a lavish bath with dual vanities, a separate shower and walk-in closets. The upper level is comprised of a gallery and a loft open to the great room and foyer below. This home is designed with a basement foundation.

© 1996 Donald A. Gardner Architects, Inc.

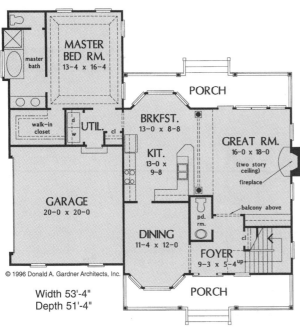

MASTER BED RM.
13-4 x 16-4

master bath

walk-in closet

UTIL.

GARAGE
20-0 x 20-0

BRKFST.
13-0 x 8-8

KIT.
13-0 x 9-8

PORCH

GREAT RM.
16-0 x 18-0
(two story ceiling)
fireplace

balcony above

pd. rm.

DINING
11-4 x 12-0

FOYER
9-3 x 5-4 up

cl

PORCH

© 1996 Donald A. Gardner Architects, Inc.

Width 53'-4"
Depth 51'-4"

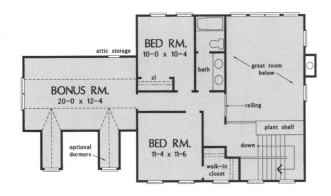

attic storage

BED RM.
10-0 x 10-4

cl

bath

great room below

railing

BONUS RM.
20-0 x 12-4

optional dormers

BED RM.
11-4 x 11-6

plant shelf

down

walk-in closet

Design 7611

First Floor: 1,395 square feet
Second Floor: 502 square feet
Total: 1,897 square feet

This traditional plan blends a country exterior with a stylish, entirely livable interior plan. The foyer opens to a U-shaped staircase on the right and a bay-windowed formal dining room on the left. Directly ahead is a stunning, two-story great room with centered fireplace and views to the rear property as well as access to a covered porch, perfect for warm summer evenings. A columned archway joins the great room to the kitchen and bay-windowed breakfast nook, creating an open, spacious living area. The secluded master suite enjoys a raised ceiling and a pampering bath with a windowed garden tub. Two family or guest bedrooms share a full bath on the second floor, which provides a balcony overlook to the family room below. A bonus room offers space for a hobby room or for additional storage.

DESIGN BY

Donald A. Gardner, Architects, Inc.

55

Design HPT440061

First Floor: 1,784 square feet
Second Floor: 660 square feet
Total: 2,444 square feet

DESIGN BY
Stephen Fuller, Inc.

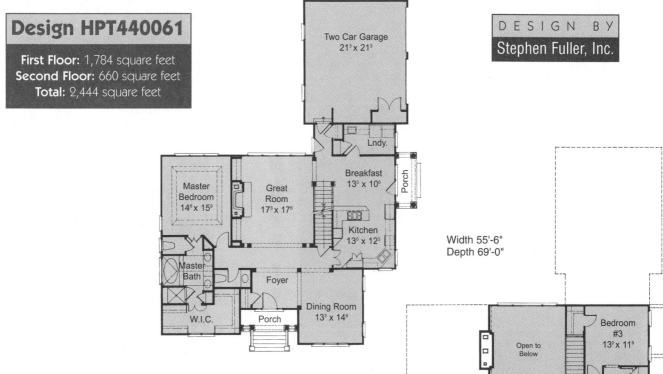

Two Car Garage
21³ x 21³

Lndy.

Breakfast
13⁰ x 10⁰

Porch

Master
Bedroom
14⁶ x 15⁹

Great
Room
17³ x 17⁶

Kitchen
13⁰ x 12³

Master
Bath

Foyer

Width 55'-6"
Depth 69'-0"

W.I.C.   Porch

Dining Room
13³ x 14⁹

Open to
Below

Bedroom
#3
13⁰ x 11⁹

Bath

Attic
Storage

Open to
Below

Bedroom
#2
11³ x 12³

Wood siding, shuttered windows and a covered front porch enhance this home's exterior. Built-ins abound in the great room with a full wall of bookshelves and a fireplace. The kitchen includes a breakfast room that accesses a side porch. The first floor also includes a master suite with a private bath and two walk-in closets. The second floor contains two family bedrooms. This home is designed with a basement foundation.

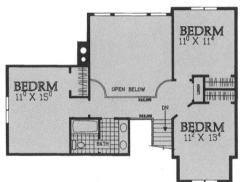

Quote One®

Cost to build? See page 214
to order complete cost estimate
to build this house in your area!

Design 3458

First Floor: 1,617 square feet
Second Floor: 725 square feet
Total: 2,342 square feet

L D

Brick veneer and horizontal siding blend beautifully with radial head windows and five gables to create this transitional exterior. The interior plan offers generous second-floor bedroom space for "visiting" family members and guests. Informal and formal living areas are perfectly blended in the first-floor plan, with living and dining rooms just off the foyer, and the two-story family room directly ahead, offering a dramatic view of the rear grounds. This is a comfortable area, open to the breakfast room, with built-in bookcases flanking the centered fireplace with tile hearth, and rear terrace access. In the U-shaped kitchen, a snack bar caters to on-the-run meals. The upstairs balcony hall offers an overlook to the family room below. Bonus space is available in the basement, should the development of a recreational or hobby area be desired.

DESIGN BY
Home Planners

Width 62'
Depth 41'

This cozy English cottage might be found hidden away in a European garden. All the charm of gables, stonework and multi-level roof lines combine to create this home. To the left of the foyer you will see the sunlit dining room, highlighted by a dramatic tray ceiling and expansive windows with transoms. This room and the living room flow together to form one large entertainment area. In the gourmet kitchen are a work island, an oversized pantry and a bright adjoining octagonal breakfast room with a gazebo ceiling. The great room features a pass-through wet bar, a fireplace and bookcases or an entertainment center. The master suite enjoys privacy at the rear of the home. An open-rail loft above the foyer leads to additional bedrooms with walk-in closets, private vanities and a shared bath. This home is designed with a basement foundation.

QUOTE ONE®

Cost to build? See page 214 to order complete cost estimate to build this house in your area!

DESIGN BY
Stephen Fuller, Inc.

DECK

BREAKFAST
10'-4" X 10'-4"

MASTER SITTING
10'-4" X 6'-0"

GREAT ROOM
17'-0" X 17'-0"

MASTER BEDROOM
15'-4" X 13'-0"

KITCHEN
13'-4" X 17'-0"

DINING ROOM
12'-10" X 10'-6"

FOYER
5'-0" X 13'-6"

MASTER BATH
12'-2" X 12'-8"

POWDER

LAUNDRY
6'-0" X 6'-10"

W.I.C.

LIVING ROOM
11'-4" X 10'-8"

STOOP

TWO CAR GARAGE
21'-4" X 21'-4"

Width 47'-10"
Depth 63'-10"

ATTIC STORAGE

CLOSET

OPEN TO BELOW

BEDROOM NO. 2
11'-2" X 13'-2"

LOFT
8'-4" X 9'-2"

BATH

BEDROOM NO. 3
10'-8" X 14'-0"

CLOSET

Design 9813

First Floor: 1,724 square feet
Second Floor: 700 square feet
Total: 2,424 square feet

BREAKFAST
11'-4" X 7'-4"

DECK

DN

W.I.C.

GREAT ROOM
14'-0" X 19'-6"

MASTER
BEDROOM
12'-6" X 16'-0"

MASTER
BATH

KITCHEN
11'-4" X 12'-0"

W.I.C.

W.I.C.

UP

DN

DINING ROOM
11'-4" X 12'-6"

FOYER
5'-0" X 8'-8"

POWDER

COAT

LAUNDRY

BEDROOM NO. 3
12'-0" X 11'-0"

STOOP

BATH

BEDROOM NO. 2
12'-9" X 11'-9"

DESIGN BY
Stephen Fuller, Inc.

Width 48'
Depth 47'-5"

Design 9914

Square Footage: 1,770

Perfect for a sloping lot, this European one-story plan offers privacy for the sleeping quarters by placing them a few steps up from the living area. The master suite is secluded off the central hallway, partitioned by double doors which are echoed by lovely French doors to the rear deck and by doors leading to a sumptuous bath with a windowed garden tub. Secondary bedrooms or guest quarters share a full bath with a double-bowl vanity. A spacious great room with centered fireplace offers rear deck access and opens to the breakfast room with a boxed window. The well-appointed U-shaped kitchen easily serves both formal and casual eating areas. The lower level offers bonus space that may be developed for recreational use. This home is designed with a basement foundation.

QUOTE ONE®

Cost to build? See page 214
to order complete cost estimate
to build this house in your area!

Design 2964

First Floor: 1,441 square feet
Second Floor: 621 square feet
Total: 2,062 square feet

Tudor houses offer their own unique exterior design features—gable roofs, simulated beam work, diamond-lite windows, muntins, panelled doors, varying roof planes and hefty cornices. This exquisite two-story home boasts a sensational first-floor master bedroom as well as generous guest quarters with a hallway balcony and lounge above. The master suite affords privacy in style with a whirlpool tub, knee-space vanity, walk-in closet and its own access to the rear terrace. The grand, two-story foyer leads to a spacious living room with sloped ceiling, warming fireplace and stunning views as well as access to the rear grounds. The formal dining area, breakfast room and U-shaped kitchen, conveniently clustered nearby, offer two additional glass doors to the rear terrace, which further enhance the bright, cheerful atmosphere of this area. Bonus space is available in the basement for development if desired.

Width 55'
Depth 59'-8"

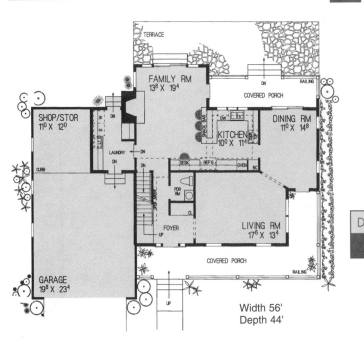

TERRACE

FAMILY RM
13⁸ X 19⁴

COVERED PORCH

DN

RAILING

SHOP/STOR
11⁰ X 12⁰

DINING RM
11⁰ X 14⁸

KITCHEN
10⁰ X 11⁴

LAUNDRY

DN

CURB

DN

FOYER
UP

LIVING RM
17⁶ X 13⁴

DESK REF'G OVEN BC

POR RM

CL

COVERED PORCH

RAILING

GARAGE
19⁸ X 23⁴

UP

Width 56'
Depth 44'

C overed porches front and rear are the first signal that this is a fine example of Folk Victorian styling. Complementing the exterior is a grand plan for family living. A formal living room and attached dining room provide space for entertaining guests. The large family room with fireplace is a gathering room for everyday. Both areas have access to outdoor spaces. Four bedrooms occupy the second floor. The master suite features two lavatories, a window seat and three closets. One of the family bedrooms has its own private balcony and could be used as a study. Note the open staircase and linen storage.

DESIGN BY
Home Planners

RAILING

BALCONY

ROOF

ROOF

BEDROOM/ STUDY
12⁰ X 10⁸

BATH

SEAT

MASTER BEDROOM
12⁰ X 14⁰

SEAT

RAILING

DN

BATH

LINEN

BEDROOM
11⁰ X 10⁰

BEDROOM
11⁰ X 10⁰

ROOF

ROOF

ROOF OVERHANG

ROOF

Design 3385

First Floor: 1,096 square feet
Second Floor: 900 square feet
Total: 1,996 square feet

L **D**

QUOTE ONE®
Cost to build? See page 214
to order complete cost estimate
to build this house in your area!

*This home, as shown in the photograph, may differ from the actual blueprints.
For more detailed information, please check the floor plans carefully.*

Photo by Bob Greenspan

BALCONY

MASTER BED RM.
18⁰ x 13⁶

VANITY

DRESSING RM.

BATH

WALK-IN CLOSET

SHELVES

CL. CL.

WALK-IN CLOSET

RAIL

DN.

LINEN

BED RM.
12⁰ x 11⁰

TWL.S.

BATH

BED RM.
11⁰ x 17⁶

Width 40'-4"
Depth 52'-0"

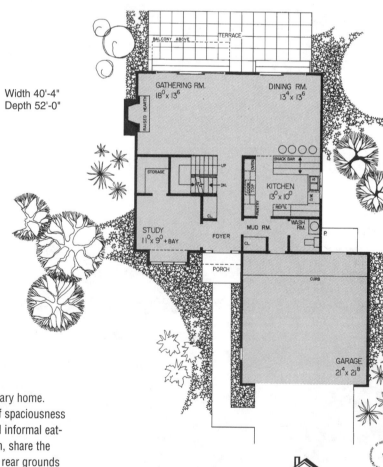

BALCONY ABOVE   TERRACE

GATHERING RM.
18⁰ x 13⁶

DINING RM.
13⁴ x 13⁶

RAISED HEARTH

STORAGE

UP

COOK TOP

OVEN

SNACK BAR

KITCHEN
13⁰ x 10⁰

DN.

PANTRY

REF'G.

D.W.

CL.

MUD RM.

WASH RM.

STUDY
11⁰ x 9⁰ + BAY

FOYER

CL.

P.

PORCH

CURB

GARAGE
21⁴ x 21⁸

Design HPT440006

First Floor: 975 square feet
Second Floor: 1,024 square feet
Total: 1,999 square feet

L **D**

Sleek, modern lines define this two-story contemporary home. Open planning in the living areas creates a sense of spaciousness found in much larger plans. The formal dining area and informal eating counter, both easily served by the U-shaped kitchen, share the cozy warmth of the centered fireplace and views to the rear grounds offered by the gathering room. Amenities abound in the second-floor owners suite with a private balcony, walk-in closet, separate dressing area and knee-space vanity. Two secondary bedrooms and a full bath complete this floor, perfect for guests or visiting relatives—or make one room a study or hobby room.

DESIGN BY
Home Planners

QUOTE ONE®

Cost to build? See page 214
to order complete cost estimate
to build this house in your area!

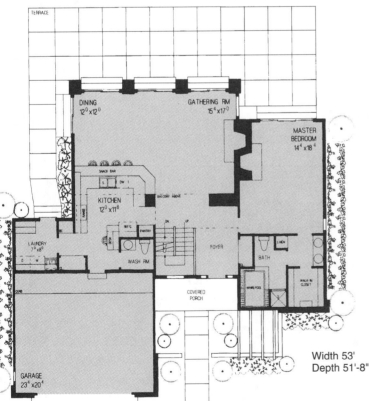

TERRACE

DINING
12⁰ x12⁰

GATHERING RM
15⁴ x17⁰

MASTER
BEDROOM
14⁴ x18⁴

SNACK BAR

BALCONY ABOVE

KITCHEN
12⁰ x11⁸

LAUNDRY
7⁰ x8⁰

WASH RM

FOYER

BATH

LINEN

WHIRLPOOL

WALK-IN
CLOSET

COVERED
PORCH

GARAGE
23⁶ x20⁶

Width 53'
Depth 51'-8"

Design 2490

First Floor: 1,414 square feet
Second Floor: 620 square feet
Total: 2,034 square feet

A sloping roof and visible skylights entice you to look closer into this contemporary home. Split-bedroom planning makes the most of this plan; the first-floor master suite pampers with a lavish bath and a fireplace while two family bedrooms reside upstairs and share a full bath. The living areas are open and have easy access to the rear terrace. The U-shaped kitchen is convenient to the dining room via a casual snack bar. A fireplace brings warmth to the gathering room, making the area cheerful.

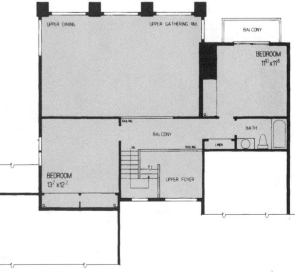

UPPER DINING

UPPER GATHERING RM.

BALCONY

BEDROOM
11¹⁰ x11⁸

BALCONY

RAILING

BATH

RAILING

LINEN

BEDROOM
13² x12²

UPPER FOYER

Design HPT440059

First Floor: 1,831 square feet
Second Floor: 651 square feet
Total: 2,482 square feet
Bonus Room: 394 square feet

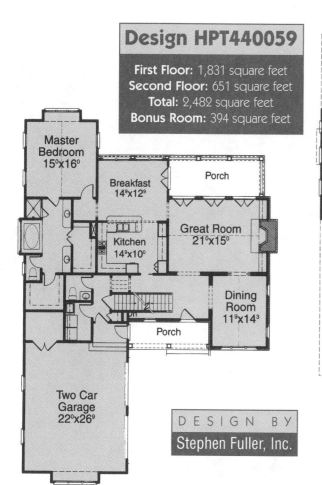

Master Bedroom 15⁰x16⁰

Breakfast 14⁹x12⁹

Porch

Kitchen 14⁹x10⁰

Great Room 21⁰x15⁰

Dining Room 11⁹x14³

Porch

Two Car Garage 22⁰x26⁹

DESIGN BY
Stephen Fuller, Inc.

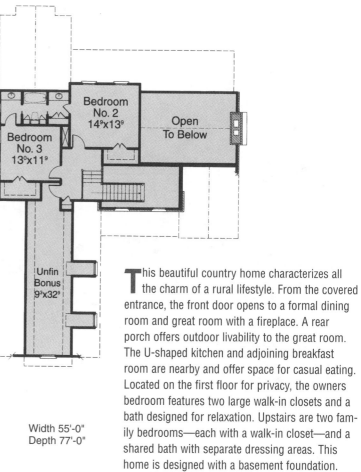

Bedroom No. 2 14⁹x13⁹

Open To Below

Bedroom No. 3 13⁰x11⁹

Unfin Bonus 9⁹x32⁹

Width 55'-0"
Depth 77'-0"

This beautiful country home characterizes all the charm of a rural lifestyle. From the covered entrance, the front door opens to a formal dining room and great room with a fireplace. A rear porch offers outdoor livability to the great room. The U-shaped kitchen and adjoining breakfast room are nearby and offer space for casual eating. Located on the first floor for privacy, the owners bedroom features two large walk-in closets and a bath designed for relaxation. Upstairs are two family bedrooms—each with a walk-in closet—and a shared bath with separate dressing areas. This home is designed with a basement foundation.

ESSENTIAL SPACE

Distinctive Designs For Modern Families

Designs that offer an esthetic, treatment of space honor the homeowner's longing for repose and create rooms that work to make our lives easier and more pleasurable. An impromptu after-dinner gathering, a quiet evening of reading or catching up on correspondence all want space that feels cozy and private; open, but not overwhelming.

Professional couples and smaller families consider plans that offer style, versatility, and—because they usually command a broader discretionary budget—more than a hint of luxury. Whether hosting a Sunday afternoon football gathering or a formal dinner party, today's entertainers want a design that measures up to the occasion: formal dining rooms and casual breakfast nooks, private master suites and gourmet kitchens. Design 9661 (page 114) is filled with great ideas—casually elegant, this home offers plenty of natural light, good inside to outside flow, and a living area that loves a crowd as well as intimate gatherings. Our modern Prairie-style home, Design 2826 (page 117), blends traditional-style architecture with a high, wide and handsome look—it's worth a second glance.

These designs reflect simplicity in shape and space with elegance, drama and style in good measure. And though our up-to-date floor plans offer modern amenities—vaulted ceilings, lots of windows and spacious bathrooms—we know buyers don't want merely a contemporary home, they want a *timeless* home they'll love living in for years.

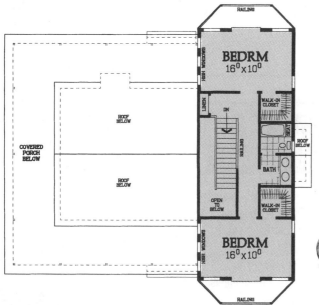

Design 3687

First Floor: 1,374 square feet
Second Floor: 600 square feet
Total: 1,974 square feet

L D

DESIGN BY
Home Planners

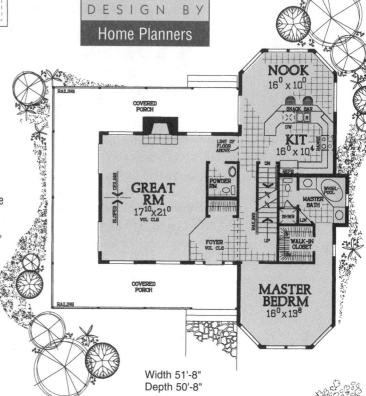

Width 51'-8"
Depth 50'-8"

Balustrades and brackets, dual balconies and a wraparound porch create a country-style exterior reminiscent of soft summer evenings spent watching fireflies and sipping sun tea. Indeed, an aura of hospitality prevails throughout the well-planned interior, starting with a tiled foyer that opens to an expansive two-story great room filled with light from six windows, a fireplace with tiled hearth and a sloped ceiling. A sunny, bayed nook invites casual dining and shares its natural light with a snack counter and a well-appointed U-shaped kitchen. A spacious master suite occupies the bay on the opposite side of the plan and offers a sumptuous bath with corner whirlpool, dual lavatories and walk-in closet. Upstairs, two family bedrooms, each with a private balcony and a walk-in closet, share a full bath with twin lavs.

This home, as shown in the photograph, may differ from the actual blueprints.
For more detailed information, please check the floor plans carefully.

Photo by Bob Greenspan

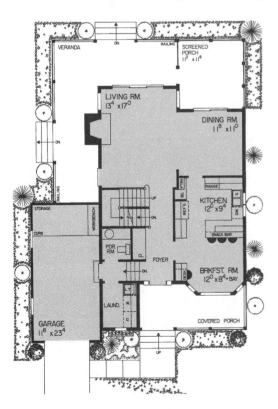

Width 38'
Depth 52'

DESIGN BY
Home Planners

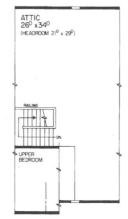

Design 2974

First Floor: 911 square feet
Second Floor: 861 square feet
Total: 1,772 square feet
Attic: 1,131 square feet

L

Cost to build? See page 214
to order complete cost estimate
to build this house in your area!

Victorian homes are well known for their orientation on narrow building sites. This house is 38' wide, but the livability is tremendous. From the front covered porch, the foyer directs traffic all the way to the back of the house with its open living and dining rooms. The U-shaped kitch-en conveniently services both the dining room and the front breakfast room. Both the veranda and the screened porch in the rear living area highlight the outdoor livability in this design. Three bedrooms account for the second floor; the third floor provides ample storage space.

Design 9060

First Floor: 1,326 square feet
Second Floor: 1,086 square feet
Total: 2,412 square feet

The oval-glass front door of this elegant Queen Anne home opens into the foyer, which showcases the bannistered stairs. The spacious family room enjoys a bay-windowed alcove and a fireplace. French doors lead to the game room, which can easily become guest quarters with a private bath. The kitchen offers a walk-in pantry and abundant cabinet and counter space. Adjacent to the bay-windowed breakfast room is a utility area with room for a washer, a dryer, a freezer and a small counter top with cabinets above. A door from this area can provide access to the two-car, detached garage for which plans are included. Upstairs, Bedrooms 2 and 3 each feature walk-in closets, along with built-in bookcases. The master area, with its sitting alcove and special bath, is the perfect retreat.

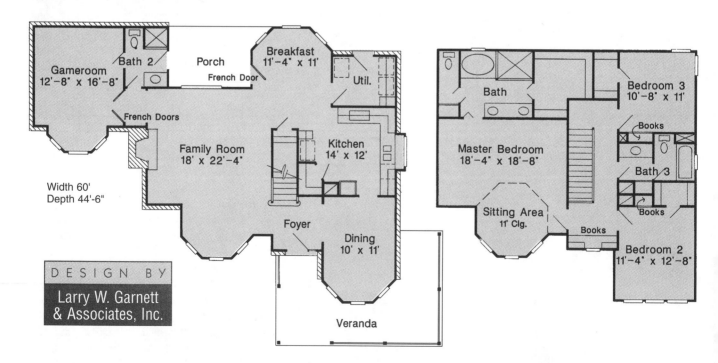

Width 60'
Depth 44'-6"

Gameroom 12'-8" x 16'-8"
Bath 2
Porch
French Door
Breakfast 11'-4" x 11'
Util.
French Doors
Family Room 18' x 22'-4"
Kitchen 14' x 12'
Foyer
Dining 10' x 11'
Veranda

Bath
Master Bedroom 18'-4" x 18'-8"
Bedroom 3 10'-8" x 11'
Books
Bath 3
Books
Sitting Area 11' Clg.
Books
Bedroom 2 11'-4" x 12'-8"

DESIGN BY
Larry W. Garnett & Associates, Inc.

Design 9063

First Floor: 1,236 square feet
Second Floor: 835 square feet
Total: 2,071 square feet

The living area of this spectacular Queen Anne Style home features a fireplace and a bay-windowed alcove. The centrally located kitchen overlooks a dining area with full-length windows and a French door. The master bedroom features a large walk-in closet and French doors opening to the rear veranda. The master bath provides additional closet space, along with a glass-enclosed shower and an oval tub in an octagon-shaped alcove. Upstairs, French doors open into a game room with octagonal bay, which offers views of the front property. Family bedrooms include walk-in closets and raised ceilings, with a raised octagon-shaped ceiling in Bedroom 3. Plans are included for a detached two-car garage and an optional screen porch.

Bedroom 3
10' x 12'-4"
10' Ceiling

Slope Ceiling

Bath

Linen

Books

French Doors

Gameroom
10' x 12'-8"

10' Ceiling

Bedroom 2
14'-4" x 12'-10"
10' Vaulted Ceiling

D E S I G N   B Y
Larry W. Garnett & Associates, Inc.

Cost to build? See page 214 to order complete cost estimate to build this house in your area!

Leaded Glass Transom Windows

11' Ceiling

Bath
Linen

Master Bedroom
14' x 15'

Veranda
French Doors

Dining
10' x 12'

French Door

Pantry

42" Bar

Kitchen
10' x 10'

Screened Porch
10'-8" x 15'
Cathedral Ceiling

Living Room
14'-4" x 17'

Veranda

Width 40'-4"
Depth 62'-10"

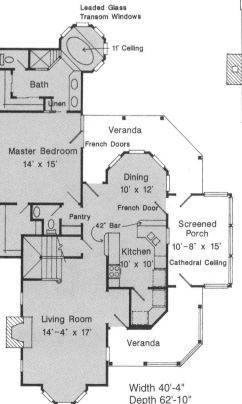

KOIZUMI BUTLER

Design 3620

First Floor: 1,295 square feet
Second Floor: 600 square feet
Total: 1,895 square feet

DESIGN BY

Home Planners

This Southern country farmhouse seems to reach right out and greet you, extending a warm welcome. The octagonal entry hall is balanced by two bay windows—one belonging to the master bedroom, the other to the formal dining room. Inside, Colonial columns and pilasters provide a charming entrance to a two-story family/great room enhanced by a fireplace and three sets of French doors opening onto the rear wraparound porch. An arched opening leads to the L-shaped country kitchen highlighted by a bay-windowed eating area with a window seat. The spacious first-floor master suite is complemented by French doors opening onto the porch and a wealth of closet space. A bay window in the master bath effectively surrounds an old fashioned claw-foot tub. The second floor holds two secondary bedrooms and a full bath. Plans for an optional indoor swimming pool/spa and detached garage are included.

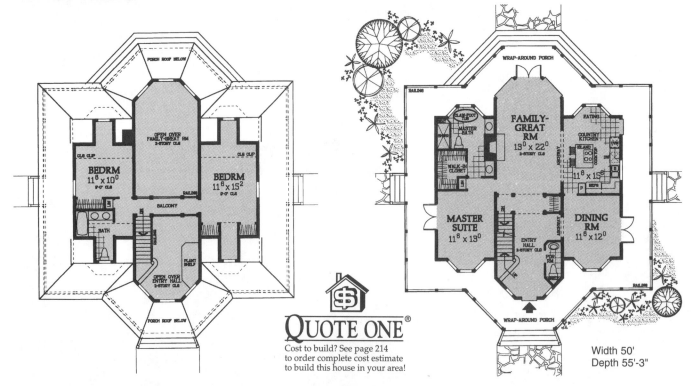

QUOTE ONE®

Cost to build? See page 214
to order complete cost estimate
to build this house in your area!

Width 50'
Depth 55'-3"

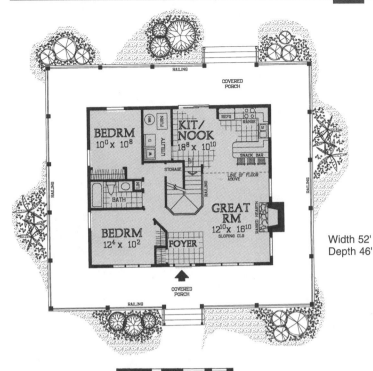

BEDRM
10⁰ x 10⁸

KIT/
NOOK
18⁸ x 10¹⁰

COVERED
PORCH

RAILING

REFG
RANGE

SNACK BAR

UTILITY

FURN

STORAGE

LINE OF FLOOR
ABOVE

BATH
LIN

RAILING

BEDRM
12⁴ x 10²

FOYER

GREAT
RM
12¹⁰ x 16¹⁰
SLOPING CLG

RAISED HEARTH

RAILING

RAILING

COVERED
PORCH

RAILING

Width 52'
Depth 46'

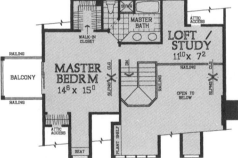

MASTER
BEDRM
14⁶ x 15⁰

WALK-IN
CLOSET

MASTER
BATH

LOFT /
STUDY
11¹⁰ x 7²

ATTIC
ACCESS

BALCONY

RAILING

RAILING

SLOPES CLG

DN

RAILING

OPEN TO
BELOW

ATTIC
ACCESS

PLANT SHELF

SEAT

SLOPES CLG

Design 3681

First Floor: 1,093 square feet
Second Floor: 576 square feet
Total: 1,669 square feet

L **D**

Here's a great country farmhouse with a lot of contemporary appeal—Palladian and arch-topped windows make a sweet complement to the fine details of this classic wraparound porch. The generous use of windows—including two sets of triple muntin windows in the front—adds exciting visual elements to the exterior as well as plenty of natural light to the interior. An impressive tiled entry opens to a two-story great room with a raised hearth and views to the front and side grounds. The U-shaped kitchen conveniently combines with this area and offers a snack counter in addition to a casual dining nook with rear porch access. The family bedrooms reside on the main floor, while an expansive master suite with adjacent study creates a resplendent retreat upstairs, complete with a private balcony, walk-in closet and pampering bath.

QUOTE ONE®
Cost to build? See page 214
to order complete cost estimate
to build this house in your area!

DESIGN BY
Home Planners

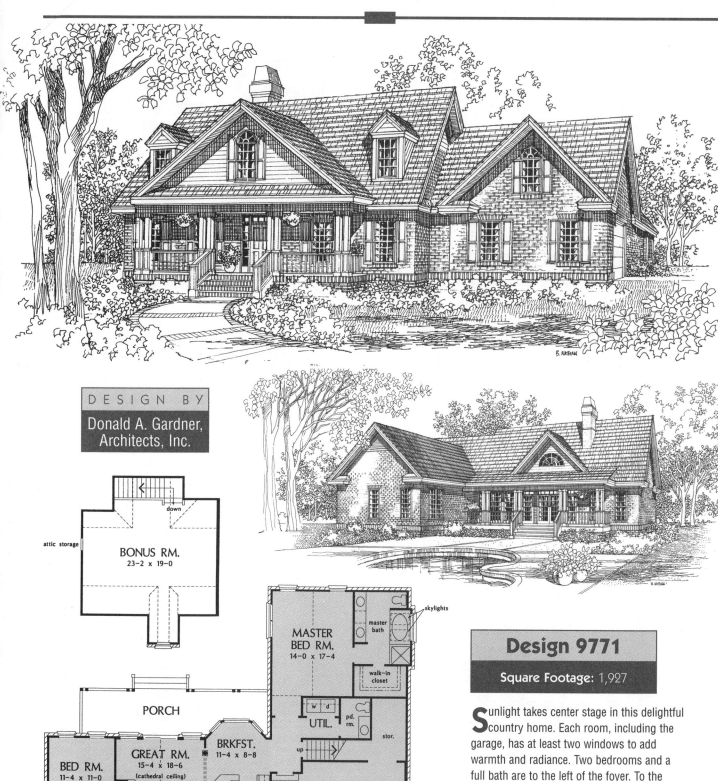

BONUS RM.
23-2 x 19-0

attic storage

down

skylights

master bath

MASTER BED RM.
14-0 x 17-4

walk-in closet

w d

UTIL.

pd. rm.

stor.

up

PORCH

GREAT RM.
15-4 x 18-6
(cathedral ceiling)

BRKFST.
11-4 x 8-8

BED RM.
11-4 x 11-0

cl

lin.

bath

fireplace

KIT.
11-4 x 12-10

GARAGE
23-2 x 22-8

BED RM.
13-8 x 11-8

cl

FOYER
7-4 x 11-8

DINING
14-8 x 11-8

cl

© 1994 Donald A. Gardner Architects, Inc.

PORCH

Width 64'-7"
Depth 64'-2"

Design 9771

Square Footage: 1,927

Sunlight takes center stage in this delightful country home. Each room, including the garage, has at least two windows to add warmth and radiance. Two bedrooms and a full bath are to the left of the foyer. To the right is the dining room which leads into the L-shaped kitchen, which has a peninsular cooktop and adjoining breakfast area with a bay window. The central great room offers a cathedral ceiling, a fireplace and access to the rear porch. The master suite is separated for privacy and features two walls of windows, a large walk-in closet and a luxurious whirlpool bath with skylights. Additional storage space is available in the garage and in the attic.

©1993 Donald A. Gardner Architects, Inc.

B. NATHAN

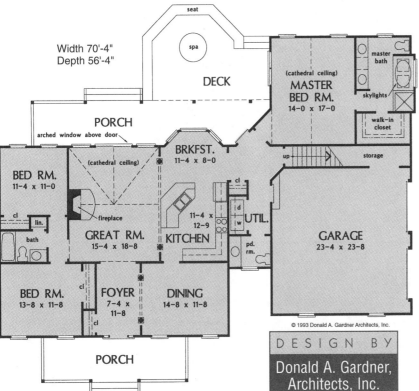

Width 70'-4"
Depth 56'-4"

seat

spa

DECK

PORCH

arched window above door

(cathedral ceiling)

BED RM.
11-4 x 11-0

cl
lin.

bath

fireplace

GREAT RM.
15-4 x 18-8

KITCHEN

11-4 x
12-9

BRKFST.
11-4 x 8-0

(cathedral ceiling)

MASTER
BED RM.
14-0 x 17-0

master
bath

skylights

walk-in
closet

up

storage

cl

d
w

UTIL.

pd.
rm.

GARAGE
23-4 x 23-8

BED RM.
13-8 x 11-8

cl

FOYER
7-4 x
11-8

cl

DINING
14-8 x 11-8

PORCH

© 1993 Donald A. Gardner Architects, Inc.

DESIGN BY
Donald A. Gardner, Architects, Inc.

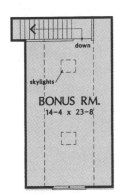

down

skylights

BONUS RM.
14-4 x 23-8

Design 9749

Square Footage: 1,864
Bonus Room: 420 square feet

Quaint and cozy on the outside with front and rear porches, this three-bedroom country home surprises with an open floor plan featuring a large great room with a cathedral ceiling. Nine-foot ceilings add volume throughout the home. A central kitchen with an angled counter opens to the breakfast and great rooms for easy entertaining. The master bedroom is carefully positioned for privacy and offers a cathedral ceiling, garden tub with skylights, roomy walk-in closet and access to the rear deck. Two secondary bedrooms share a full hall bath. A bonus room with skylights may be developed later. Please specify basement or crawlspace foundation when ordering.

This compact design has all the amenities available in larger plans. In addition, a wraparound covered porch, a front Palladian window, dormers and rear arched windows provide exciting visual elements to the exterior. The spacious great room has a fireplace, a cathedral ceiling and clerestory windows. A second-level balcony overlooks this gathering area. The kitchen is centrally located for maximum flexibility in layout and features a pass-through to the great room. Besides the generous master suite with a full bath, there are two family bedrooms located on the second level sharing a full bath with a double vanity. Please specify basement or crawlspace foundation when ordering.

DECK 41-10 x 13-4
spa
seat
seat
GREAT RM. 15-4 x 19-2
BRKFST. 9-0 x 9-2
wash dry cl
UTILITY 7-8 x 6-8
MASTER BED RM. 11-4 x 15-6
fireplace
pass-thru
balcony above
KIT. 12-4 x 12-0
cl
walk-in closet
cl
pd. rm.
DINING 11-4 x 12-8
master bath
FOYER 9-10 x 7-2
up
PORCH
© 1991 Donald A. Gardner Architects, Inc.

clerestory with windows
great room below (cathedral ceiling)
storage
railing
BED RM. 11-4 x 10-2
down
BED RM. 11-4 x 10-2
cl
cl
bath
cl
cl
foyer below
clerestory with palladian window

Design 9621

First Floor: 1,325 square feet
Second Floor: 453 square feet
Total: 1,778 square feet

Width 48'-4"
Depth 51'-10"

QUOTE ONE®
Cost to build? See page 214 to order complete cost estimate to build this house in your area!

DESIGN BY
Donald A. Gardner, Architects, Inc.

This home, as shown in the photograph, may differ from the actual blueprints. For more detailed information, please check the floor plans carefully.

Photo by Jon Riley

Quote One®

Cost to build? See page 214 to order complete cost estimate to build this house in your area!

Design 9645

First Floor: 1,356 square feet
Second Floor: 542 square feet
Total: 1,898 square feet
Bonus Room: 393 square feet

The welcoming charm of this country farmhouse is expressed by its many windows and its covered, wraparound porch. A two-story entrance foyer is enhanced by a Palladian window in a clerestory dormer above to allow natural lighting. A first-floor master suite allows privacy and accessibility. The master bath includes a whirlpool tub, a shower and double-bowl vanity along with a walk-in closet. The first floor features nine-foot ceilings throughout with the exception of the kitchen area, which features an eight-foot ceiling. The second floor provides two additional bedrooms, a full bath and plenty of storage space. An unfinished basement and bonus room provide room to grow. Please specify basement or crawlspace foundation when ordering.

BONUS RM.
23-8 × 14-4

© 1991 Donald A. Gardner Architects, Inc.

Width 59'
Depth 64'

DECK
34-8 × 12-0

GARAGE
20-4 × 21-8

DINING
13-0 × 12-0

KIT.
10-4 × 12-0

BRKFST.
10-8 × 9-8

pd. rm.

UTIL.
dry wash

walk-in closet

master bath

GREAT RM.
13-4 × 19-4

fireplace

FOYER

MASTER BED RM.
13-4 × 13-0

PORCH

© 1991 Donald A. Gardner Architects, Inc.

attic storage — bath — attic storage

BED RM.
13-4 × 10-8

BED RM.
17-0 × 10-8

foyer below

clerestory with palladian window

DESIGN BY
Donald A. Gardner, Architects, Inc.

Photo by Andrew D. Lautman

This home, as shown in the photograph, may differ from the actual blueprints. For more detailed information, please check the floor plans carefully.

Design 3316

First Floor: 1,111 square feet
Second Floor: 886 square feet
Total: 1,997 square feet

L

Don't be fooled by a small-looking exterior. This plan offers three bedrooms and plenty of living space. Notice that the screened porch leads to a rear terrace with access to the breakfast room. A living room/dining room combination adds spaciousness to the floor plan. Other welcome amenities include: boxed-bay windows in the breakfast room and dining room, fireplace in the living room, planning desk and pass-through snack bar in the kitchen, whirlpool tub in the master bath and an open two-story foyer. The thoughtfully placed flower box, outside the kitchen window above the sink, adds a homespun touch to this already comfortable design.

DESIGN BY
Home Planners

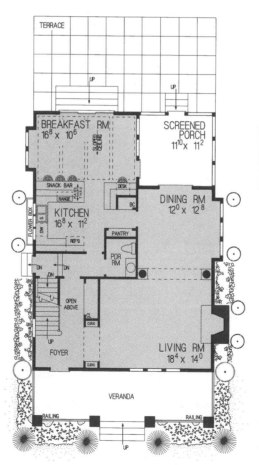

Width 34'-1"
Depth 50'

QUOTE ONE®

Cost to build? See page 214 to order complete cost estimate to build this house in your area!

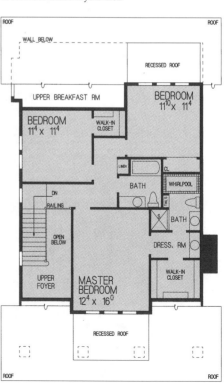

Design HPT440014

Square Footage: 1,925

This three-bedroom farmhouse offers classic style and an up-to-date floor plan. The slope-ceilinged living room offers a fireplace and French-door access to a covered rear porch. The kitchen features a large pantry and is located between the casual eating area and the formal dining room. Two family bedrooms, one with built-in bookshelves and a walk-in closet, share a full bath to the left of the living room. To the right, the master suite includes a dressing room and a full bath with a walk-in closet. Please specify crawlspace or slab foundation when ordering.

DESIGN BY
Breland & Farmer Designers, Inc.

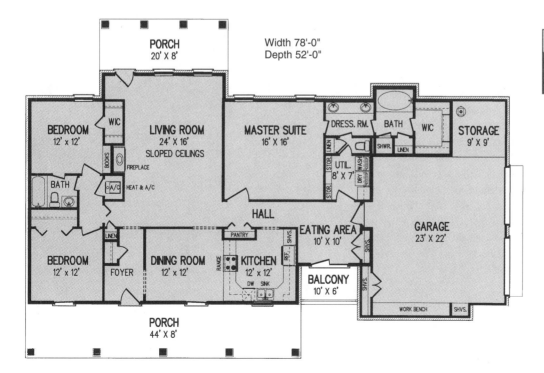

Width 78'-0"
Depth 52'-0"

PORCH 20' X 8'

BEDROOM 12' x 12'
WIC
LIVING ROOM 24' X 16' SLOPED CEILINGS
fireplace
BOOKS
HEAT & A/C
A/C

MASTER SUITE 16' X 16'
DRESS. RM.
BATH
WIC
STORAGE 9' X 9'
LINEN
SHWR.
LINEN

BATH

STOR.
UTIL. 8' X 7'
DRY
WASH

HALL
LINEN
FOYER
PANTRY
SHVS.

BEDROOM 12' x 12'
DINING ROOM 12' x 12'
RANGE
KITCHEN 12' x 12'
DW   SINK
REF.

EATING AREA 10' X 10'
SHVS.
GARAGE 23' X 22'

BALCONY 10' X 6'
SHVS.

WORK BENCH
SHVS.

PORCH 44' X 8'

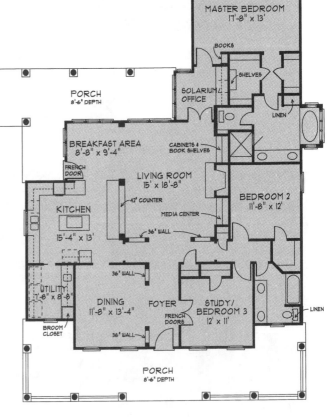

2 - CAR GARAGE
21'-4" x 23'-4"

PORCH
8'-6" DEPTH

MASTER BEDROOM
17'-8" x 13'

BOOKS

SHELVES

SOLARIUM/
OFFICE

LINEN

BREAKFAST AREA
8'-8" x 9'-4"

CABINETS &
BOOK SHELVES

FRENCH
DOOR

LIVING ROOM
15' x 18'-8"

BEDROOM 2
11'-8" x 12'

42" COUNTER

KITCHEN
15'-4" x 13'

MEDIA CENTER

36" WALL

36" WALL

UTILITY
7'-8" x 8'-8"

DINING
11'-8" x 13'-4"

FOYER

STUDY/
BEDROOM 3
12' x 11'

LINEN

BROOM
CLOSET

FRENCH
DOORS

36" WALL

PORCH
8'-6" DEPTH

This is not just an average farmhouse plan. It was designed to delight and cater to those looking for special details. The full front porch greets all comers and leads to a center-hall foyer. On the left is a formal dining room accented by half-walls. On the right is a study or bedroom that is accessed through French doors. The main living area has a fireplace, built in bookshelves and cabinets and a media center. It is open to the breakfast area and island kitchen. The master suite features a small solarium/office. A pampering bath containing two large walk-in closets, a bumped-out tub, a shower and dual vanities enhance the master suite. An additional family bedroom also has a walk-in closet. The two-car garage can be reached via the rear covered porch.

Design 8997

Square Footage: 2,077

Width 50'-4"
Depth 69'-10"

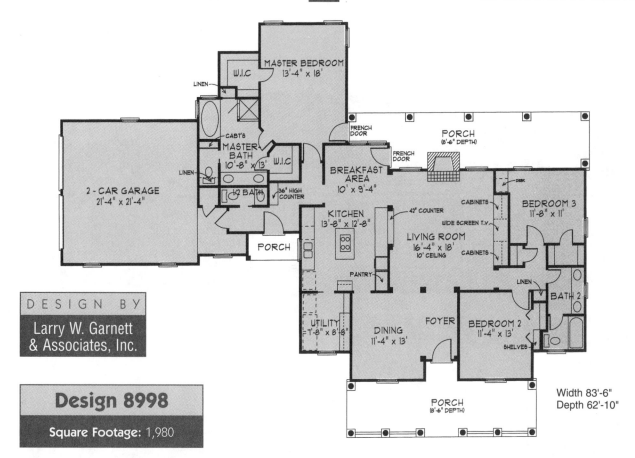

MASTER BEDROOM
13'-4" x 18'

W.I.C

LINEN

FRENCH DOOR

PORCH
(8'-6" DEPTH)

CABT'S

MASTER BATH
10'-8" x 13'

LINEN

W.I.C

BREAKFAST AREA
10' x 9'-4"

DESK

CABINETS

BEDROOM 3
11'-8" x 11'

1/2 BATH

36" HIGH COUNTER

42" COUNTER

WIDE SCREEN T.V.

2 - CAR GARAGE
21'-4" x 21'-4"

KITCHEN
13'-8" x 12'-8"

LIVING ROOM
16'-4" x 18'
10' CEILING

CABINETS

PORCH

PANTRY

LINEN

BATH 2

UTILITY
7'-8" x 8'-8"

DINING
11'-4" x 13'

FOYER

BEDROOM 2
11'-4" x 13'

SHELVES

PORCH
(8'-6" DEPTH)

Width 83'-6"
Depth 62'-10"

DESIGN BY
Larry W. Garnett & Associates, Inc.

Design 8998

Square Footage: 1,980

Encompassing just one floor, this farmhouse plan provides excellent livability. From the large covered porch, the foyer opens to a dining room on the left and a center living room with space for a wide-screen TV flanked by cabinets and a fireplace with a scenic view on each side. The large kitchen sports an island cooktop and easy accessibility to the rear breakfast

area, the utility room, and the dining room. While the family bedrooms reside on the right side of the plan and share a full bath with twin vanities, the master bedroom takes advantage of its secluded rear location. It features twin walk-in closets and vanities, a windowed corner tub, a separate shower and private access to the rear covered porch.

Design 3461

First Floor: 1,391 square feet
Second Floor: 611 square feet
Total: 2,002 square feet

L

Muntin windows, shutters and flower boxes add exterior appeal to this well-designed family farmhouse. The high ceiling, open staircase and wide, columned opening to the living room all lend themselves to an impressive entry foyer. In the living room, a long expanse of windows and two, long blank walls for effective furniture placement set the pace. Informal living takes off in the open kitchen and family room. An island cooktop will be a favorite feature, as will the fireplace. On the way to the garage, with its workshop area, is the laundry room and its handy closet. Sleeping accommodations are defined by the master bedroom where a bay window provides a perfect sitting nook. The master bath has a large, walk-in closet, a vanity, twin lavatories, a stall shower and a whirlpool tub. Three family bedrooms reside upstairs.

Width 64'
Depth 44'

DESIGN BY

Home Planners

Cost to build? See page 214 to order complete cost estimate to build this house in your area!

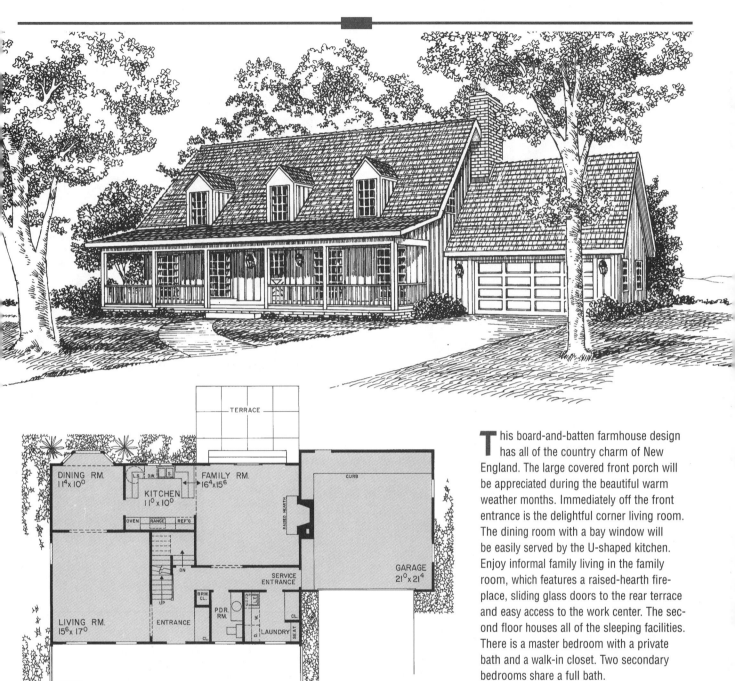

TERRACE

DINING RM.
11⁴ x 10⁰

KITCHEN
11⁰ x 10⁰

FAMILY RM.
16⁴ x 15⁶

CURB

OVEN RANGE REF'G

RAISED HEARTH

GARAGE
21⁰ x 21⁴

DN

SERVICE ENTRANCE

UP

BRM. CL.

PDR. RM.

LIVING RM.
15⁶ x 17⁰

ENTRANCE

CL.

LAUNDRY

CL.

SEAT

PORCH

Width 61'-4"
Depth 38'

This board-and-batten farmhouse design has all of the country charm of New England. The large covered front porch will be appreciated during the beautiful warm weather months. Immediately off the front entrance is the delightful corner living room. The dining room with a bay window will be easily served by the U-shaped kitchen. Enjoy informal family living in the family room, which features a raised-hearth fireplace, sliding glass doors to the rear terrace and easy access to the work center. The second floor houses all of the sleeping facilities. There is a master bedroom with a private bath and a walk-in closet. Two secondary bedrooms share a full bath.

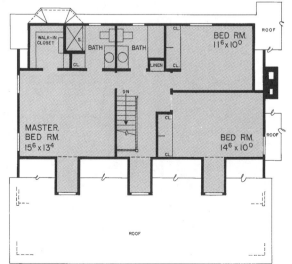

WALK-IN CLOSET

BATH

BATH

LINEN

CL.

CL.

BED RM.
11⁶ x 10⁰

ROOF

MASTER. BED RM.
15⁶ x 13⁴

DN

CL.

BED RM.
14⁶ x 10⁰

ROOF

ROOF

Design 2776

First Floor: 1,134 square feet
Second Floor: 874 square feet
Total: 2,008 square feet

L D

DESIGN BY

Home Planners

QUOTE ONE®

Cost to build? See page 214
to order complete cost estimate
to build this house in your area!

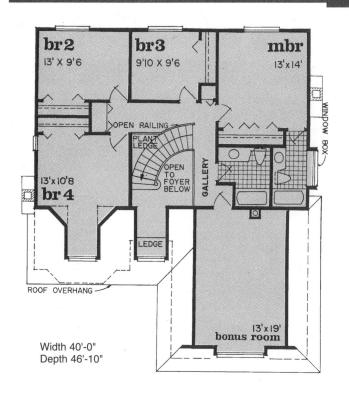

br 2
13' X 9'6

br 3
9'10 X 9'6

mbr
13'x14'

OPEN RAILING

PLANT LEDGE

OPEN TO FOYER BELOW

GALLERY

WINDOW BOX

13'x10'8
br 4

LEDGE

ROOF OVERHANG

Width 40'-0"
Depth 46'-10"

13'x19'
bonus room

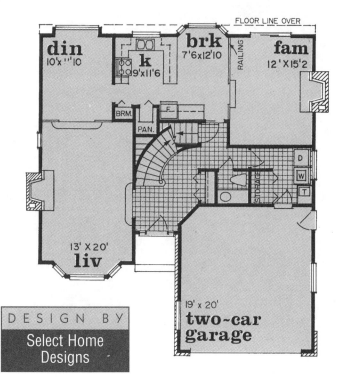

din
10'x''10

k
9'x11'6

brk
7'6x12'10

fam
12'X15'2

FLOOR LINE OVER

BRM.

PAN.

RAILING

STORAGE

D

W

T

13' X 20'
liv

19' x 20'
two~car garage

Dormer windows, a Palladian window over the garage and a bumped-out bay add to this home's quaint appeal. Inside, a sweeping, curved staircase dominates the two-story foyer. The spacious, sunken living room features a front-view bay and a fireplace. The attached dining room has a box-bay overlooking the rear yard. The U-shaped kitchen is appointed with a walk-in pantry and a broom closet. The attached breakfast nook overlooks the sunken family room. On the second level are three family bedrooms and a master bedroom, which has a private bath.

Design HPT440015

First Floor: 1,167 square feet
Second Floor: 1,095 square feet
Total: 2,262 square feet
Bonus Room: 260 square feet

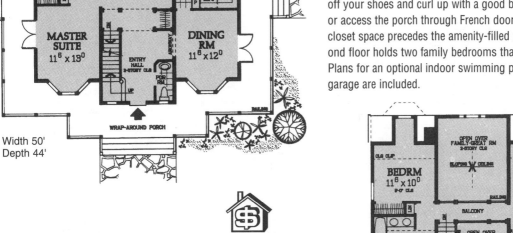

There's nothing that tops gracious Southern hospitality—unless it's offered Southern farmhouse style! The entry hall opens through an archway on the right to a formal dining room. Nearby, the efficient country kitchen shares space with a bay-windowed eating area. The two-story family/great room is warmed by a fireplace in the winter and open to outdoor country comfort in the summer via double French doors. The first floor master suite offers room to kick off your shoes and curl up with a good book by the bay window or access the porch through French doors. An abundance of closet space precedes the amenity-filled master bath. The second floor holds two family bedrooms that share a full bath. Plans for an optional indoor swimming pool/spa and detached garage are included.

Design 3619

First Floor: 1,171 square feet
Second Floor: 600 square feet
Total: 1,771 square feet

L **D**

Width 50'
Depth 44'

The exterior of this three-bedroom country-style home is enhanced by its many gables, arched windows and wrap-around porch. A large great room with an impressive fireplace leads to both the dining room and screened porch. Sized for entertaining, the deck wraps to provide room for a spa and outdoor dining space adjacent to the dining room and the informal breakfast area. An open kitchen offers a country-kitchen atmosphere. The second-level master suite has two walk-in closets and an impressive bath enhanced with a bumped-out tub. Two family bedrooms share a full bath and plenty of storage. Bonus space over the garage can be developed for future use.

SCREENED PORCH
13-0 × 11-0

DECK

DINING
12-0 × 12-4

KITCHEN
11-4 × 11-4

DECK

fireplace

storage

BRKFST.
11-4 × 8-4

GREAT RM.
13-0 × 22-4

FOYER

balcony above

up

UTILITY
9-0 × 7-4

d

w

PORCH

storage

GARAGE
20-8 × 24-0

© 1991 Donald A. Gardner Architects, Inc.

Width 53'-8"
Depth 67'-8"

master bath

closet

closet

cl

BED RM.
11-0 × 12-4

BED RM.
10-0 × 12-4

down

walk-in closet

sto.   storage

MASTER BED RM.
13-0 × 14-4

balcony

foyer below

bath

sto.

BONUS RM.
12-4 × 24-0

Design 9662

First Floor: 1,025 square feet
Second Floor: 911 square feet
Total: 1,936 square feet

QUOTE ONE®

Cost to build? See page 214 to order complete cost estimate to build this house in your area!

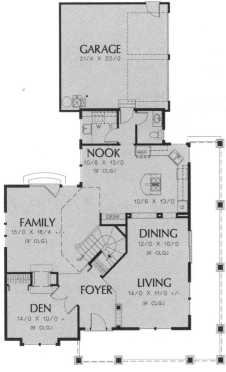

GARAGE
21/4 X 20/0

NOOK
10/6 X 13/0
(9' CLG.)

10/6 X 13/0

FAMILY
15/0 X 16/4
(9' CLG.)

DESK

DINING
12/0 X 10/0
(9' OLG.)

FOYER

LIVING
14/0 X 11/0 +/-
(9' CLG.)

DEN
14/0 X 10/0 +
(9' CLG.)

UP

REF.

W   D

Width 43'
Depth 69'

BR. 3
10/6 X 13/0

FAMILY
BELOW

PLANT
SHELF

BR. 2
12/4 X 11/0

LINEN

DN

VAULTED
MASTER
12/0 X 15/0

DESIGN BY

Alan Mascord
Design Associates, Inc.

Design 9557

First Floor: 1,371 square feet
Second Floor: 916 square feet
Total: 2,287 square feet

The decorative pillars and the wrap-around porch are just the beginning of this comfortable home. Inside, an angled, U-shaped stairway leads to the second-floor sleeping zone. On the first floor, French doors lead to a bay-windowed den that shares a see-through fireplace with the two-story family room. The large island kitchen includes a writing desk, a corner sink, a breakfast nook and access to the laundry room, the powder room and the two-car garage. The master suite provides ultimate relaxation with its French-door access, vaulted ceiling and luxurious bath. Two other bedrooms and a full bath complete the second floor.

Photo by Riley & Riley Photography, Inc.

This home, as shown in the photograph, may differ from the actual blueprints. For more detailed information, please check the floor plans carefully.

Width 70'-0"
Depth 79'-2"

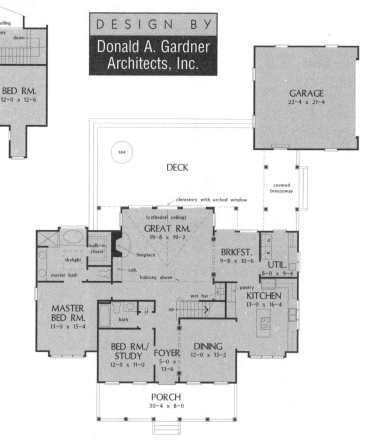

Design HPT440016

First Floor: 1,783 square feet
Second Floor: 611 square feet
Total: 2,394 square feet

Onlookers will delight in the symmetry of this facade's arched windows and dormers. The interior offers a great room with a cathedral ceiling. This open plan is packed with the latest design features, including a kitchen with a large island, a wet bar, a bedroom/study combo on the first floor and a gorgeous master suite with a spa-style bath. Upstairs, two family bedrooms share a compartmented hall bath. An expansive rear deck and generous covered front porch offer maximum outdoor livability.

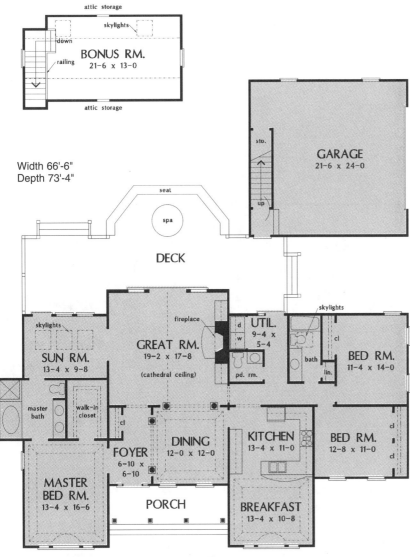

attic storage

skylights

down

BONUS RM.
21-6 x 13-0

railing

attic storage

Width 66'-6"
Depth 73'-4"

seat

spa

GARAGE
21-6 x 24-0

sto.

up

DECK

skylights

fireplace

d w

UTIL.
9-4 x
5-4

skylights

bath

cl

lin.

BED RM.
11-4 x 14-0

GREAT RM.
19-2 x 17-8

(cathedral ceiling)

pd. rm.

SUN RM.
13-4 x 9-8

skylights

master
bath

walk-in
closet

cl

cl

FOYER
6-10 x
6-10

DINING
12-0 x 12-0

KITCHEN
13-4 x 11-0

BED RM.
12-8 x 11-0

cl

**MASTER
BED RM.**
13-4 x 16-6

PORCH

BREAKFAST
13-4 x 10-8

© 1997 Donald A Gardner Architects, Inc.

Design HPT440017

Square Footage: 2,058
Bonus Room: 349 square feet

DESIGN BY
**Donald A. Gardner
Architects, Inc.**

This three-bedroom country home lets the light shine in through skylights, transoms and Palladian windows, while special ceiling treatments in key rooms add distinction and an air of spaciousness. The great room features a cathedral ceiling and a fireplace flanked by built-in cabinets, while French doors encourage outdoor living on the expansive rear deck. The practical U-shaped kitchen is open to the breakfast room, creating the feel of a big country kitchen. The master suite provides a generous walk-in closet and a bath with access to the skylit sun room. Two more bedrooms, located on the opposite side of the house, share another full bath.

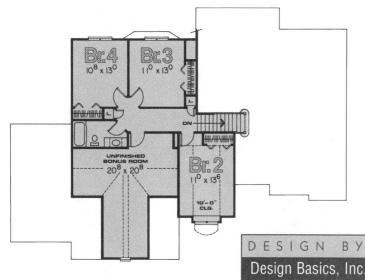

Design HPT440018

First Floor: 1,597 square feet
Second Floor: 685 square feet
Total: 2,282 square feet
Bonus Room: 337 square feet

DESIGN BY
Design Basics, Inc.

Width 65'-4"
Depth 48'-8"

A comfortable family atmosphere is created by the warmth of the covered front porch of this 1½-story home. The entry leads to the formal dining room, which offers hutch space. A well-organized kitchen boasts a central food-preparation island, efficient cabinet space, an ample pantry and a windowed sink. The breakfast area shares a through-fireplace with the spacious great room, which offers three transom windows. The master bedroom features a tray ceiling and a relaxing private bath with a window seat and tiled whirlpool tub area. Upstairs, three secondary bedrooms share a full bath and a hall that leads to a generous bonus space. Please specify basement or slab foundation when ordering.

Design HPT440019

First Floor: 1,369 square feet
Second Floor: 1,111 square feet
Total: 2,480 square feet

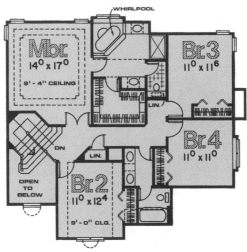

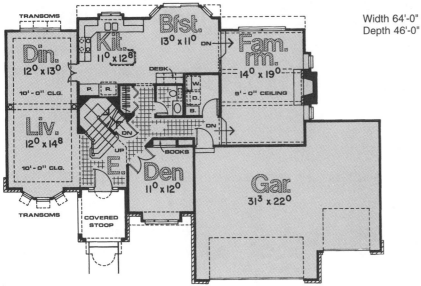

Width 64'-0"
Depth 46'-0"

This delightful plan offers the best in transitional design. Combined dining and living areas provide abundant space for formal entertaining or holiday gatherings. Or if preferred, escape to the den for quiet time with a book—built-in bookshelves fill out one wall of this room. The kitchen makes use of island counter space and a breakfast nook. Take a step down into the large family room and enjoy the ambiance of a cozy fireplace and beam ceiling. A laundry room and powder room round out the first floor. The master bedroom—with a tiered ceiling and a bath with a whirlpool tub—highlights the second floor. Three additional bedrooms and another full bath complete the design.

DESIGN BY
Design Basics, Inc.

Design 3340

Square Footage: 1,611

L

A skylit covered porch extends an invitation to enjoy all seasons in comfort. The interior provides its own special appeal. Bedrooms are effectively arranged to the front of the plan, out of the traffic flow of the house. One bedroom could double nicely as a TV room or study. The adjacent master bedroom provides the ultimate in relaxation and features a large walk-in closet and a private bath. The living room/dining area features a fireplace, sliding glass doors to the skylit porch, and an open staircase with a built-in planter. The breakfast room provides a built-in desk—making it a breeze to get organized—and also accesses the rear covered porch for extended outdoor dining. An efficient U-shaped kitchen and a laundry room complete the plan.

QUOTE ONE®

Cost to build? See page 214 to order complete cost estimate to build this house in your area!

DESIGN BY
Home Planners

Width 58'
Depth 52'-6"

© 1985 Donald A. Gardner Architects, Inc.

Design 9619

Square Footage: 2,021

DESIGN BY
Donald A. Gardner, Architects, Inc.

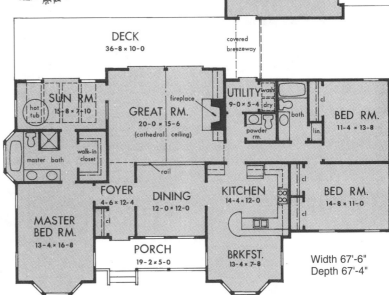

Multi-pane windows, dormers, bay windows and a delightful covered porch provide a neighborly welcome into this delightful country cottage. The great room contains a fireplace, a cathedral ceiling and sliding glass doors with an arched window above to allow for natural illumination. A sunroom with a hot tub leads to an adjacent deck. This space can also be reached from the master bath. The generous master suite is filled with amenities that include a walk-in closet and a spacious bath with a double-bowl vanity, a shower and a garden tub. Two additional bedrooms are located at the other end of the house for privacy. The garage is connected to the house by a breezeway. Please specify basement or crawlspace foundation when ordering.

GARAGE
20-4 × 20-4

DECK
36-8 × 10-0

covered breezeway

SUN RM.
15-8 × 7-10

hot tub

GREAT RM.
20-0 × 15-6
(cathedral ceiling)

fireplace

UTILITY
9-0 × 5-4

wash
dry

bath

powder rm.

BED RM.
11-4 × 13-8

lin.

cl

walk-in closet

master bath

rail

FOYER
4-6 × 12-4

DINING
12-0 × 12-0

KITCHEN
14-4 × 12-0

cl

BED RM.
14-8 × 11-0

cl

MASTER BED RM.
13-4 × 16-8

PORCH
19-2 × 5-0

BRKFST.
13-4 × 7-8

Width 67'-6"
Depth 67'-4"

An eclectic mix of building materials—stone, stucco and siding—sing in tune with the European charm of this one-story home. Decorative columns set off the formal dining room and foyer from the vaulted family room, while the formal living room is quietly tucked behind French doors. The master bedroom has an elegant tray ceiling, bay sitting area and a lush bath. Two family bedrooms located on the right side of the plan include walk-in closets and share a dual-basin bath. Please specify basement, crawlspace or slab foundation when ordering.

DESIGN BY
Frank Betz
Associates, Inc.

QUOTE ONE®
Cost to build? See page 214 to order complete cost estimate to build this house in your area!

Width 62'-0"
Depth 61'-0"

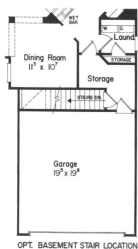

OPT. BASEMENT STAIR LOCATION

Design HPT440020

Square Footage: 2,322

DESIGN BY
Stephen Fuller, Inc.

QUOTE ONE®
Cost to build? See page 214
to order complete cost estimate
to build this house in your area!

PORCH

BEDROOM/
OFFICE
10'-4" X 11'-0"

BREAKFAST
13'-4" X 9'-0"

KITCHEN
13'-4" X 10'-6"

GREAT ROOM
17'-0" X 17'-8"

MASTER
BATH

MASTER BEDROOM
16'-4" X 13'-6"

BEDROOM NO. 2
10'-4" X 12'-0"

BATH

LAUNDRY

DN.

BATH

TWO CAR GARAGE
20'-6" X 19'-6"

DINING ROOM
11'-4" X 12'-10"

FOYER
5'-4" X
12'-10"

BEDROOM/
STUDY
11'-2" X 12'-0"

PORCH

Width 61'
Depth 70'-6"

Design 9853

Square Footage: 2,090

This traditional home features board-and-batten and cedar shingles in an attractively proportioned exterior. Finishing touches include a covered entrance and porch with column detailing and an arched transom, flower boxes and shuttered windows. The foyer opens to both the dining room and the great room, with French doors opening onto the porch. Through the double doors to the right of the foyer is the combination bedroom/study. A short hallway leads to a full bath and a secondary bedroom with ample closet space. The master bedroom is spacious, with walk-in closets on both sides of the entrance to the master bath. With separate vanities, a shower and a toilet, the master bath forms a private retreat at the rear of the home. Convenient to both the great room and dining room, the kitchen opens to an attractive breakfast area featuring a bay window. An additional room is remotely located off the kitchen, providing a retreat for today's at-home office or for guests. This home is designed with a basement foundation.

Design 9088

Square Footage: 1,994

This design offers an abundance of space and style at a budget-conscious price. A well-lit formal dining area with a ten-foot ceiling is just off the decorative foyer, which opens ahead to a grand living room designed for formal as well as informal entertaining. This area offers a centered fireplace with flanking French doors and leads to a sunny bayed nook for casual dining. An angled, peninsular counter leaves the kitchen open to the living area. Sleeping quarters define the left side of the plan. The master suite features a corner tub and a glass-enclosed shower with seat. A large utility room and storage area occupy space in the garage.

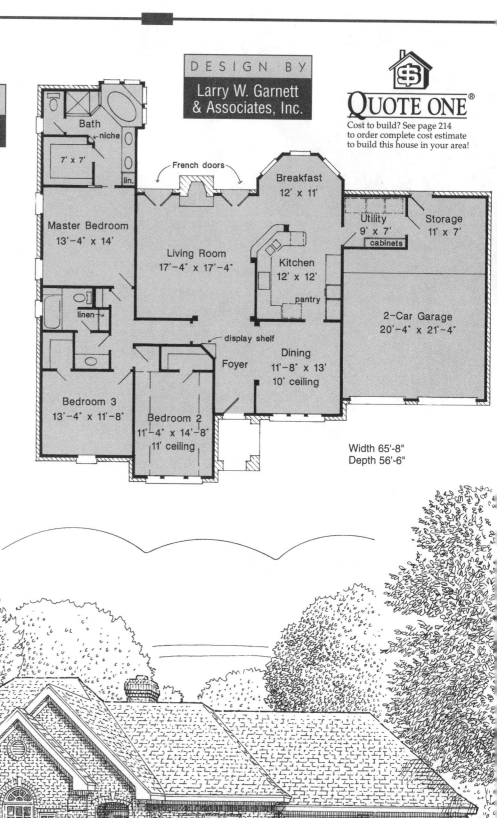

DESIGN BY
Larry W. Garnett & Associates, Inc.

QUOTE ONE®
Cost to build? See page 214
to order complete cost estimate
to build this house in your area!

Bath

niche

7' x 7'

French doors

lin.

Master Bedroom
13'-4" x 14'

Living Room
17'-4" x 17'-4"

Breakfast
12' x 11'

Utility
9' x 7'

Storage
11' x 7'

cabinets

Kitchen
12' x 12'

pantry

2-Car Garage
20'-4" x 21'-4"

linen

display shelf

Foyer

Dining
11'-8" x 13'
10' ceiling

Bedroom 3
13'-4" x 11'-8"

Bedroom 2
11'-4" x 14'-8"
11' ceiling

Width 65'-8"
Depth 56'-6"

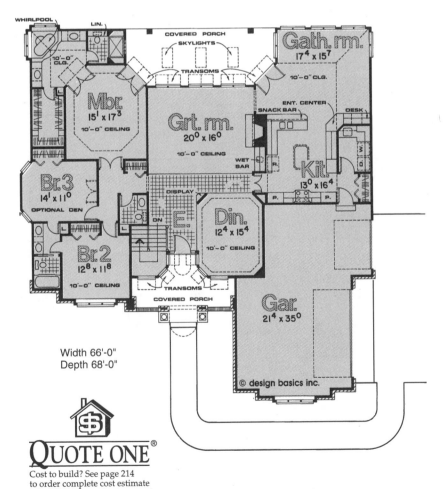

WHIRLPOOL
LIN.

COVERED PORCH
SKYLIGHTS
TRANSOMS

Gath. rm.
17⁴ x 15⁷

10'-0" CLG.

10'-0" CLG.

Mbr.
15¹ x 17³
10'-0" CEILING

Grt. rm.
20⁰ x 16⁰
10'-0" CEILING

ENT. CENTER
SNACK BAR

DESK

Kit.
13⁰ x 16⁴

WET BAR

Br. 3
14¹ x 11⁰
OPTIONAL DEN

DISPLAY

Din.
12⁴ x 15⁴
10'-0" CEILING

Br. 2
12⁸ x 11⁸
10'-0" CEILING

DN

E.

Gar.
21⁴ x 35⁰

TRANSOMS
COVERED PORCH

© design basics inc.

Width 66'-0"
Depth 68'-0"

Design HPT440021

Square Footage: 2,456

Gently tapered columns set off an elegant arched entry framed by multi-pane windows. Inside, an open great room features a wet bar, fireplace, tall transom windows and access to a covered porch with skylights. The gourmet kitchen boasts a food-preparation island and a snack bar, and overlooks the gathering room. Double doors open to the master suite, where French doors lead to a private bath with an angled whirlpool tub and a sizable walk-in closet. One of two nearby family bedrooms could serve as a den, with optional French doors opening from a hall central to the sleeping wing.

DESIGN BY
Design Basics, Inc.

Design 9894

Square Footage: 1,733

Delightfully different, this brick one-story home has everything for the active family. The foyer opens to a formal dining room accented with decorative columns, and to a great room with a warming fireplace and lovely French doors to the rear deck. The efficient kitchen has an attached, light-filled breakfast nook. A split bedroom plan offers a secluded master suite with coffered ceiling, His and Hers walk-in closets, double vanity and garden tub. Two family bedrooms, or one and a study, have separate access to a full bath on the left side of the plan. This home is designed with a basement foundation.

DESIGN BY
Stephen Fuller, Inc.

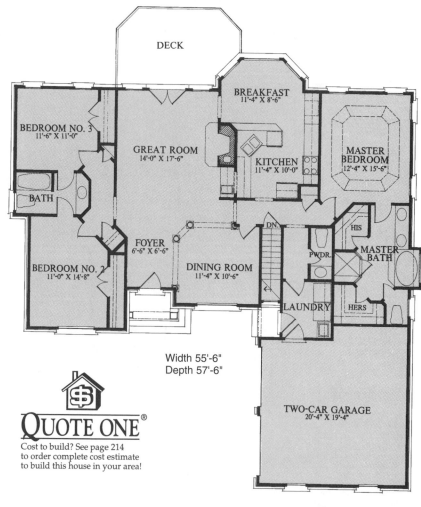

Width 55'-6"
Depth 57'-6"

QUOTE ONE®

Cost to build? See page 214
to order complete cost estimate
to build this house in your area!

Design HPT440022

Square Footage: 2,276

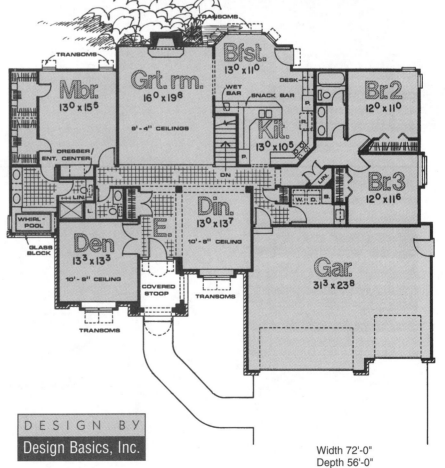

Drama and harmony are expressed by utilizing a variety of elegant exterior materials. An expansive entry views the private den with French doors and an open dining room—both rooms have extra-high ceilings. The great room, with a window-framed fireplace, is conveniently located next to the eat-in kitchen with its bayed breakfast area. Special amenities include a wet bar/servery, two pantries, a planning desk and snack bar. Two secluded secondary bedrooms enjoy easy access to a compartmented bath with a twin vanity. His and Hers closets and a built-in armoire that could be an entertainment center or a dresser grace the master bedroom.

DESIGN BY
Design Basics, Inc.

Width 72'-0"
Depth 56'-0"

Design 9840

Square Footage: 1,684
(without basement)

Charmingly compact, this one-story home is as beautiful as it is practical. The grace of an impressive arch over the double front door is echoed by an arched window in the formal dining room. The theme continues with columned archways that open the dining area to the great room, where lovely double doors lead to the rear deck. A handsome fireplace with extended hearth warms this area in the winter. Nearby a well-appointed kitchen with adjoining bayed breakfast nook with its own access to the rear deck offers an informal gathering space. Split bedrooms create privacy for the master suite with a splendid bath and His and Hers walk-in closets. Additional space in the basement may be developed later.

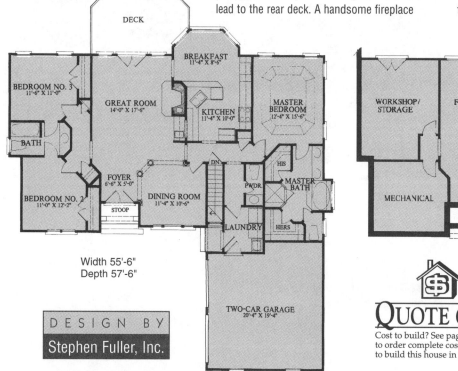

Width 55'-6"
Depth 57'-6"

DESIGN BY
Stephen Fuller, Inc.

QUOTE ONE®

Cost to build? See page 214
to order complete cost estimate
to build this house in your area!

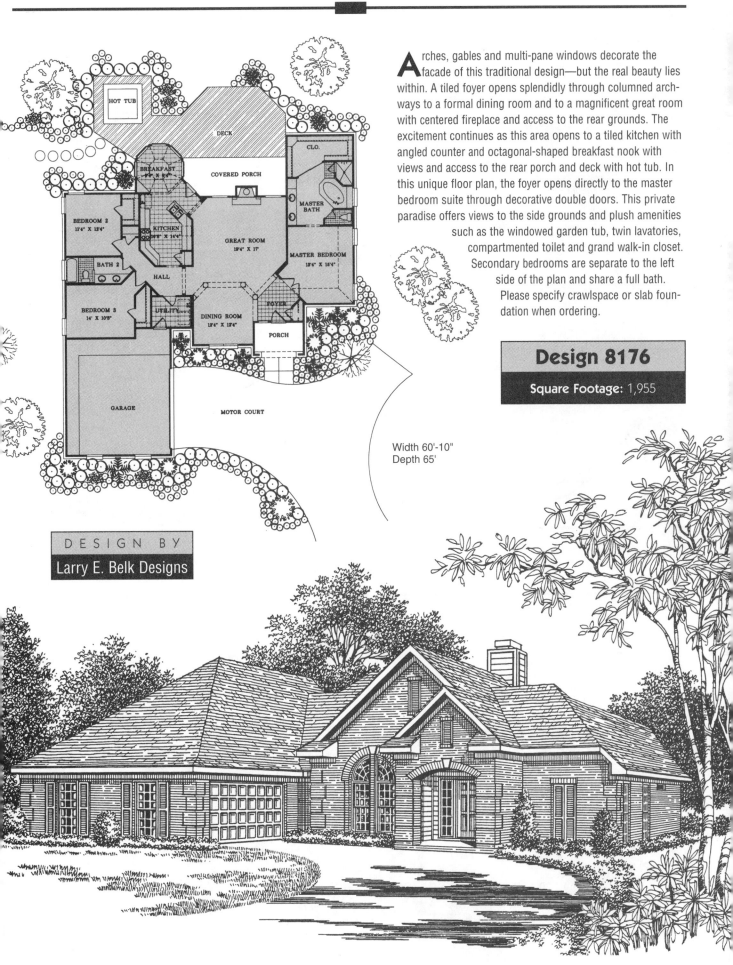

Arches, gables and multi-pane windows decorate the facade of this traditional design—but the real beauty lies within. A tiled foyer opens splendidly through columned archways to a formal dining room and to a magnificent great room with centered fireplace and access to the rear grounds. The excitement continues as this area opens to a tiled kitchen with angled counter and octagonal-shaped breakfast nook with views and access to the rear porch and deck with hot tub. In this unique floor plan, the foyer opens directly to the master bedroom suite through decorative double doors. This private paradise offers views to the side grounds and plush amenities such as the windowed garden tub, twin lavatories, compartmented toilet and grand walk-in closet. Secondary bedrooms are separate to the left side of the plan and share a full bath. Please specify crawlspace or slab foundation when ordering.

Design 8176
Square Footage: 1,955

Width 60'-10"
Depth 65'

DESIGN BY
Larry E. Belk Designs

HOT TUB

DECK

BREAKFAST

COVERED PORCH

CLO.

MASTER BATH

BEDROOM 2
11'4" X 12'4"

KITCHEN
10'8" X 14'4"

GREAT ROOM
19'4" X 17'

MASTER BEDROOM
15'4" X 15'4"

BATH 2

HALL

BEDROOM 3
14' X 10'8"

UTILITY

DINING ROOM
12'4" X 12'4"

FOYER

PORCH

GARAGE

MOTOR COURT

DESIGN BY

Breland & Farmer
Designers, Inc.

Width 56'-0"
Depth 93'-0"

Design HPT440023

Square Footage: 2,259

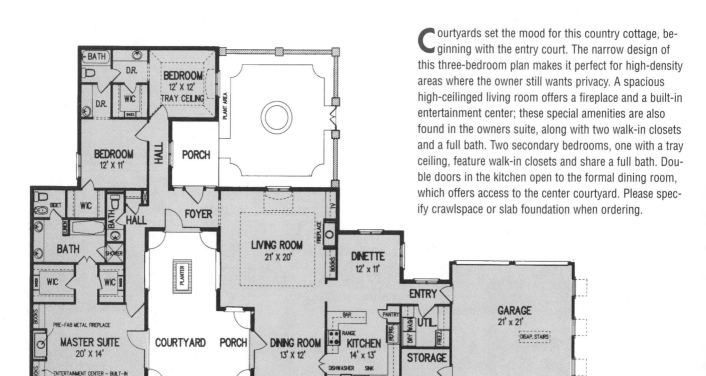

Courtyards set the mood for this country cottage, beginning with the entry court. The narrow design of this three-bedroom plan makes it perfect for high-density areas where the owner still wants privacy. A spacious high-ceilinged living room offers a fireplace and a built-in entertainment center; these special amenities are also found in the owners suite, along with two walk-in closets and a full bath. Two secondary bedrooms, one with a tray ceiling, feature walk-in closets and share a full bath. Double doors in the kitchen open to the formal dining room, which offers access to the center courtyard. Please specify crawlspace or slab foundation when ordering.

Quote One®

Cost to build? See page 214
to order complete cost estimate
to build this house in your area!

Design 8923

Square Footage: 2,361

Floor plan labels:

- Bath
- linen
- Master Bedroom 13' x 18' 10' stepped ceiling
- Living Area 16' x 20'
- Screened Porch
- sliding French doors
- French doors
- Breakfast 10' x 10' 13' ceiling
- display niche
- French doors
- Bedroom 2 12'-8" x 14'-4"
- Bath
- Kitchen 12' x 12'
- Foyer 10' clg.
- Gallery 10' clg.
- Bath
- books
- Study/Br 4 11'-4" x 13' 10' ceiling
- Dining 12' x 14' 13' clg.
- Util.
- books
- Bedroom 3 14'-4" x 12'
- Storage 10' x 5'
- 2-Car Garage 21'-4" x 19'
- Width 62'
- Depth 67'-10"

The combination of finely detailed brick and shingle siding recalls some of the distinctive architecture of the East Coast during the early part of this century. A dramatic columned foyer opens to a central gallery and to the formal dining room. The expansive living area offers a corner fireplace and access to the rear porch through lovely French doors. The bayed breakfast nook, though, is going to be the family's favorite area of the home—in the summer, fling wide open the French doors leading to the screened porch and take in the sunshine and the sounds of birds. A master suite with coffered ceiling and windowed garden tub adjoins a study or guest room with its own bath. Family bedrooms are to the right of the plan—Bedroom 2 offers private access to the screened porch through French doors.

DESIGN BY

Larry W. Garnett & Associates, Inc.

Design 9201

Square Footage: 1,996

This stately brick facade conceals an interior that offers all of the essential amenities, plus a few surprises—it's a perfect plan for small, active families. The tiled entry extends to a central hallway that connects living areas and sleeping quarters. The formal living room can become a third bedroom if you choose. A magnificent great room with a fireplace and views to the rear grounds serves nicely as the main living area. A coffered ceiling, His and Hers walk-in closets and a sumptuous bath with skylights and corner whirlpool tub highlight the luxurious master suite. One family bedroom and a hall bath complete this side of the plan. The sunny, bayed breakfast nook with triple transomed windows, the convenient U-shaped kitchen and the formal dining room with built-in hutch and coffered ceiling are nicely clustered to the left of the plan. A tandem drive-through garage offers room for a third car, bicycles or even a hobby area.

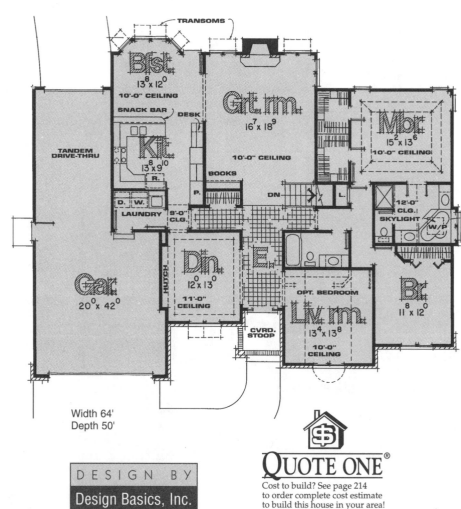

Width 64'
Depth 50'

DESIGN BY
Design Basics, Inc.

QUOTE ONE®

Cost to build? See page 214
to order complete cost estimate
to build this house in your area!

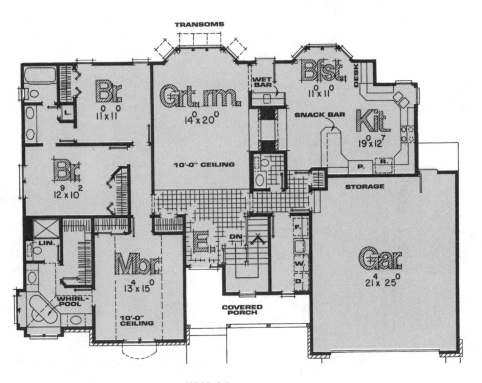

TRANSOMS

Br. 11⁰ x 11⁰

Grt. rm. 14⁰ x 20⁰

WET BAR

Bfst. 11⁰ x 11⁰

DESK

SNACK BAR

Kit. 19⁰ x 12⁷

10'-0" CEILING

Br. 12⁹ x 10²

P.   R.

STORAGE

LIN.

Mbr. 13⁴ x 15⁰

DN

F.

W.

Gar. 21⁴ x 25⁰

WHIRL-POOL

10'-0" CEILING

COVERED PORCH

Width 64'
Depth 44'

Design 9202

Square Footage: 1,808

Discriminating buyers will love the refined yet inviting look of this three-bedroom ranch plan. A tiled entry with ten-foot ceilings leads into the spacious great room with large bay window. An open-hearth fireplace warms both the great room and kitchen. The sleeping area features a large master suite with a dramatic arched window and a bath with whirlpool, His and Hers vanities and walk-in closet. Don't miss the storage space in the oversized garage.

D E S I G N   B Y
Design Basics, Inc.

Design 9884

Square Footage: 2,120

Graceful arches accent this traditional facade and announce a floor plan that's just a little different than the rest. The foyer, formal dining room and an expansive family room with centered fireplace flanked by picture windows, are open to one another through columned archways. To the right of this central living area are the master suite with coffered ceiling and plush bath with dressing area, as well as a private den. On the opposite side of the living area, a superb arrangement of the island kitchen, the breakfast room with views of the side courtyard and a spectacular sun room create a casual place for family and guests to gather. Two family bedrooms and a full bath are to the rear of the plan, connected by a hall just off the sun room. This home is designed with a basement foundation.

Quote One®

Cost to build? See page 214
to order complete cost estimate
to build this house in your area!

DESIGN BY
Stephen Fuller, Inc.

BATH

BEDROOM NO. 3
11'-6" X 11'-0"

BEDROOM NO. 2
11'-4" X 11'-0"

SUN ROOM
12'-0" X 13'-9"

MASTER BATH

W.I.C.

PORCH

BREAKFAST
10'-0" X 9'-0"

FAMILY ROOM
18'-0" X 14'-0"

MASTER BEDROOM
13'-4" X 15'-8"

LAUNDRY

KITCHEN
12'-0" X 13'-9"

DN.

BATH

TWO CAR GARAGE
20'-4" X 20'-8"

DINING ROOM
10'-6" X 13'-6"

FOYER

DEN
11'-4" X 12'-6"

STOOP

Width 62'
Depth 62'-6"

DESIGN BY
Stephen Fuller, Inc.

DECK

BREAKFAST
11'-4" X 9'-4"

BATH

BEDROOM NO. 2
11'-0" X 12'-0"

KITCHEN
10'-8" X 12'-2"

FAMILY ROOM
17'-8" X 15'-4"

MASTER BEDROOM
13'-8" X 15'-4"

BEDROOM NO. 3
11'-0" X 12'-0"

DN.

LAUNDRY

POWDER

MASTER
BATH

FOYER
6'-0" X 12'-0"

LIVING ROOM
11'-4" X 14'-0"

W.I.C.

DINING ROOM
11'-8" X 15'-0"

STOOP

TWO CAR GARAGE
20'-4" X 19'-10"

Width 65'
Depth 55'-11"

Design 9874

Square Footage: 2,095

QUOTE ONE®
Cost to build? See page 214
to order complete cost estimate
to build this house in your area!

Flared eaves, multi-pane windows and graceful arches decorate the outside of this spectacular home and introduce a theme for an interior that offers just a little more. An elegant foyer opens to both the living room and the formal dining room—which features dramatic window detail—and leads through a central hallway to an expansive family room. This versatile area is great for formal as well as informal gatherings, offering a sloped ceiling, fireplace with extended hearth, built-in bookcases and rear deck access. A beautiful, bayed breakfast nook with views to the rear grounds opens to a spacious kitchen with a peninsula cooktop counter. A butler's pantry is strategically located just off the kitchen for easy access when entertaining. The secluded master suite with coffered ceiling, dual vanities, jacuzzi tub and separate shower is complete with a roomy walk-in closet. To the rear of the plan are two family bedrooms; each have private access to a full bath which offers each room its own vanity area. This home is designed with a basement foundation.

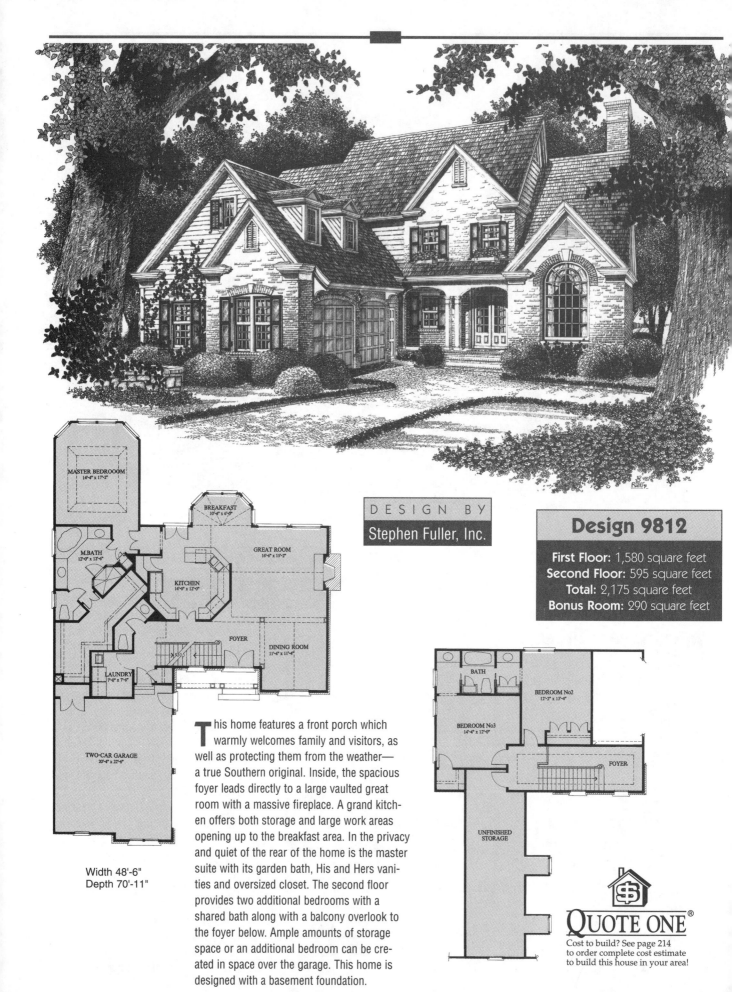

MASTER BEDROOM
14'-4" x 17'-2"

M.BATH
12'-0" x 12'-6"

BREAKFAST
10'-8" x 6'-8"

GREAT ROOM
16'-6" x 15'-2"

KITCHEN
14'-0" x 12'-0"

FOYER

DINING ROOM
11'-4" x 11'-4"

LAUNDRY
7'-0" x 7'-6"

TWO-CAR GARAGE
20'-4" x 22'-6"

Width 48'-6"
Depth 70'-11"

DESIGN BY
Stephen Fuller, Inc.

Design 9812

First Floor: 1,580 square feet
Second Floor: 595 square feet
Total: 2,175 square feet
Bonus Room: 290 square feet

BATH

BEDROOM No2
12'-2" x 13'-4"

BEDROOM No3
14'-4" x 12'-0"

FOYER

UNFINISHED
STORAGE

This home features a front porch which warmly welcomes family and visitors, as well as protecting them from the weather— a true Southern original. Inside, the spacious foyer leads directly to a large vaulted great room with a massive fireplace. A grand kitchen offers both storage and large work areas opening up to the breakfast area. In the privacy and quiet of the rear of the home is the master suite with its garden bath, His and Hers vanities and oversized closet. The second floor provides two additional bedrooms with a shared bath along with a balcony overlook to the foyer below. Ample amounts of storage space or an additional bedroom can be created in space over the garage. This home is designed with a basement foundation.

QUOTE ONE®

Cost to build? See page 214 to order complete cost estimate to build this house in your area!

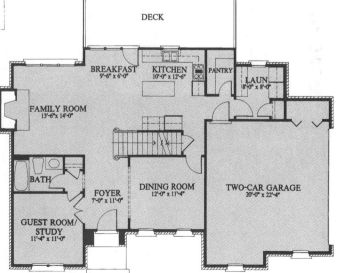

Brick takes a bold stand in grand style in this traditional design. From the front entry to rear deck, the floor plan serves family needs in just over 2,000 square feet. The front study has a nearby full bath, making it a handy guest bedroom. The family room with fireplace opens to a cozy breakfast area. For more formal entertaining there's a dining room just off the entry. The kitchen features a preparation island and a walk-in pantry. Upstairs, a luxurious master suite opens from a balcony hall and features a coffered ceiling, windowed sitting area and a spacious bath with garden tub, twin lavatories and walk-in closet. Two family bedrooms share a full bath. This home is designed with a basement foundation.

Width 52'
Depth 34'

Design 9842

First Floor: 1,053 square feet
Second Floor: 1,053 square feet
Total: 2,106 square feet
Bonus Room: 212 square feet

Quote One®
Cost to build? See page 214 to order complete cost estimate to build this house in your area!

DESIGN BY
Stephen Fuller, Inc.

This stately two-story Georgian home echoes tradition with the use of brick and jack-arch detailing. Once inside, the foyer is flanked by a spacious dining room to the right and living room on the left; with the addition of French doors this room can also function as a guest room, if needed. Beyond the foyer lies a two-story family room accented by a warming fireplace and open railing staircase. This room flows casually into the spacious breakfast room and well-planned kitchen with access to the laundry room and garage. The secluded master bedroom with a tray ceiling and master bath including His and Hers vanities, a garden tub and walk-in closet completes the main level of this home. Upstairs, two additional bedrooms with roomy closets and two baths combine to finish this traditional country home. A future bedroom can be finished later if desired. This home is designed with a basement foundation.

Design 9877

First Floor: 1,660 square feet
Second Floor: 665 square feet
Total: 2,325 square feet
Bonus Room: 240 square feet

Width 64'
Depth 48'-6"

DESIGN BY
Stephen Fuller, Inc.

QUOTE ONE®

Cost to build? See page 214 to order complete cost estimate to build this house in your area!

This European design offers ample space for formal and informal occasions. An impressive foyer opens to a fabulous two-story family room with fireplace and views to the rear yard. The adjacent windowed breakfast room with access to the rear covered porch is easily served by the kitchen with angled counter. Formal rooms flank the foyer—each enjoys a stunning bay window and opens to the foyer through decorative archways. An expansive master suite is secluded to the rear of the first-floor plan and offers a coffered ceiling, corner vanity, garden tub and roomy walk-in closet. Upstairs, Bedroom 2 features a bay window and has its own bath. Bedroom 3 offers a walk-in closet and full bath which leads to future bedroom space. This home is designed with a basement foundation.

Width 64'
Depth 48'-6"

Design 9893

First Floor: 1,660 square feet
Second Floor: 665 square feet
Total: 2,325 square feet

DESIGN BY

Stephen Fuller, Inc.

Design 9907

First Floor: 1,720 square feet
Second Floor: 545 square feet
Total: 2,265 square feet

This French country cottage is a charming example of European architecture. Stucco and stone blend with multiple gables and hipped rooflines to establish the character of the design. A two-story foyer opens to an even more impressive two-story family room with fireplace. To the right, a formal living area opens to a dining room through decorative columns.

This room is easily served by a generous kitchen with island cooktop counter. The master suite is also located on the first floor and is well appointed with a coffered ceiling, a walk-in closet and a double-bowl vanity in the bath. The second floor holds two family bedrooms, a full bath, space for an additional bedroom and future bath, and bonus storage space. This home is designed with a basement foundation.

DESIGN BY
Stephen Fuller, Inc.

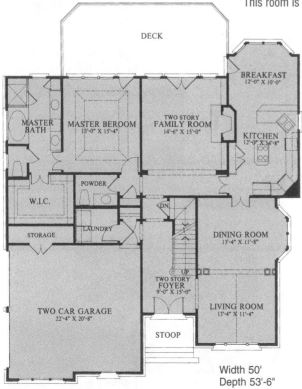

DECK

MASTER BATH

MASTER BEROOM
13'-0" X 15'-4"

TWO STORY FAMILY ROOM
14'-6" X 15'-0"

BREAKFAST
12'-0" X 10'-0"

KITCHEN
12'-0" X 14'-8"

W.I.C.

POWDER

LAUNDRY

STORAGE

DN

UP

TWO STORY FOYER
9'-0" X 15'-0"

DINING ROOM
13'-4" X 11'-8"

LIVING ROOM
13'-4" X 11'-4"

TWO CAR GARAGE
22'-4" X 20'-8"

STOOP

Width 50'
Depth 53'-6"

UNFIN. STORAGE

OPEN TO BELOW

BEDROOM NO. 3
11'-10" X 12'-0"

BATH

BALCONY

FUTURE BEDROOM NO. 4
13'-6" X 12'-0"

DN

FUTURE BATH

FUTURE STORAGE

OPEN TO BELOW

BEDROOM NO. 2
13'-0" X 12'-0"

Width 52'-6"
Depth 43'-6"

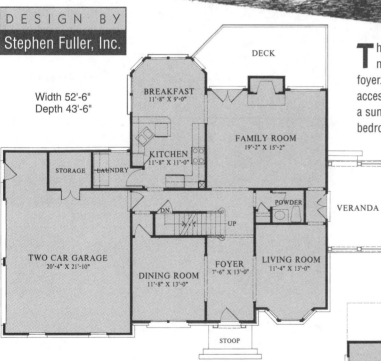

DECK

BREAKFAST
11'-8" X 9'-0"

FAMILY ROOM
19'-2" X 15'-2"

KITCHEN
11'-8" X 11'-0"

STORAGE LAUNDRY

POWDER

VERANDA

DN. UP

TWO CAR GARAGE
20'-4" X 21'-10"

DINING ROOM
11'-8" X 13'-0"

FOYER
7'-6" X 13'-0"

LIVING ROOM
11'-4" X 13'-0"

STOOP

This charming exterior conceals a perfect family plan. The formal dining and living rooms are located to either side of the foyer. At the rear of the home is a family room with a fireplace and access to a deck and a side veranda. The modern kitchen features a sunlit breakfast area. The second floor provides room for four bedrooms, one of which may be finished at a later date and used as a guest suite. The master bedroom includes a pampering bath and a walk-in closet. Note the extra storage space in the garage. This home is designed with a basement foundation.

MASTER
BATH

MASTER BEDROOM
19'-2" X 13'-8"

W.I.C.

W.I.C.

BATH

UNFIN.
BEDROOM NO. 4
13'-0" X 13'-0"

DN.

W.I.C. W.I.C.

BEDROOM NO. 3
11'-8" X 13'-0"

OPEN TO
BELOW

BEDROOM NO. 2
11'-4" X 13'-0"

BATH

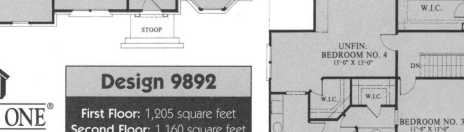

Design 9892

First Floor: 1,205 square feet
Second Floor: 1,160 square feet
Total: 2,365 square feet

Design HPT440024

First Floor: 1,829 square feet
Second Floor: 657 square feet
Total: 2,486 square feet

DESIGN BY
Design Basics, Inc.

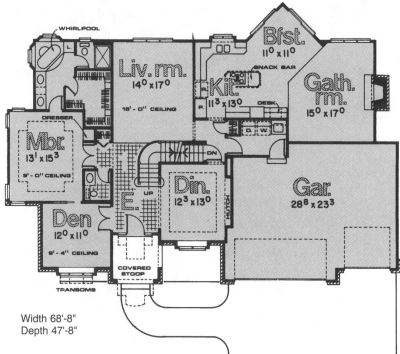

Width 68'-8"
Depth 47'-8"

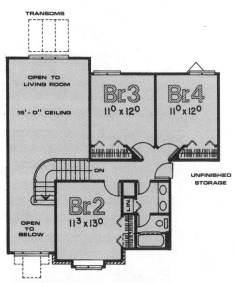

Elegant windows and trim details highlight the exterior of this traditional home. In the living room, transom windows let in plenty of light. The formal dining room features hutch space. Casual living is the focus in the heartwarming kitchen and gathering room. Long wrapping counters, a cooktop island with a snack bar, and an angular breakfast nook nicely balance the large gathering room that's accented with a fireplace. The secluded master suite includes a nine-foot ceiling, a pocket door to the den, a corner whirlpool tub and a walk-in closet.

Design HPT440025

First Floor: 1,093 square feet
Second Floor: 1,038 square feet
Total: 2,131 square feet

DESIGN BY

Design Basics, Inc.

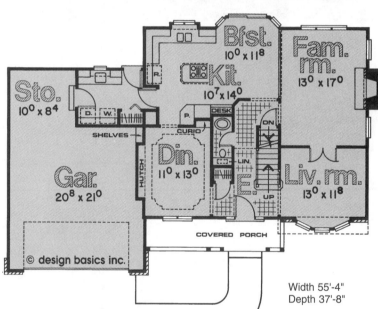

Width 55'-4"
Depth 37'-8"

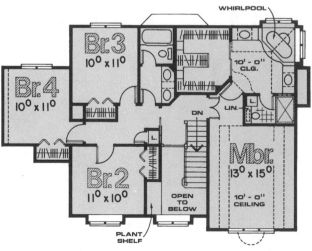

Bay windows, French doors and a fireplace are just some of the amenities offered in this delightful family plan. A covered front porch offers a warm welcome, while the two-story foyer provides a grand entry to a comfortable interior. The formal dining room has a built-in hutch and a curio cabinet, and enjoys a patterned tray ceiling. A bay window highlights the formal living room, and double French doors lead to the spacious family area, which includes a fireplace. Upstairs, the sumptuous master suite features a walk-in closet, a whirlpool tub and ten-foot ceilings.

Photo by Jon Riley

Design 9661

First Floor: 1,416 square feet
Second Floor: 445 square feet
Total: 1,861 square feet
Bonus Room: 284 square feet

An arched entrance and windows provide a touch of class to the exterior of this plan. The foyer leads to all areas of the house, minimizing corridor space. The dining room displays round columns at the entrance while the great room boasts a cathedral ceiling, fireplace and arched window over exterior doors to the deck. The large kitchen is open to the breakfast nook, and sliding glass doors present a second access to the deck. In the master suite are two walk-in closets and a lavish bath. On the second level are two bedrooms and a full bath. Bonus space over the garage can be developed later. Please specify basement or crawlspace foundation when ordering.

Width 58'-3"
Depth 68'-9"

DECK

seat

spa

arched window above door

GREAT RM.
15-4 × 18-0
(cathedral ceiling)

fireplace

KIT./BRKFST.
16-8 × 16-0

master bath

walk-in closet

walk-in closet

pd. rm.

cl

up

sto.

MASTER BED RM.
13-0 × 13-6

FOYER
7-8 × 9-0

DINING
12-4 × 12-4

UTILITY
10-0 × 6-4

w
d

up

storage

PORCH

© 1991 Donald A. Gardner Architects, Inc.

GARAGE
20-0 × 20-0

BED RM.
10-4 × 11-9

walk-in closet

down

cl

bath

BED RM.
12-4 × 13-6

down

BONUS RM.
11-0 × 20-0

DESIGN BY
Donald A. Gardner,
Architects, Inc.

Quote One®

Cost to build? See page 214 to order complete cost estimate to build this house in your area!

This home, as shown in the photograph, may differ from the actual blueprints. For more detailed information, please check the floor plans carefully.

Photo by Andrew D. Lautman

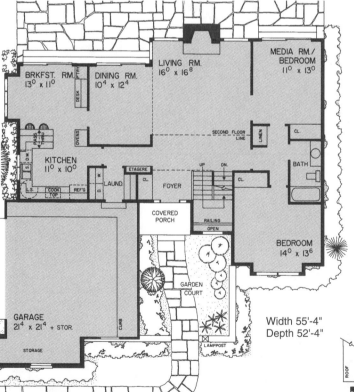

Width 55'-4"
Depth 52'-4"

Design 2927

First Floor: 1,425 square feet
Second Floor: 704 square feet
Total: 2,129 square feet

D

This charming Early American adaptation offers a warm welcome—inside and out. The first floor features a convenient kitchen with a pass-through to the breakfast room. There's also a formal dining room just steps away in the rear of the house. An adjacent rear living room enjoys its own fireplace. Other features include a rear media room (or optional third bedroom) and a complete second-floor master suite. A downstairs bedroom enjoys an excellent front view. Other features include a garden court, a covered porch and a two-car garage with extra storage.

This home, as shown in the photographs, may differ from the actual blueprints. For more detailed information, please check the floor plans carefully.

Photos by Andrew D. Lautman

Design 2822

First Floor: 1,363 square feet
Second Floor: 351 square feet
Total: 1,714 square feet

L

Tailor-made for small families, this is a one-level design with second floor possibilities. The bonus room upstairs (please see alternate layout) can be nearly anything you want it to be: lounge, guest room, playroom for the kids—partitioned or open. Downstairs, a little space goes a long way: an extensive great room with extended hearth, a formal dining room with private covered porch, and a master wing which includes a study, spacious bath with dressing area, walk-in closet and access to a hot tub/spa.

DESIGN BY
Home Planners

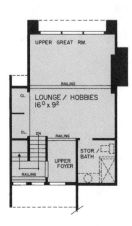

Alternate Second Floor

QUOTE ONE®
Cost to build? See page 214 to order complete cost estimate to build this house in your area!

Width 54'-8"
Depth 54'

Photos by Andrew D. Lautman

This home, as shown in the photographs, may differ from the actual blueprints.
For more detailed information, please check the floor plans carefully.

DESIGN BY

Home Planners

TERRACE

DECK

GATHERING RM.
14⁴ x 16¹⁰

STUDY
11⁸ x 11⁰

THRU
FIREPLACE

DINING RM.
11⁰ x 10⁰

SLOPED CEILING

DR. BOOKS

LAUNDRY

WASH RM.

KITCHEN
13⁰ x 10⁰

REF'G.

RANGE

FOYER

DN

SLOPED CEILING

BRKFST. RM.
11⁰ x 7⁰ + BAY

DESK

COVERED PORCH

GARAGE
22⁰ x 21⁸ + STORAGE

STORAGE

ENT. COURT

Width 49'
Depth 54'-4"

TERRACE

BRKFST. RM.
11⁰ x 7⁰

RANGE

OVEN

KITCHEN
13⁰ x 10⁰

BRM. CL.

REF'G.

DINING RM.
11⁰ x 10⁰ + BAY

This is an outstanding example of the type of informal, traditional-style architecture that has captured the modern imagination. Notice the spacious sunken gathering room with sliding glass doors to the rear terrace, which shares a through-fireplace with the quiet study that offers access to a rear deck. Formal and informal dining areas are nicely separated by a roomy U-shaped kitchen.

Upstairs, the master bedroom suite is sure to please, while two family bedrooms and a lounge fulfill the family's needs.

UPPER GATHERING ROOM

MASTER BEDROOM
11⁸ x 13⁸

BEDROOM
11⁰ x 10⁶

LOUNGE
10⁰ x 10⁴

WALK-IN CLOSET

LINEN

BATH

BATH

ATTIC

UPPER FOYER

BEDROOM
11⁰ x 10⁶

Design 2826

First Floor: 1,112 square feet
Second Floor: 881 square feet
Total: 1,993 square feet

Design 3569

Square Footage: 1,981

L D

An impressive arched entry graces this Transitional one-story design. An elegant foyer introduces an open gathering room/dining room combination. A front-facing study with sloped ceiling could easily be converted to a guest room with a full bath accessible from the rear of the room. In the kitchen, such features as an island cooktop and a built-in desk add style and convenience. A corner bedroom offers front and side views, and the nearby master suite sports a whirlpool bath and walk-in closet, and offers access to the rear terrace. Other special features of the plan include multipane windows, a warming fireplace, a cozy covered dining porch and a two-car garage. Note the handy storage closet in the laundry area.

QUOTE ONE®

Cost to build? See page 214 to order complete cost estimate to build this house in your area!

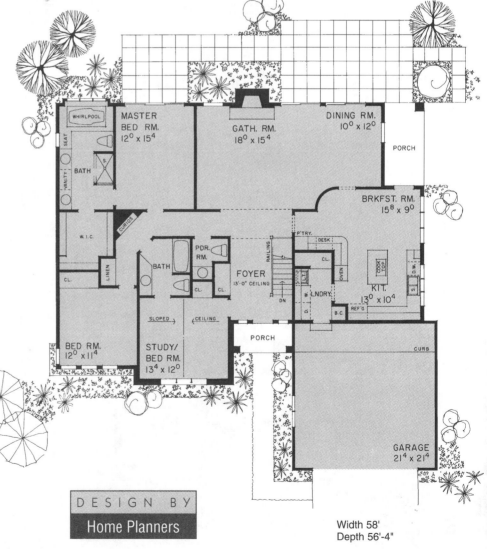

DESIGN BY
Home Planners

Width 58'
Depth 56'-4"

Covered Patio

opt.

opt.
summer
kitchen

Master Bedroom
volume ceiling
16⁸ · 12⁰

Bath

Breakfast
volume ceiling

lin

w.i.c.

Great Room
15⁸ · 14⁰

opt. media center

Kitchen

dw

volume ceiling

wall to 8'

m

Bedroom 2
volume ceiling
13⁴ · 10⁰

ref.

pan.

lin

opt. snk & stg

Utility

lin

Dining
12⁰ · 10¹⁰

Bath

w d

ac

ac

wh

Foyer

Bedroom 3
volume ceiling
13⁴ · 11⁰

Double Garage

w.i.c.

Entry

Study/ Bedroom 4
volume ceiling
14⁰ · 11⁰

Width 45'
Depth 66'

wh   ac

Foyer

Bedroom 3

Opt. 3 Car Garage

Entry

This innovative plan features an angled entry into the home, lending visual impact to the facade and giving the interior floor plan space for a fourth bedroom. A fabulous central living area with volume ceiling includes a dining area with kitchen access, a great room with built-in media center and access to the rear covered patio. The tiled kitchen shares natural light from the bayed breakfast area with volume ceiling. The kitchen and breakfast nook overlook the outdoor living space which even offers an optional summer kitchen—great for entertaining. A plush master suite opens from the great room through a privacy door and offers vistas onto the rear and side grounds. The traditional feel of the exterior and the up-to-date interior make this home a perfect design for the 90s.

Design 8633

Square Footage: 1,865

DESIGN BY
**Home Design
Services, Inc.**

Design 2948

Square Footage: 1,830

Styled for Southwest living, this home is a good choice in many areas. Among its many highlights are a gathering room/dining room combination that includes a fireplace, a snack bar pass-through and sliding glass doors to the rear terrace. The kitchen is uniquely shaped and sports a walk-in pantry plus a breakfast room with windows to the front covered porch. Bedrooms include a master suite with a sloped ceiling, access to the rear terrace, a whirlpool spa and a double vanity. Two additional bedrooms share a full bath. One of these bedrooms makes a fine study and features built-in shelves for books as well as a built-in cabinet.

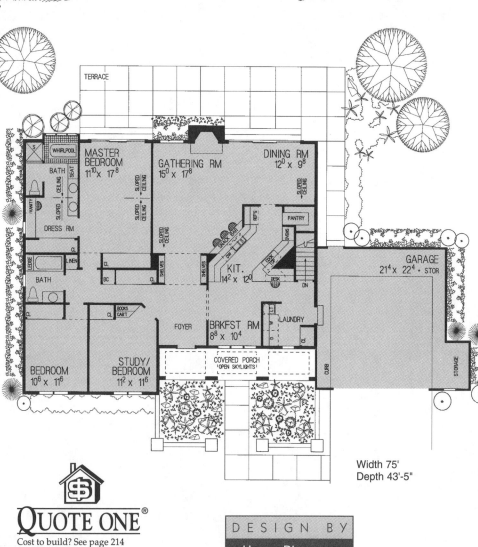

Width 75'
Depth 43'-5"

Cost to build? See page 214 to order complete cost estimate to build this house in your area!

QUOTE ONE®

DESIGN BY
Home Planners

Design 2875

Square Footage: 1,913

L **D**

This elegant Spanish design incorporates excellent indoor/outdoor living relationships for modern families who enjoy the sun and the comforts of a well-planned new home. Note the overhead openings for rain and sun to fall upon a front garden, while a twin arched entry leads to the front porch and foyer. Inside, the floor plan features a modern kitchen with pass-through to a large gathering room with fireplace. Other features include a dining room, laundry room, a study off the foyer, plus three bedrooms including a master suite with its own whirlpool.

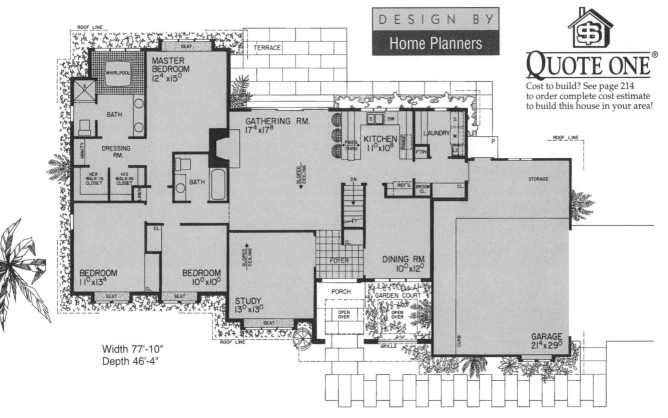

DESIGN BY
Home Planners

QUOTE ONE®

Cost to build? See page 214
to order complete cost estimate
to build this house in your area!

Width 77'-10"
Depth 46'-4"

Design 3431

Square Footage: 1,907

Graceful curves welcome you into the courtyard of this Santa Fe home. Inside, a gallery directs traffic to the work zone on the left or the sleeping zone on the right. Straight ahead lies a sunken gathering room with a beamed ceiling and a raised-hearth fireplace. A large pantry offers extra storage space for kitchen items. The covered rear porch is accessible from the dining room, gathering room and secluded master bedroom. Luxury describes the feeling in the master bath with a whirlpool tub, a separate shower, a double vanity and closet space. Two family bedrooms share a compartmented bath. The study could serve as a guest room, a media room or a home office.

Cost to build? See page 214 to order complete cost estimate to build this house in your area!

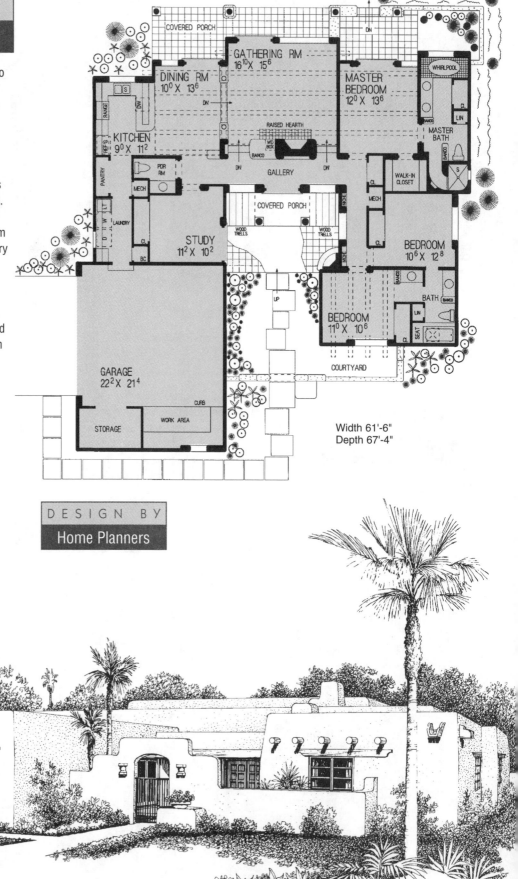

DESIGN BY
Home Planners

Width 61'-6"
Depth 67'-4"

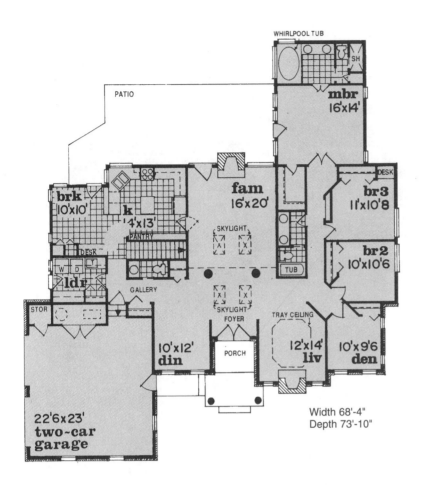

Design HPT440026

Square Footage: 2,404

This great ranch-style home features a low-maintenence brick finish, shuttered windows and a covered porch surrounded by decorative pillars. Directly in view of the skylit foyer is a spacious family room with twin sky-lights. The living room features a tray ceiling and a fireplace and opens from the foyer, across from the formal dining room. A gourmet kitchen features a center prep island, long pantry, break-fast room and built-in desk. Bedrooms are positioned away from the living areas for privacy.

Width 68'-4"
Depth 73'-10"

DESIGN BY
Select Home Designs

Design 3376

Square Footage: 1,999

L **D**

Small families will appreciate the layout of this traditional ranch. The foyer opens to the gathering room with fireplace and sloped ceiling. The dining room opens to the gathering room for entertaining ease and offers sliding glass doors to a rear terrace. The breakfast room also provides access to a covered porch for dining outdoors. The media room to the left of the home offers a bay window and a wet bar, or it can double as a third bedroom.

QUOTE ONE®

Cost to build? See page 214 to order complete cost estimate to build this house in your area!

Cost to build? See page 214

DESIGN BY
Home Planners

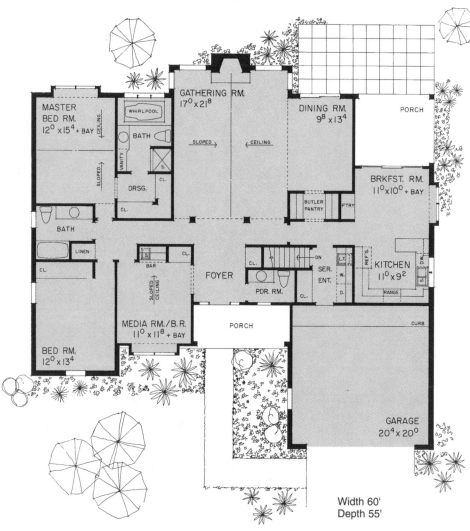

MASTER BED RM. 12⁰ x 15⁴ + BAY

WHIRLPOOL

BATH

VANITY

DRSG.

CL.

CL.

BATH

LINEN

CL.

GATHERING RM. 17⁰ x 21⁸

SLOPED CEILING

DINING RM. 9⁸ x 13⁴

PORCH

BUTLER PANTRY

PTRY

BRKFST. RM. 11⁰ x 10⁰ + BAY

BAR

SLOPED CEILING

FOYER

CL.

PDR. RM.

DN

SER. ENT.

CL.

REF'G.

RANGE

KITCHEN 11⁰ x 9²

DW

MEDIA RM./B.R. 11⁰ x 11⁸ + BAY

PORCH

BED RM. 12⁰ x 13⁴

PORCH

CURB

GARAGE 20⁴ x 20⁰

Width 60'
Depth 55'

ON THE GROW
Chic Plans For Moving Up

What will the 21st-Century home look like? The trend in home design is toward traditional values, but the discriminating demands of today's savvy home-builder will easily carry over to the next millennium—and that throws new light on the home of the future.

Trendsetting Baby Boomers are stoking the American dream with a sophisticated *savoir-vivre*. With incomes climbing and families growing, this generation wants a home plan that fits their hard-earned success as well as their lifestyles. And household arrangements today come in new flavors, so flexibility is key. Live-in grandparents, double-income parents and breadwinners who work at home entreat bright ideas for interior space.

Ergonomics and aesthetics can work together to take home design beyond style and into a comfortable, personalized way of life. Design 2973, a popular Victorian featured on page 126, offers places to kick off your shoes or put on a bash. And Design 3662 (page 152) combines traditional and *avant-garde* elements that succeed in giving it a contemporary spirit that's right at home with a rustic leitmotif.

New trends in building want well-heeled, intelligent designs that simmer with individuality and don't scrimp on style. Elegance partnered with restraint and simplicity creates homes that are impressive but not imposing, refined but not stuffy—tomorrow's home, the one you've been waiting for.

Photo by Andrew D. Lautman

This home, as shown in the photograph, may differ from the actual blueprints. For more detailed information, please check the floor plans carefully.

Design 2973

First Floor: 1,269 square feet
Second Floor: 1,227 square feet
Total: 2,496 square feet

L

A most popular feature of the Victorian house has always been its covered porches. The two finely detailed outdoor living spaces found on this home add much to formal and informal entertaining options. However, in addition to its wonderful Victorian facade, this home provides a myriad of interior features that cater to the active, growing family. Living and dining areas include a formal living room and dining room, a family room with a fireplace, a study and a kitchen with an attached breakfast nook. The second floor has three family bedrooms and a luxurious master bedroom with whirlpool spa and His and Hers walk-in closets.

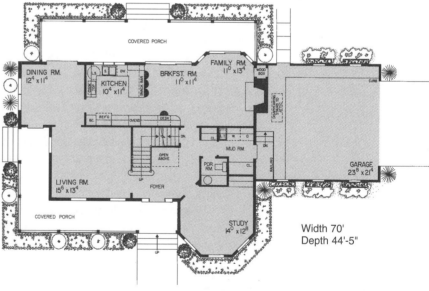

Width 70'
Depth 44'-5"

QUOTE ONE®

Cost to build? See page 214 to order complete cost estimate to build this house in your area!

DESIGN BY
Home Planners

This home, as shown in the photograph, may differ from the actual blueprints.
For more detailed information, please check the floor plans carefully.

Photo by Bob Greenspan

Design 3309

First Floor: 1,375 square feet
Second Floor: 1,016 square feet
Total 2,391 square feet

Covered porches, front and back, are a fine preview to the livable nature of this Victorian. Living areas are defined in a family room with a fireplace, formal living and dining rooms and a kitchen with a breakfast room. Note the sliding glass doors from the breakfast room to the rear veranda. An ample laundry room, a garage with storage area and a powder room round out the first floor. Three second-floor bedrooms are joined by a study and two full baths. The master suite on this floor has two closets (one a convenient walk-in), a double vanity, a whirlpool tub and a separate shower.

L

Width 62'-7"
Depth 54'

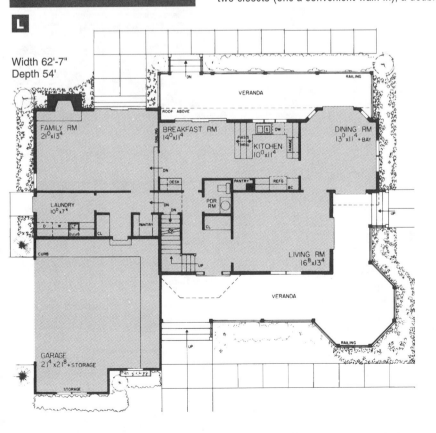

DESIGN BY
Home Planners

QUOTE ONE®

Cost to build? See page 214
to order complete cost estimate
to build this house in your area!

Photo by Andrew D. Lautman

This home, as shown in the photograph, may differ from the actual blueprints. For more detailed information, please check the floor plans carefully.

With its exceptional detail and proportions, this home is reminiscent of the Queen Anne Style. The foyer opens to a living area with a bay windowed alcove and a fireplace with flanking bookshelves. Natural light fills the breakfast area with a full-length bay window and a French door. Upstairs, the master bedroom offers unsurpassed elegance and convenience. The sitting area has an eleven-foot ceiling with arch-top windows. The bath area features a large walk-in closet, His and Hers lavatories and plenty of linen storage. Plans for a two-car detached garage are included.

Design 9055

First Floor: 997 square feet
Second Floor: 1,069 square feet
Total: 2,066 square feet

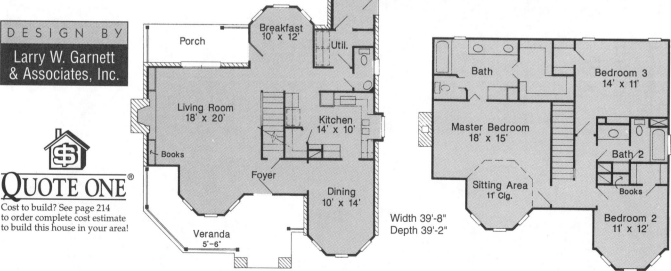

Optional 2-Car Attached Garage 21'-4" x 22'-4"

(plans for a detached 2-car garage are also included)

Porch

Breakfast 10' x 12'

Util.

Living Room 18' x 20'

Kitchen 14' x 10'

Books

Foyer

Dining 10' x 14'

Veranda 5'-6"

Width 39'-8"
Depth 39'-2"

Bath

Bedroom 3 14' x 11'

Master Bedroom 18' x 15'

Sitting Area 11' Clg.

Bath 2

Books

Bedroom 2 11' x 12'

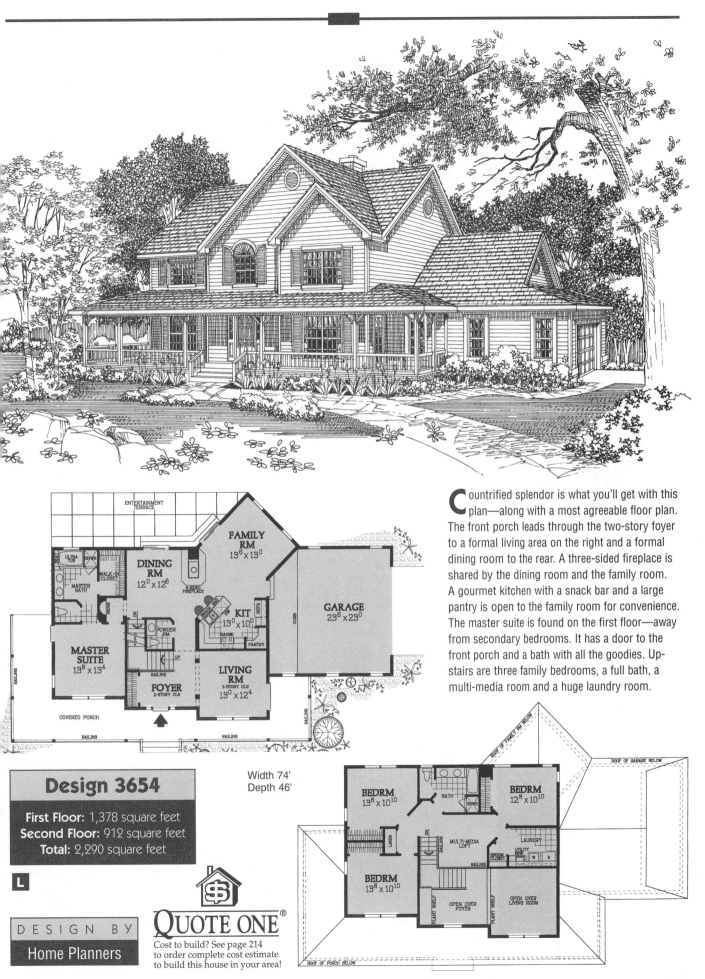

Countrified splendor is what you'll get with this plan—along with a most agreeable floor plan. The front porch leads through the two-story foyer to a formal living area on the right and a formal dining room to the rear. A three-sided fireplace is shared by the dining room and the family room. A gourmet kitchen with a snack bar and a large pantry is open to the family room for convenience. The master suite is found on the first floor—away from secondary bedrooms. It has a door to the front porch and a bath with all the goodies. Upstairs are three family bedrooms, a full bath, a multi-media room and a huge laundry room.

Width 74'
Depth 46'

Design 3654

First Floor: 1,378 square feet
Second Floor: 912 square feet
Total: 2,290 square feet

L

A wraparound veranda with delicate spindlework and a raised turret with leaded-glass windows recall the Queen Anne-style Victorians of the late 1880s. Double doors open from the two-story foyer to a study with built-in bookcases and a bay window. A fireplace adds warmth to the breakfast area and the island kitchen. Above the two-car garage is an optional area that is perfect for a home office or guest quarters. Upstairs, the balcony overlooks the foyer below. An octagon-shaped ceiling and leaded-glass windows define a cozy sitting area in the master suite. A raised alcove in the master bath contains a garden tub and glass-enclosed shower. An optional exercise loft and plant shelves complete this elegant master bath. Two additional bedrooms, one with a private deck, and the other with a cathedral ceiling share a dressing area and bath.

Design 9012

First Floor: 1,357 square feet
Second Floor: 1,079 square feet
Total: 2,436 square feet

QUOTE ONE®
Cost to build? See page 214 to order complete cost estimate to build this house in your area!

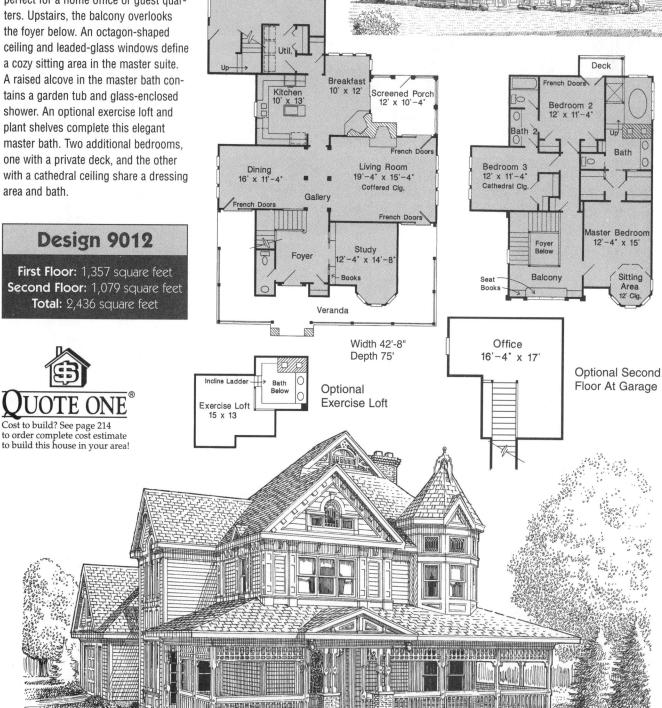

DESIGN BY
Larry W. Garnett & Associates, Inc.

2-Car Garage

Up

Util.

Kitchen 10' x 13'

Breakfast 10' x 12'

Screened Porch 12' x 10'-4"

French Doors

Dining 16' x 11'-4"

Living Room 19'-4" x 15'-4" Coffered Clg.

Gallery

French Doors

French Doors

French Doors

Foyer

Study 12'-4" x 14'-8"

Books

Veranda

Width 42'-8"
Depth 75'

Deck

French Doors

Bedroom 2 12' x 11'-4"

Bath 2

Up

Bath

Bedroom 3 12' x 11'-4" Cathedral Clg.

Master Bedroom 12'-4" x 15'

Foyer Below

Seat Books

Balcony

Sitting Area 12' Clg.

Incline Ladder

Bath Below

Exercise Loft 15 x 13

Optional Exercise Loft

Office 16'-4" x 17'

Optional Second Floor At Garage

Design 9585

First Floor: 1,337 square feet
Second Floor: 1,025 square feet
Total: 2,362 square feet

An octagonal tower, a wraparound porch and a wealth of amenities combine to give this house its charming Victorian appeal. The tower furnishes more than a pretty face, containing a sunny den on the first floor and a delightful bedroom on the second floor. To the right of the foyer, the formal living room and dining room unite to provide a wonderful place to celebrate special occasions and holidays. A large kitchen featuring an island cooktop easily serves both the formal dining room and the adjoining nook. Here, family members will appreciate the built-in desk for use in meal planning or paying bills. The spacious family room completes the casual living area and supplies easy access to the rear porch. Upstairs, two bedrooms share a full hall bath while the master bedroom revels in its own luxurious private bath. A two-car garage accommodates the family vehicles.

Width 50'-6"
Depth 72'-6"

DESIGN BY
Alan Mascord Design Associates, Inc.

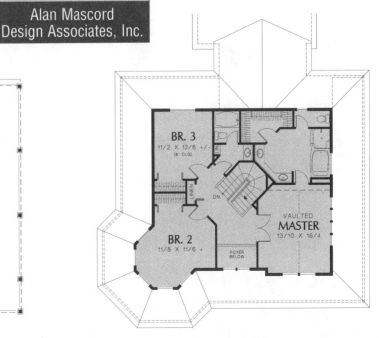

131

Design 9252

First Floor: 1,113 square feet
Second Floor: 965 square feet
Total: 2,078 square feet

Elegant detail, a charming veranda and a tall brick chimney make a pleasing facade on this four-bedroom, two-story Victorian home. Yesterday's simpler lifestyle is reflected throughout this plan. From the large bayed parlor with sloped ceiling to the sunken gathering room with fireplace, there's plenty to appreciate about the floor plan. The formal dining room opens to the parlor for convenient entertaining. An L-shaped kitchen with attached breakfast room is nearby. Upstairs quarters include a master suite with private dressing area and whirlpool, and three family bedrooms.

DESIGN BY
Design Basics, Inc.

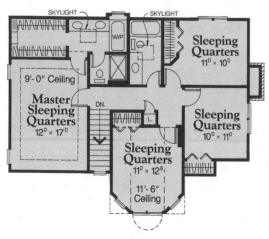

QUOTE ONE®

Cost to build? See page 214
to order complete cost estimate
to build this house in your area!

Width 46'
Depth 41'-5"

Design 9251

First Floor: 1,653 square feet
Second Floor: 700 square feet
Total: 2,353 square feet

Beautiful arches and elaborate detail give the elevation of this four-bedroom, 1½-story home an unmistakable elegance. Inside the floor plan is equally appealing. Note the formal dining room with bay window, visible from the entrance hall. The large great room shares a pass-through fireplace with the hearth room, which offers built-in bookshelves for favorite family cookbooks. The private, first-floor master suite features a pampering bath that contains a large whirlpool and double lavatories. Upstairs quarters share a full bath with compartmented sinks.

QUOTE ONE®

Cost to build? See page 214 to order complete cost estimate to build this house in your area!

Width 54'
Depth 50'

DESIGN BY
Design Basics, Inc.

133

Design 9206

First Floor: 1,421 square feet
Second Floor: 578 square feet
Total: 1,999 square feet

Growing families will love this unique plan which combines all the essentials with an abundance of stylish touches. Start with the living areas—a spacious great room with high ceilings, windows overlooking the back yard, a through-fireplace to the kitchen and access to the rear yard. A dining room with hutch space accommodates formal occasions. The hearth kitchen features a well-planned work area and a bay-windowed breakfast area. The master suite with whirlpool and a walk-in closet is found downstairs while three family bedrooms are upstairs.

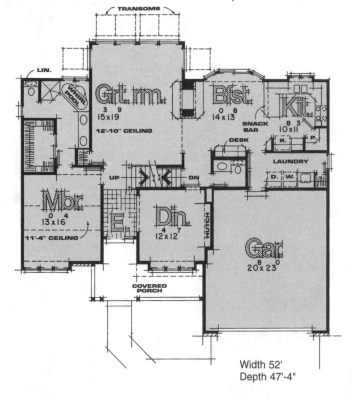

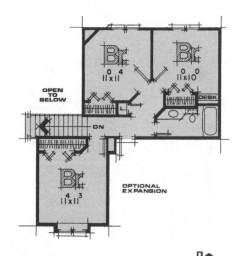

Width 52'
Depth 47'-4"

DESIGN BY
Design Basics, Inc.

Cost to build? See page 214
to order complete cost estimate
to build this house in your area!

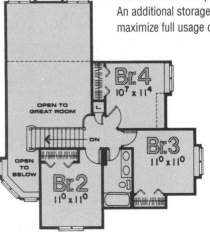

Design 7236

First Floor: 1,413 square feet
Second Floor: 563 square feet
Total: 1,976 square feet

Charming shutter treatments and an angled porch with balustrade inspire a country mood with this traditional design. An extended tiled entry opens to a majestic great room, where an aura of spaciousness beckons with a high ceiling and sunny, transomed windows which frame the centered fireplace. Nearby, a well-designed kitchen offers daily cooking ease and shares a snack counter with a bright breakfast room with triple transoms. The spacious master bath features an angled whirlpool, dual lavatories, separate shower and spacious walk-in closet. Upstairs, three family bedrooms and a hall bath complete the livable floor plan. An additional storage area in the garage helps maximize full usage of the home.

Width 54'
Depth 51'-8"

DESIGN BY
Design Basics, Inc.

Design 9310

First Floor: 1,505 square feet
Second Floor: 610 square feet
Total: 2,115 square feet

Many windows, lap siding and a covered porch give this elevation a welcoming country flair. The formal dining room with hutch space is conveniently located near the island kitchen. A main floor laundry room with a sink is discreetly located next to the bright breakfast area with desk and pantry. Highlighting the spacious great room are a raised-hearth fireplace, a cathedral ceiling and trapezoid windows. Special features in the master suite include a large dressing area with a double vanity, a skylight, a step-up corner whirlpool and a generous walk-in closet. Upstairs, the three secondary bedrooms are well separated from the master bedroom and share a hall bath.

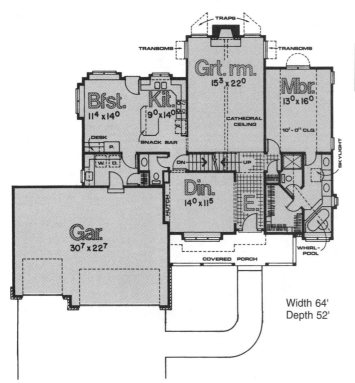

Width 64'
Depth 52'

DESIGN BY
Design Basics, Inc.

QUOTE ONE®

Cost to build? See page 214 to order complete cost estimate to build this house in your area!

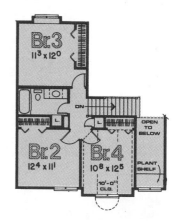

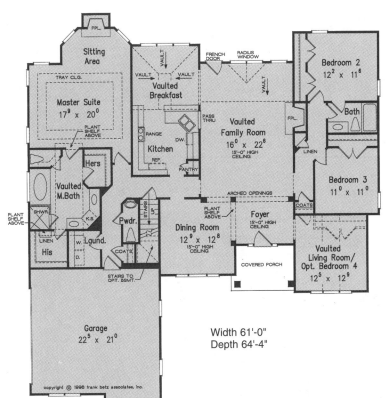

With elegant hipped rooflines, stucco-and-stone detailing, arched windows and gabled roofs, this home presents its European heritage with pride. The covered entryway leads to a formal dining room defined by graceful columns and arched openings. Columns and arched openings also lead into the vaulted family room, where a welcoming fireplace waits to warm cool evenings, while radius windows flood the room with light. The kitchen is sure to please with its angled counter and accessibility to the bayed breakfast nook. Two family bedrooms are to the right of the design, while the master bedroom is to the left. Please specify basement or crawlspace foundation when ordering.

Width 61'-0"
Depth 64'-4"

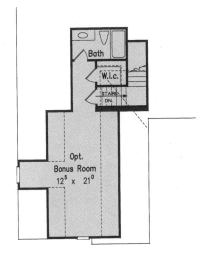

Design HPT440027

Square Footage: 2,311
Bonus Room: 425 square feet

Design 8064

Square Footage: 1,742

DESIGN BY
Larry E. Belk Designs

This traditional design warmly welcomes both family and visitors with a delightful bay window, a Palladian window and shutters. The entry introduces a beautiful interior plan, starting with the formal dining room and the central great room with fireplace, and views and access to outdoor spaces. Ten-foot ceilings in the major living areas give the home an open, spacious feel. The kitchen features an angled eating bar, a pantry and lots of cabi-net and counter space. Comfort and style abound in the distinctive master suite, offering a high ceiling, corner whirlpool tub, knee-space vanity and compartmented toilet. An ample walk-in closet with a window for natural light completes this owner's retreat. Bedrooms 2 and 3 are nearby and share a hall bath, and bedroom 3 offers a raised ceiling. Please specify basement or crawlspace foundation when ordering.

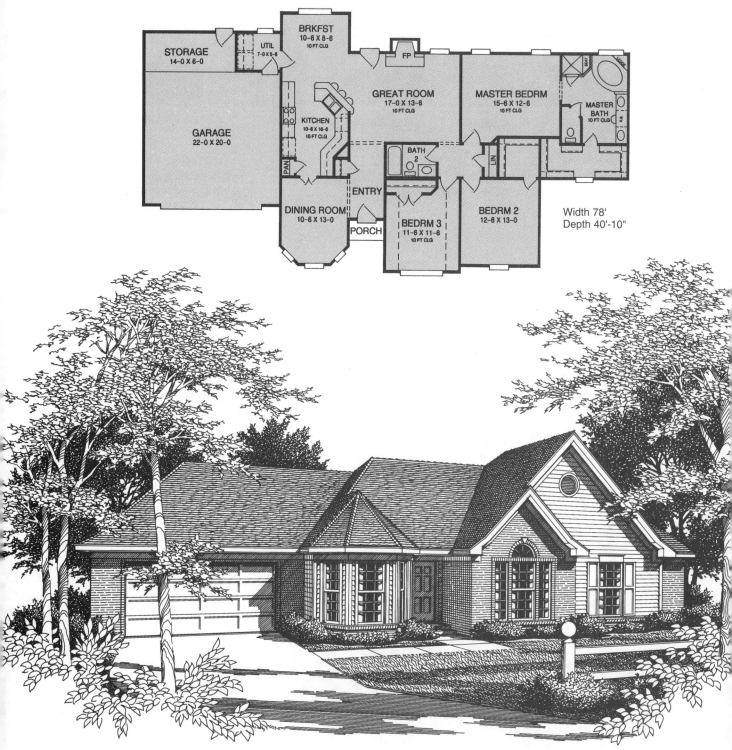

Width 78'
Depth 40'-10"

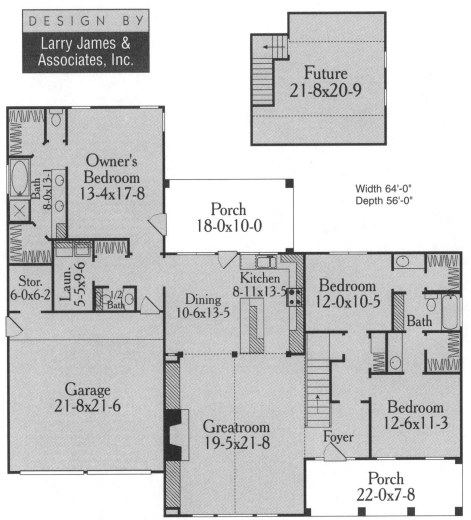

DESIGN BY
Larry James & Associates, Inc.

Future
21-8x20-9

Design HPT440028

Square Footage: 1,927
Bonus Room: 400 square feet

Owner's Bedroom
13-4x17-8

Bath
8-0x13-1

Stor.
6-0x6-2

Laun.
5-5x9-6

1/2 Bath

Garage
21-8x21-6

Porch
18-0x10-0

Width 64'-0"
Depth 56'-0"

Kitchen
8-11x13-5

Dining
10-6x13-5

Bedroom
12-0x10-5

Bath

Greatroom
19-5x21-8

Foyer

Bedroom
12-6x11-3

Porch
22-0x7-8

A Palladian window and an inviting porch grace the front of this design. Inside, the foyer allows entry to the vast great room with its vaulted ceiling and warming fireplace. The kitchen opens to the great room and the dining room. A covered rear porch can be reached from the dining room as well as the large owners suite. The owners suite is secluded behind the two-car garage for increased privacy. His and Hers walk-in closets flank the bath that's complete with a dual-vanity sink and separate shower. The family bedrooms occupy the opposite end of the home. Two bedrooms each enjoy a large walk-in closet and private vanity while sharing a bath. Storage needs are provided for with an extra room adjacent to the garage and future space above the family bedrooms. Please specify basement, crawlspace or slab foundation when ordering.

©1994 Donald A. Gardner Architects, Inc.

Design 9742

Square Footage: 1,954
Bonus Room: 436 square feet

This beautiful brick country home has all the amenities needed for today's active family. Covered front and back porches along with a rear deck provide plenty of room for outdoor enjoyment. Inside, the focus is on the large great room with its cathedral ceiling and welcoming fireplace. To the right, columns separate the kitchen and breakfast area while keeping this area open. Resident gourmets will certainly appreciate the convenience of the kitchen with its center island and additional eating space. The master bedroom provides a splendid private retreat, featuring a cathedral ceiling and a large walk-in closet. A double-bowl vanity, a separate shower and a skylit whirlpool tub enhance the luxurious master bath. At the opposite end of the plan, two additional bedrooms share a full bath. A skylit bonus room above the garage allows for additional living space.

D E S I G N   B Y
Donald A. Gardner, Architects, Inc.

Width 71'-3"
Depth 62'-6"

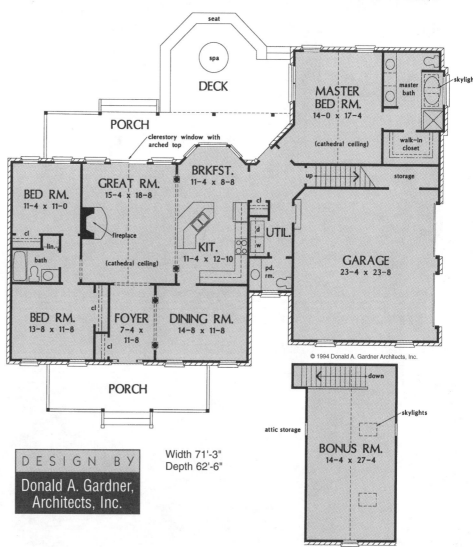

© 1994 Donald A. Gardner Architects, Inc.

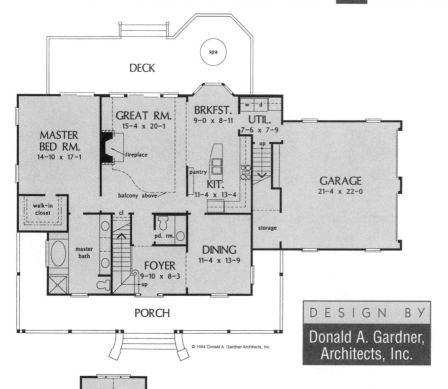

DECK

spa

GREAT RM.
15-4 x 20-1

BRKFST.
9-0 x 8-11

UTIL.
7-6 x 7-9

w d

MASTER
BED RM.
14-10 x 17-1

fireplace

up

pantry

balcony above

KIT.
11-4 x 13-4

GARAGE
21-4 x 22-0

walk-in
closet

cl

master
bath

pd. rm.

storage

FOYER
9-10 x 8-3

DINING
11-4 x 13-9

up

PORCH

© 1994 Donald A. Gardner Architects, Inc.

Design 9773

First Floor: 1,499 square feet
Second Floor: 665 square feet
Total: 2,164 square feet

The warm, down-home appeal of this country house is as apparent inside as it is out. A wraparound front porch and a rear deck with a spa provide plenty of space to enjoy the surrounding scenery. Inside, a two-story foyer and a great room give the home an open feel. The great room leads to a breakfast area and an efficient kitchen with an island work area and a large pantry. The master bedroom is situated on the left side of the house for privacy. It features deck access, a large walk-in closet and a bath that includes dual vanities, a whirlpool tub and a separate shower. Three bedrooms, a full bath and bonus space are located upstairs.

DESIGN BY
Donald A. Gardner, Architects, Inc.

cl

BED RM.
11-4 x 10-0

great room
below

attic storage

lin.

BONUS RM.
22-10 x 13-4

railing

down

BED RM.
11-4 x 10-0

down

bath

BED RM.
11-4 x 13-8

cl

foyer
below

cl

attic storage

Width 69'-8"
Depth 40'-6"

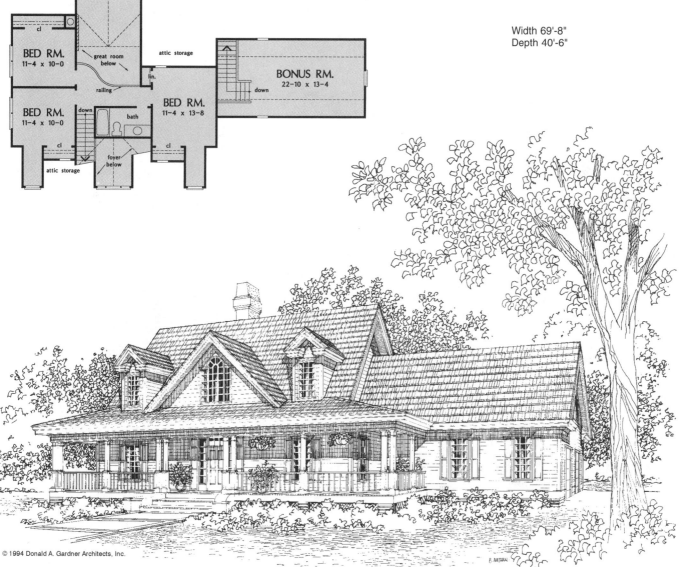

B. NATHAN

© 1994 Donald A. Gardner Architects, Inc.

Gabled dormers accent the facade of this classic farmhouse. The covered front porch is a perfect spot for enjoying cool evening breezes. Inside, this home's layout provides privacy for both the homeowner and the family. The children's bedrooms are found on the left of the foyer and share a full bath with dual vanities. To the right of the foyer is the formal dining room. The great room offers an angled, raised-hearth fireplace with an accommodating media shelf. The central, U-shaped kitchen is easily accessible from any room and opens to a sun-drenched morning room. The private master suite is impressive with its access to the sun patio, large walk-in closet and luxurious bath.

Width 76'
Depth 64'

Design 3677

Square Footage: 2,090

L D

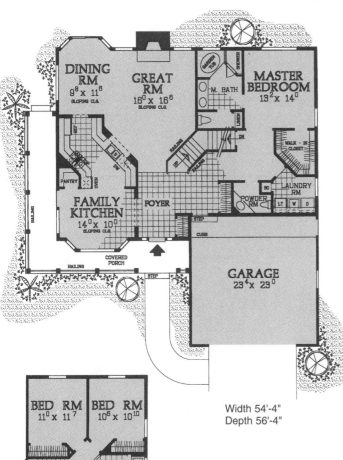

DINING RM
9⁸ x 11⁸
SLOPING CLG.

GREAT RM
18⁰ x 18⁶
SLOPING CLG.

MASTER BEDROOM
13² x 14⁰

M. BATH

WALK - IN CLOSET

FAMILY KITCHEN
14⁰ x 10⁰
SLOPING CLG.

FOYER

PANTRY

LAUNDRY RM

POWDER RM

STEP

CURB

COVERED PORCH

RAILING

STEP

GARAGE
23⁴ x 29⁰

BED RM
11⁰ x 11⁷

BED RM
10⁶ x 10¹⁰

BATH

RAILING

COMPUTER

STUDY

DESK

DESK

Width 54'-4"
Depth 56'-4"

DESIGN BY
Home Planners

Design 3609

First Floor: 1,624 square feet
Second Floor: 596 square feet
Total: 2,220 square feet

L **D**

This home's front-projecting garage allows utilization of a narrow, less expensive building site. The wrap-around porch provides sheltered entrances and outdoor living access from the family kitchen. Open planning, sloping ceilings and an abundance of windows highlight the formal dining room/great room area. Notice the second bay window in the dining room. The great room has a centered fireplace as its focal point. The master bedroom has a big walk-in closet and the master bath has twin lavatories, a garden tub, a stall shower and a compartmented toilet with a linen closet. Upstairs are two bedrooms, a bath with twin lavatories, plus an outstanding computer/study area.

QUOTE ONE®

Cost to build? See page 214
to order complete cost estimate
to build this house in your area!

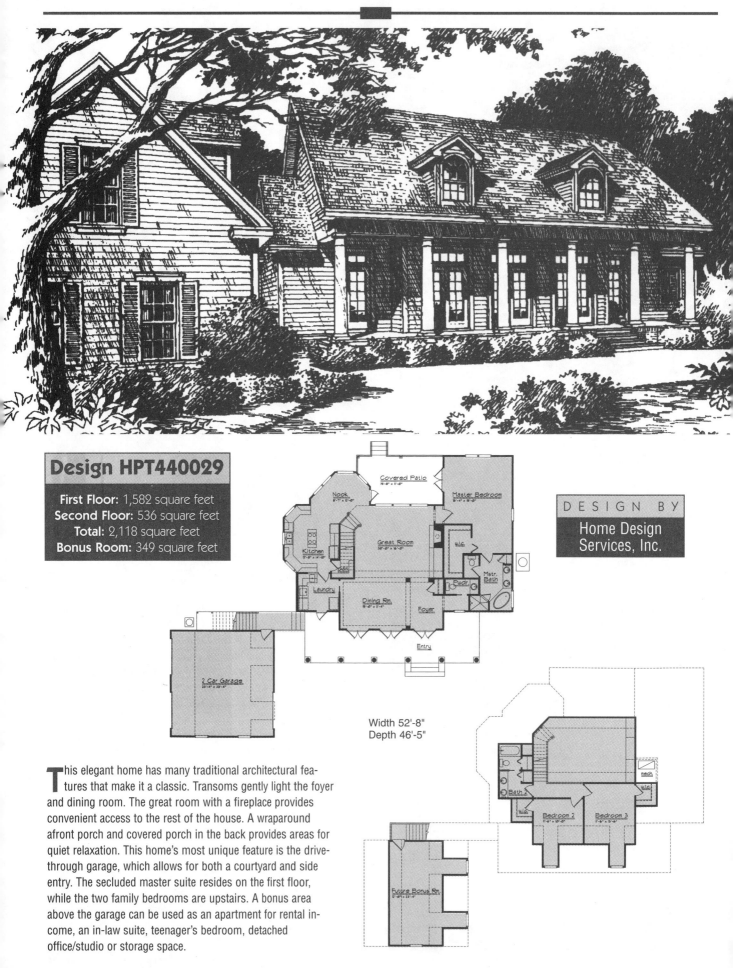

Design HPT440029

First Floor: 1,582 square feet
Second Floor: 536 square feet
Total: 2,118 square feet
Bonus Room: 349 square feet

DESIGN BY
Home Design Services, Inc.

Width 52'-8"
Depth 46'-5"

This elegant home has many traditional architectural features that make it a classic. Transoms gently light the foyer and dining room. The great room with a fireplace provides convenient access to the rest of the house. A wraparound afront porch and covered porch in the back provides areas for quiet relaxation. This home's most unique feature is the drive-through garage, which allows for both a courtyard and side entry. The secluded master suite resides on the first floor, while the two family bedrooms are upstairs. A bonus area above the garage can be used as an apartment for rental income, an in-law suite, teenager's bedroom, detached office/studio or storage space.

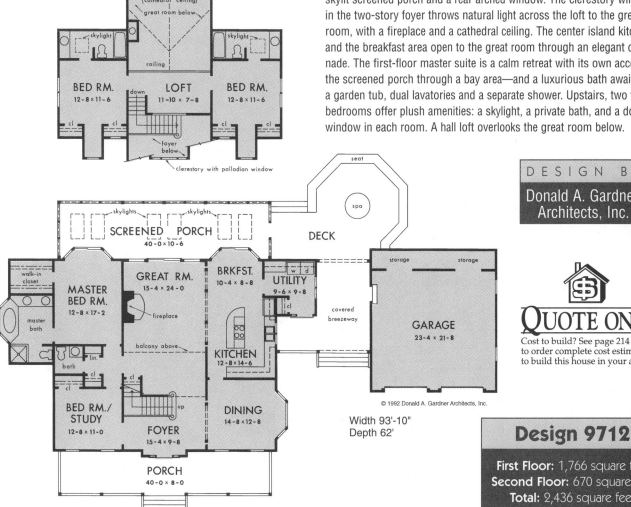

clerestory with arched window

(cathedral ceiling)
great room below

skylight

skylight

railing

BED RM.
12-8 × 11-6

LOFT
11-10 × 7-8

BED RM.
12-8 × 11-6

down

cl   cl

cl   cl

foyer
below

clerestory with palladian window

With an elegant but casual exterior, this four-bedroom farmhouse celebrates sunlight with a Palladian window and triple dormers, a skylit screened porch and a rear arched window. The clerestory window in the two-story foyer throws natural light across the loft to the great room, with a fireplace and a cathedral ceiling. The center island kitchen and the breakfast area open to the great room through an elegant colonnade. The first-floor master suite is a calm retreat with its own access to the screened porch through a bay area—and a luxurious bath awaits with a garden tub, dual lavatories and a separate shower. Upstairs, two family bedrooms offer plush amenities: a skylight, a private bath, and a dormer window in each room. A hall loft overlooks the great room below.

seat

spa

skylights   skylights

SCREENED   PORCH
40-0 × 10-6

DECK

walk-in
closet

**MASTER
BED RM.**
12-8 × 17-2

GREAT RM.
15-4 × 24-0

BRKFST.
10-4 × 8-8

w d

UTILITY
9-6 × 9-8

cl

storage   storage

master
bath

fireplace

balcony above

covered
breezeway

GARAGE
23-4 × 21-8

bath

lin

cl

KITCHEN
12-8 × 14-6

cl

**BED RM./
STUDY**
12-8 × 11-0

cl

up

DINING
14-8 × 12-8

FOYER
15-4 × 9-8

© 1992 Donald A. Gardner Architects, Inc.

Width 93'-10"
Depth 62'

PORCH
40-0 × 8-0

DESIGN BY
**Donald A. Gardner,
Architects, Inc.**

Quote One®
Cost to build? See page 214
to order complete cost estimate
to build this house in your area!

Design 9712

First Floor: 1,766 square feet
Second Floor: 670 square feet
Total: 2,436 square feet

Design HPT440030

Square Footage: 2,308

This home offers the ultimate in family entertaining by featuring a huge great room with a fireplace/media wall as its centerpiece, and an open and airy dining room. Off the great room is a den/study that can also double as a bedroom for guests. The master suite is generously appointed with sliding glass doors leading to the covered patio. The sumptuous bath includes His and Hers walk-in closets and vanities, a large soaking tub, a walk-in shower and private toilet chamber. The kitchen overlooks the nook with views of the covered patio through bayed walls of mitered glass. The secondary bedrooms share an ample bath, and the "kids" door off the hallway to the patio is a great feature. This plan is completed with a nicely sized walk-in pantry near the utility room, and a two-car garage.

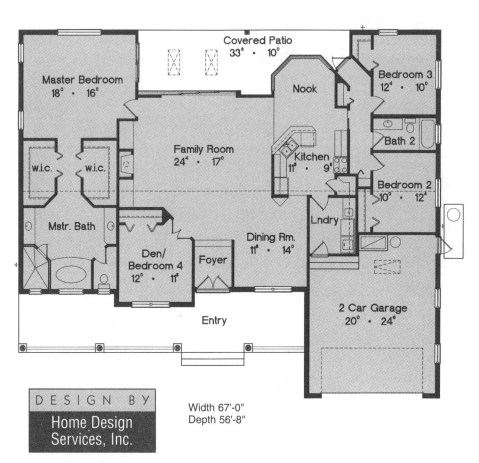

DESIGN BY

Home Design Services, Inc.

Width 67'-0"
Depth 56'-8"

Photo by Carl Socolow

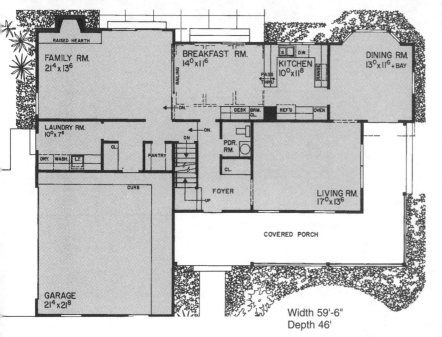

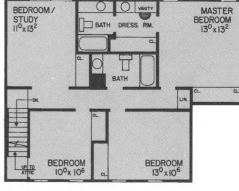

FAMILY RM.
21⁴x13⁶
RAISED HEARTH

BREAKFAST RM.
14⁰x11⁶

KITCHEN
10⁰x11⁸

DINING RM.
13⁰x11⁶ + BAY

PASS THRU

LAUNDRY RM.
10⁰x7⁶

DRY. WASH.

CL.

PANTRY

DESK REF'G OVEN

PDR. RM.

CL.

FOYER

LIVING RM.
17⁰x13⁶

GARAGE
21⁴x21⁸

CURB

COVERED PORCH

Width 59'-6"
Depth 46'

BEDROOM/
STUDY
11⁰x13²

BATH DRESS. RM.

VANITY

MASTER
BEDROOM
13⁰x13²

BATH

DN.

UP TO ATTIC

BEDROOM
10⁰x10⁶

BEDROOM
13⁰x10⁶

LIN.

Design 2774

First Floor: 1,366 square feet
Second Floor: 969 square feet
Total: 2,335 square feet

L **D**

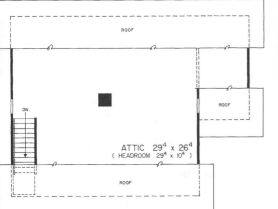

ROOF

DN.

ATTIC 29⁴ x 26⁴
(HEADROOM 29⁴ x 10⁴)

ROOF

ROOF

QUOTE ONE®
Cost to build? See page 214
to order complete cost estimate
to build this house in your area!

Here's a great farmhouse adaptation with many of the most up-to-date features. There is the quiet corner living room which opens to the sizable dining room. This room enjoys plenty of natural light from the delightful bay window overlooking the rear yard and is conveniently located near the efficient U-shaped kitchen. The kitchen features many built-ins and a pass-through to the beam-ceilinged nook. Sliding glass doors to the terrace are found in both the family room and nook. The service entrance to the garage is flanked by a clothes closet and a large, walk-in pantry. Recreational activities and hobbies can be pursued in the basement area. Four bedrooms and two baths are located on the second floor. The master bedroom has a dressing room and double vanity.

DESIGN BY
Home Planners

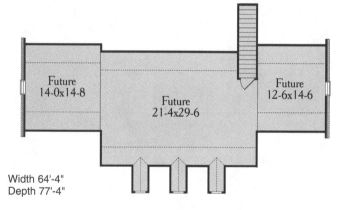

Width 64'-4"
Depth 77'-4"

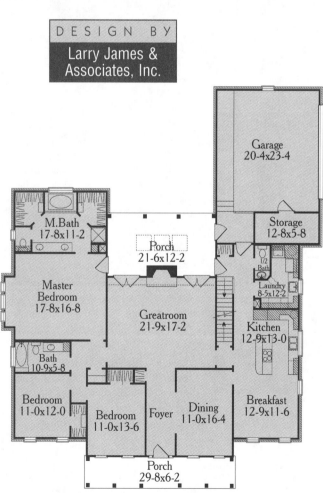

Garage
20-4x23-4

Storage
12-8x5-8

1/2
Bath

Laundry
8-5x12-2

M.Bath
17-8x11-2

Porch
21-6x12-2

Master
Bedroom
17-8x16-8

Greatroom
21-9x17-2

Kitchen
12-9x13-0

Bath
10-9x5-8

Bedroom
11-0x12-0

Bedroom
11-0x13-6

Foyer

Dining
11-0x16-4

Breakfast
12-9x11-6

Porch
29-8x6-2

Future
14-0x14-8

Future
21-4x29-6

Future
12-6x14-6

Three dormers in a row bring charm, while the porch colonnade adds elegance to this home. The dining room has plenty of room for formal gatherings and provides ease of service with the island kitchen close by. A bumped-out sitting bay, twin walk-in closets, dual vanities and a compartmented toilet highlight the spacious master bedroom. Two family bedrooms share a dual-vanity bath. The second floor holds abundant space for future development. Please specify basement, crawlspace or slab foundation when ordering.

Design HPT440031

Square Footage: 2,410
Bonus Space: 1,123 square feet

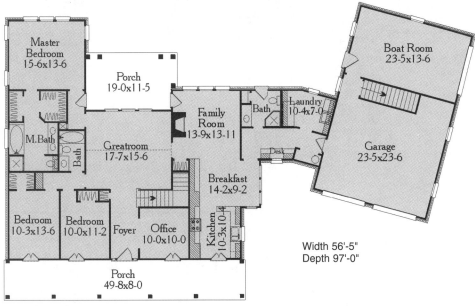

Master
Bedroom
15-6x13-6

Porch
19-0x11-5

M.Bath

Greatroom
17-7x15-6

Bath

Bedroom
10-3x13-6

Bedroom
10-0x11-2

Foyer

Office
10-0x10-0

Kitchen
10-3x10-4

Breakfast
14-2x9-2

Family
Room
13-9x13-11

Bath

Laundry
10-4x7-0

Desk

Boat Room
23-5x13-6

Garage
23-5x23-6

Porch
49-8x8-0

Width 56'-5"
Depth 97'-0"

Design HPT440032

Square Footage: 2,144
Bonus Space: 1,667 square feet

There is plenty of space to be developed on the second level of both the house and the garage, making this an ideal country home. An office to the right of the foyer is another added bonus. The great room and family room are separated by a warming fireplace and the family room accesses the rear porch. The hyphen bridging the garage and the central block houses a laundry room, desk and half-bath. The breakfast area features a bank of windows while the kitchen, office and two family bedrooms boast French-door access to the front porch. Please specify basement, crawlspace or slab foundation when ordering.

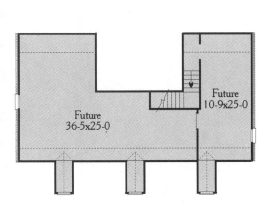

Future
36-5x25-0

Future
10-9x25-0

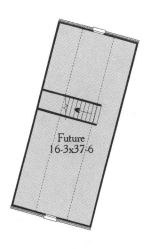

Future
16-3x37-6

DESIGN BY
**Larry James &
Associates, Inc.**

This open country plan boasts front and rear covered porches and a bonus room for future expansion. The foyer with a sloped ceiling contains a Palladian window clerestory to let in natural light. The spacious great room boasts a fireplace, cathedral ceiling and clerestory with arched windows. The second-floor balcony overlooks the great room. A U-shaped kitchen provides the ideal layout for food preparation. For flexibility, access is provided to the bonus room from both the first and second floors. The first-floor master bedroom features a bath with dual lavatories, a separate tub and shower and a walk-in closet.

Design HPT440033

First Floor: 1,632 square feet
Second Floor: 669 square feet
Total: 2,301 square feet
Bonus Room: 528 square feet

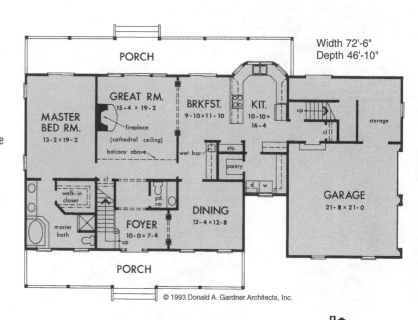

Width 72'-6"
Depth 46'-10"

© 1993 Donald A. Gardner Architects, Inc.

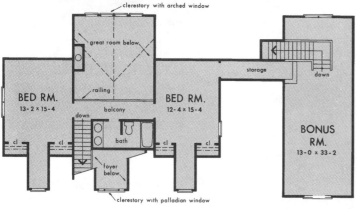

DESIGN BY
Donald A. Gardner Architects, Inc.

QUOTE ONE®

Cost to build? See page 214 to order complete cost estimate to build this house in your area!

B. NATHAN

DECK

GREAT RM.
16-0 x 18-10
(cathedral ceiling)

fireplace

BED RM.
12-2 x 13-4

cl

sto.

bath

lin.

cl

BED RM.
11-0 x 11-6

cl

sto.

FOYER
9-6 x 6-8

up

STUDY/
LIVING RM.
11-0 x 12-0

porch

DINING
12-0 x 12-4

KIT.
12-0 x 11-6

BRKFST.
12-0 x 9-8

MASTER
BED RM.
14-0 x 16-0

skylight

master
bath

lin.

w   d

UTIL.   cl

walk-in
closet

up

storage

GARAGE
22-8 x 19-8

(optional door location)

Width 68'-10"
Depth 57'-4"

Brick accents and bright, arch-topped windows highlight the facade of this appealing home. The foyer introduces a clever interior design, starting with stylish formal living and dining rooms flanking the entry, each with a coffered ceiling and an arched, multi-pane window. The elegance continues with a cathedral ceiling in the great room which features a warming fireplace as well as rear deck access and opens to a sunny breakfast room through a columned archway. A convenient kitchen with food preparation island easily serves casual and formal dining areas. The dramatic master suite is carefully positioned to the rear of the plan for privacy and offers a coffered ceiling and access to the rear deck. A skylit bath with twin lavs, garden tub, separate shower and walk-in closet complete this lavish retreat. The second story offers 615 square feet of bonus space and a balcony overlook to the great room below.

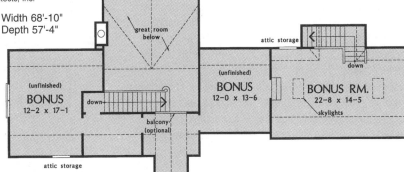

great room
below

attic storage

down

BONUS
12-2 x 17-1
(unfinished)

down

balcony
(optional)

BONUS
12-0 x 13-6
(unfinished)

BONUS RM.
22-8 x 14-5

skylights

attic storage

Design 9799

Square Footage: 2,170
Bonus Room: 615 square feet

DESIGN BY

**Donald A. Gardner,
Architects, Inc.**

Design 3662

Square Footage: 1,937
Bonus Room: 414 square feet

L

This transitional design wears a winsome, country look but delivers contemporary appeal. Arch-top and multi-pane windows complement gables, dormers and a columned, covered porch to create an inviting exterior. An angled entry introduces a refreshingly unique interior design, and opens to the principal living area. The great room offers a sloped ceiling, a fireplace with extended hearth, access to a patio deck retreat and built-in shelves for an entertainment center—or "build" a library. The kitchen shares a lovely feature with this room: an angled desk set against a curved half-wall with display below. Gourmet features in the kitchen includes a cooktop island, double sink and pantry—the outdoors compliments the morning nook with plenty of natural light. A satisfying master suite with sloped ceiling affords privacy and repose with a secluded sitting area and a relaxing bath with windowed garden tub, dual lavatories, compartmented toilet and walk-in closet with extra linen storage. Two family bedrooms share a full bath and a gallery hall off the living area. Plans for an optional bonus room are included.

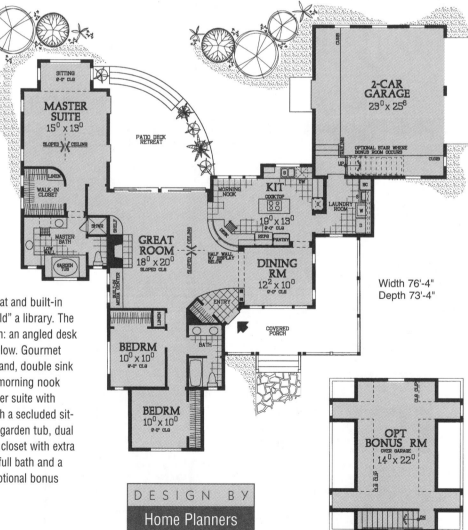

Width 76'-4"
Depth 73'-4"

DESIGN BY
Home Planners

© 1994 Donald A. Gardner Architects, Inc.

B. NATHAN

seat

spa

DECK

skylights

SCREEN PORCH
16-0 x 11-0

wet bar

BED RM.
12-4 x 11-8

cl

GREAT RM.
16-0 x 17-4

fireplace

cabinets

lin.

bath

cl

FOYER
12-4 x 5-6

cl

BED RM./ STUDY
12-0 x 12-0

PORCH

BRKFST.
12-0 x 8-6

KITCHEN
12-0 x 12-8

DINING
12-0 x 13-8

up

MASTER BED RM.
13-4 x 18-8

skylights

master bath

UTIL.

d w

lin.

storage

walk-in closet

GARAGE
22-0 x 20-4

storage

© 1994 Donald A. Gardner Architects, Inc.

Width 69'-8"
Depth 67'-6"

attic storage

down

up

BONUS RM.
18-0 x 19-0

skylights

Design 9734

Square Footage: 1,977
Bonus Room: 430 square feet

A two-story foyer with a Palladian window above sets the tone for this sunlit home. Columns mark the passage from the foyer to the great room, which features a centered fireplace and built-in cabinets. This room offers views and access to a rear screen porch with four skylights and a wet bar—and just a few steps away is a deck with spa. The nearby breakfast room offers a separate entrance to the rear deck and shares light from outdoor areas with the kitchen. The formal dining room offers a coffered ceiling and a Palladian window with views to the front property. A secluded master suite offers comfort and style to spare, with a skylit bath, corner whirlpool tub, generous walk-in closet and private access to the rear deck and spa. On the opposite side of the plan, a front bedroom with coffered ceiling and Palladian window could be a study. This room shares a hall bath with a secondary bedroom.

DESIGN BY
Donald A. Gardner, Architects, Inc.

Design 8126

Square Footage: 2,127
Bonus Room: 338 square feet

DESIGN BY
Larry E. Belk Designs

Three arched windows, shutters, and a brick facade provide just the right touch of elegance and give this home a picturesque appeal. Ten-foot ceilings in the living areas lend an open, spaciousness inside. A corner fireplace in the great room offers warmth and light to the main living areas. Guests and family alike will enjoy the rear covered patio with access to a sunny breakfast area and adjoining kitchen with snack counter. The formal dining room sits just off the foyer and opens to the great room through decorative columns. Luxurious accomodations abound in the master suite: a bath with coffered ceiling, large His and Hers closets, a whirlpool tub, a shower with a seat and knee-space vanity. Bedrooms 2 and 3 on the opposite side of the plan share a hall bath. Stairs at the front of the plan lead to an expandable area on the second floor. Please specify crawlspace or slab foundation when ordering.

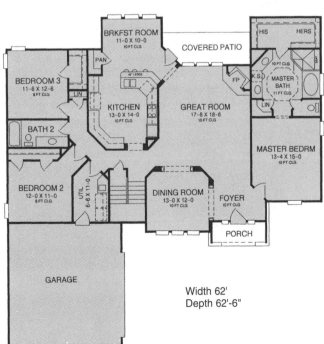

Width 62'
Depth 62'-6"

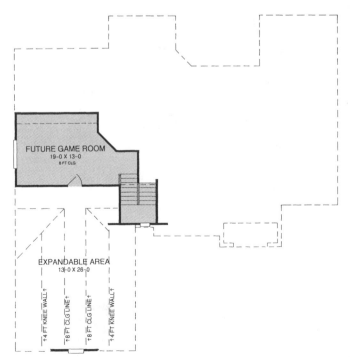

Design HPT440034

Square Footage: 2,127
Bonus Space: 1,095 square feet

This home's facade employs an elegant balance of country comfort and traditional grace. Inside, the foyer opens to the formal dining room that features a coffered ceiling. Straight ahead, the great room offers a warm fireplace and open flow to the breakfast and kitchen areas. Two secondary bedrooms and a full bath can be found just off the kitchen. A bonus room, near the owners suite, can be used as a nursery or den. The owners bath enjoys dual vanities, two walk-in closets and a compartmented toilet. Upstairs, unfinished space is ready for expansion. Please specify basement, crawlspace or slab foundation when ordering.

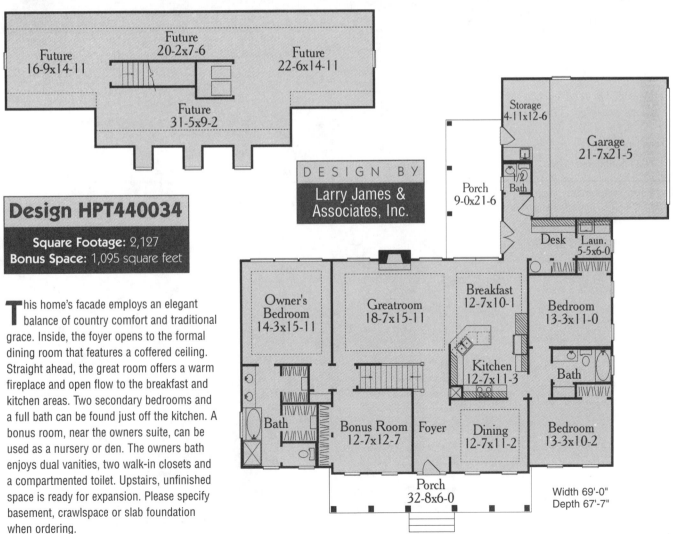

DESIGN BY
Larry James & Associates, Inc.

Future 16-9x14-11

Future 20-2x7-6

Future 22-6x14-11

Future 31-5x9-2

Storage 4-11x12-6

Garage 21-7x21-5

Porch 9-0x21-6

Bath ½

Desk

Laun. 5-5x6-0

Owner's Bedroom 14-3x15-11

Greatroom 18-7x15-11

Breakfast 12-7x10-1

Bedroom 13-3x11-0

Kitchen 12-7x11-3

Bath

Bath

Bonus Room 12-7x12-7

Foyer

Dining 12-7x11-2

Bedroom 13-3x10-2

Porch 32-8x6-0

Width 69'-0"
Depth 67'-7"

This stately brick Colonial-style home features an elegant recessed entry and a ribbon of windows topped by a keystone accent. A paneled door crowned by a fanlight opens to an entry hall with a powder room and coat closet. Double doors open to a versatile, well-lit room that serves as a study with built-in bookshelves or a formal dining room. The unique great room also provides built-in shelves as well as a fireplace. An island kitchen adjoins a breakfast area/sun room with access to the rear deck. The owners suite, thoughtfully placed away from traffic flow, includes a spacious bath with two walk-in closets and separate vanities. This home is designed with a basement foundation.

Deck

Master
Bedroom
17⁰ x 13⁶

Sunroom/
Breakfast
18⁹ x 9³

Great
Room
15⁹ x 19⁰

Kitchen
12⁶ x 15³

Study/
Dining
Room
11⁸ x 13³

Three Car Garage
22⁹ x 30³

Bedroom #2
11⁰ x 10³

Bedroom #3
17⁰ x 11⁰

Bedroom #4
10⁰ x 15⁶

Width 46'-6"
Depth 72'-0"

DESIGN BY
Stephen Fuller, Inc.

Design HPT440035

First Floor: 1,652 square feet
Second Floor: 543 square feet
Total: 2,195 square feet
Bonus Room: 470 square feet

Design 9831

Square Footage: 2,150
Expandable Lower Level:
2,150 square feet

QUOTE ONE®
Cost to build? See page 214
to order complete cost estimate
to build this house in your area!

DESIGN BY
Stephen Fuller, Inc.

Width 64'
Depth 64'-4"

This home draws its inspiration from both French and English country homes. From the foyer and across the spacious great room, French doors give a generous view of the covered rear porch. The adjoining dining room is subtly defined by the use of columns and a large triple window. The kitchen, with its generous work island, adjoins the breakfast area and keeping room with fireplace, a vaulted ceiling and an abundant use of windows. The study to the front of the first floor could be a guest room. It shares a bath with the bedroom beside it. The home is completed by a quiet master suite located at the rear. It contains a bay window, a garden tub and His and Hers vanities. Space on the lower level can be developed later.

Design 9885

Square Footage: 2,377

One-story living takes a lovely traditional turn in this brick one-story home. The foyer opens to the dining room through columned arches and to the great room, creating an extensive living area with a sense of spaciousness. To the right of the plan, this area opens to a second, more casual, living area through double doors. Gourmet cooks will fully appreciate this well-appointed kitchen with large food prepartion counter and walk-in pantry. Family and friends will gather around the fireplace in the adjacent keeping room with beautiful bayed breakfast nook. To the left of the plan, two family bedrooms and a full bath share a central hall which leads to a sizable master suite with coffered ceiling, lovely bayed sitting area, and sumptuous bath with compartmented garden tub, dressing area and walk-in closet. This home is designed with a basement foundation.

QUOTE ONE®

Cost to build? See page 214
to order complete cost estimate
to build this house in your area!

Width 69'
Depth 49'-6"

DESIGN BY
Stephen Fuller, Inc.

BEDROOM NO. 3
11'-6" X 11'-0"

BATH

BEDROOM NO. 2
11'-4" X 11'-0"

SUN ROOM
12'-0" X 13'-8"

Width 62'-4"
Depth 62'-2"

MASTER BATH

W.I.C.

PORCH

PORCH

BREAKFAST
10'-0" X 9'-0"

FAMILY ROOM
18'-0" X 14'-0"

MASTER BEDROOM
13'-4" X 15'-6"

LAUNDRY

KITCHEN
12'-0" X 13'-2"

BATH

STORAGE

DN

TWO CAR GARAGE
20'-4" X 19'-8"

DINING ROOM
11'-4" X 11'-4"

FOYER
6'-8" X 11'-10"

DEN/GUEST BEDROOM
11'-4" X 14'-0"

PORCH

DESIGN BY
Stephen Fuller, Inc.

Quote One®
Cost to build? See page 214
to order complete cost estimate
to build this house in your area!

Design 9862

Square Footage: 2,170

This classic cottage features a stone and wooden exterior with an arch-detailed porch and a box-bay window. From the foyer, double doors open to the den with built-in bookcases and a fireplace. A full bath is situated next to the den, allowing for an optional guest room. The family room is centrally located, just beyond the foyer. Its hearth is framed by windows overlooking the porch at the rear of the home. The master bedroom opens onto the rear porch. The master bath, with a large walk-in closet, double vanities, a corner tub and a separate shower, completes this relaxing retreat. Left of the family room awaits a sun room with access to the covered porch. A breakfast area complements the attractive and efficiently designed kitchen. Two secondary bedrooms with large closets share a full bath featuring double vanities. This home is designed with a basement foundation.

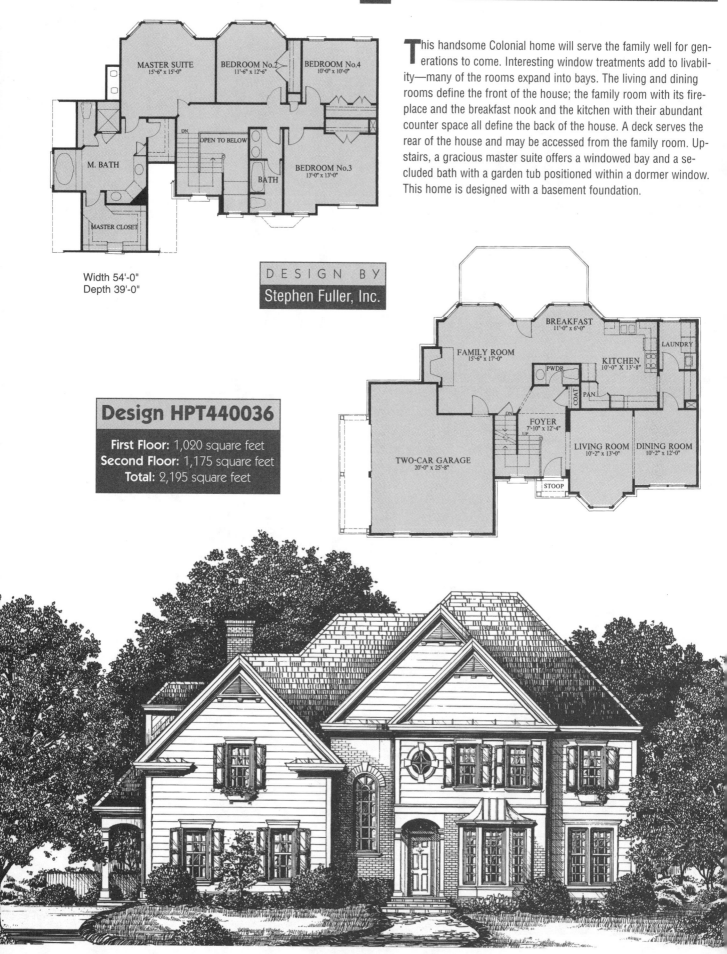

MASTER SUITE
15'-6" x 15'-0"

BEDROOM No.2
11'-6" x 12'-6"

BEDROOM No.4
10'-0" x 10'-0"

DN
OPEN TO BELOW

M. BATH

BATH

BEDROOM No.3
13'-0" x 13'-0"

MASTER CLOSET

Width 54'-0"
Depth 39'-0"

DESIGN BY
Stephen Fuller, Inc.

This handsome Colonial home will serve the family well for generations to come. Interesting window treatments add to livability—many of the rooms expand into bays. The living and dining rooms define the front of the house; the family room with its fireplace and the breakfast nook and the kitchen with their abundant counter space all define the back of the house. A deck serves the rear of the house and may be accessed from the family room. Upstairs, a gracious master suite offers a windowed bay and a secluded bath with a garden tub positioned within a dormer window. This home is designed with a basement foundation.

BREAKFAST
11'-0" x 6'-0"

FAMILY ROOM
15'-6" x 17'-0"

LAUNDRY

KITCHEN
10'-0" X 13'-8"

PWDR

COAT

PAN.

DN

FOYER
7'-10" x 12'-4"

UP

TWO-CAR GARAGE
20'-0" x 25'-8"

LIVING ROOM
10'-2" x 13'-0"

DINING ROOM
10'-2" x 12'-0"

STOOP

Design HPT440036

First Floor: 1,020 square feet
Second Floor: 1,175 square feet
Total: 2,195 square feet

Deck

Breakfast / Keeping
13³ x 13⁰

Dining Room
10⁰ x 13⁶

Great Room
13⁶ x 20⁰

Kitchen
10⁸ x 10⁶

Foyer

Two Car Garage
20⁰ x 18⁶

Stoop

Master Bedroom
17³ x 13⁶

Bedroom #2
12⁰ x10⁰

Bath

Bedroom #3
11³ x 10⁰

Master Bath

W.I.C.

Unifinished Bonus

D E S I G N   B Y
Stephen Fuller, Inc.

Design HPT440037

Width 38'-0"
Depth 43'-0"

First Floor: 915 square feet
Second Floor: 935 square feet
Total: 1,850 square feet
Bonus Room: 85 square feet

Brick and clapboard siding with pairs of double gables establish the Georgian character of this home. The front covered porch, with a Palladian window above, completes this presentation. Inside, a formal dining room opens through graceful columns to the expansive great room with an extended-hearth fireplace and French doors to the rear deck. Upstairs, the sleeping quarters include a lavish master suite with a pampering bath and a bonus room, as well as two family bedrooms that which share a full bath. This home is designed with a basement foundation.

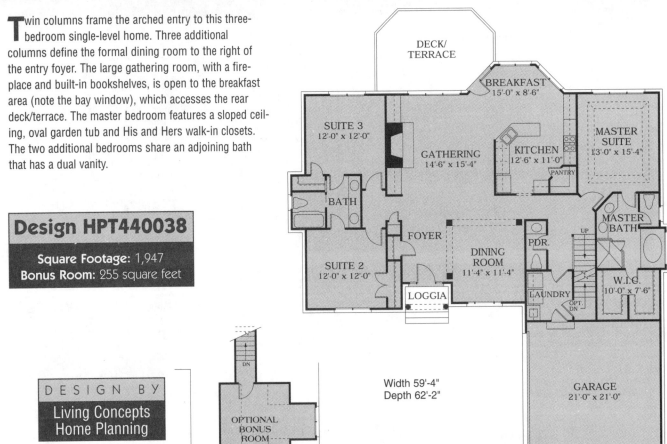

Twin columns frame the arched entry to this three-bedroom single-level home. Three additional columns define the formal dining room to the right of the entry foyer. The large gathering room, with a fireplace and built-in bookshelves, is open to the breakfast area (note the bay window), which accesses the rear deck/terrace. The master bedroom features a sloped ceiling, oval garden tub and His and Hers walk-in closets. The two additional bedrooms share an adjoining bath that has a dual vanity.

Design HPT440038

Square Footage: 1,947
Bonus Room: 255 square feet

DESIGN BY
**Living Concepts
Home Planning**

DECK/
TERRACE

BREAKFAST
15'-0" x 8'-6"

SUITE 3
12'-0" x 12'-0"

GATHERING
14'-6" x 15'-4"

KITCHEN
12'-6" x 11'-0"

MASTER
SUITE
13'-0" x 15'-4"

PANTRY

BATH

MASTER
BATH

FOYER

PDR.

DINING
ROOM
11'-4" x 11'-4"

UP

SUITE 2
12'-0" x 12'-0"

W.I.C.
10'-0" x 7'-6"

LAUNDRY

OPT.
DN

LOGGIA

Width 59'-4"
Depth 62'-2"

OPTIONAL BONUS
ROOM
12'-4" x 16'-8"

DN

GARAGE
21'-0" x 21'-0"

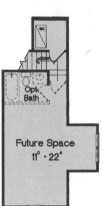

Width 64'-4"
Depth 63'-0"

Shingles, horizontal siding and columns add to the charm of this wonderful Craftsman-style home. The entry—flanked by the den/study and the formal dining room—opens to the vaulted family room. The centrally located kitchen delights with an island cooktop and a nook that leads to the greenhouse. The master suite features a large walk-in closet, double-sink vanity, garden tub, separate shower and a compartmented lavatory. Future space is found over the two-car garage. Please specify basement, crawlspace or slab foundation when ordering.

Design HPT440039

Square Footage: 1,997
Bonus Room: 310 square feet

DESIGN BY
Home Design Services, Inc.

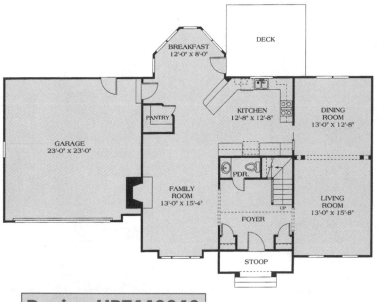

A dramatic combination of stone and horizontal siding adds style to this two-story traditional home. A grand foyer opens to the family and living rooms. The breakfast area and the formal dining room flank the versatile kitchen. The second-floor master suite features His and Hers walk-in closets, a corner whirlpool tub, a separate shower and His and Hers vanities. A laundry room, three bedrooms, a full bath and a bonus room complete this level. Please specify basement or crawlspace foundation when ordering.

BREAKFAST
12'-0" x 8'-0"

DECK

KITCHEN
12'-8" x 12'-8"

DINING ROOM
13'-0" x 12'-8"

PANTRY

GARAGE
23'-0" x 23'-0"

PDR.

FAMILY ROOM
13'-0" x 15'-4"

LIVING ROOM
13'-0" x 15'-8"

FOYER

UP

STOOP

Width 62'-6"
Depth 41'-2"

Design HPT440040

First Floor: 1,250 square feet
Second Floor: 1,225 square feet
Total: 2,475 square feet
Bonus Room: 330 square feet

DESIGN BY

Living Concepts
Home Planning

STORAGE

SUITE 2
12'-0" x 9'-4"

SUITE 4
12'-0" x 9'-4"

LAUNDRY

MASTER BATH

LIN.

W.I.C.

ACCESS

BONUS ROOM
12'-0" x 23'-4"

DN

ACCESS

BATH

DN

OPEN TO BELOW

MASTER SUITE
13'-0" x 16'-0"

SUITE 3
13'-0" x 9'-4"

W.I.C.

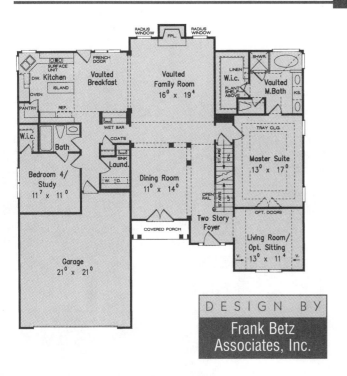

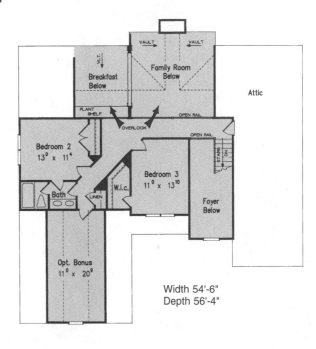

Width 54'-6"
Depth 56'-4"

DESIGN BY
Frank Betz Associates, Inc.

Design HPT440041

First Floor: 1,860 square feet
Second Floor: 612 square feet
Total: 2,472 square feet
Bonus Room: 244 square feet

Keystones, stucco arches and shutters add a French flavor to this traditional home. Inside, the formal dining room is defined by decorative columns. The gourmet kitchen has a work island and its own French door to the rear of the property. The secluded master suite features a tray ceiling, an optional sitting room and a sumptuous master bath. Two additional bedrooms share a full bath on the upper level, where an optional bonus room provides space to grow. Please specify basement or crawlspace foundation when ordering.

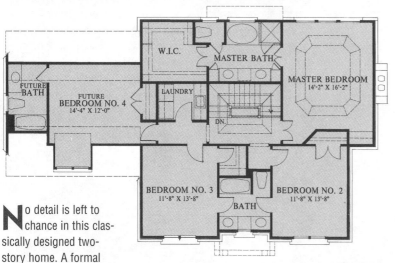

Design 9886

First Floor: 1,165 square feet
Second Floor: 1,050 square feet
Total: 2,215 square feet

DESIGN BY
Stephen Fuller, Inc.

No detail is left to chance in this classically designed two-story home. A formal entry opens to the living and dining rooms through graceful arches. For more casual entertaining, the family room provides ample space for large gatherings and features a warming fireplace and access to the rear deck through double doors. A roomy breakfast area is bathed in beautiful natural light from triple windows. The adjacent L-shaped kitchen handles any occasion with ease. Upstairs, the master suite runs the width of the house and includes a generous walk-in closet and bath with knee-space vanity, twin lavatories, garden tub and separate shower. A central hall leads to two family bedrooms and a full bath as well as bonus space which offers the possibility of a future fourth bedroom and bath. This home is designed with a basement foundation.

Width 58'
Depth 36'

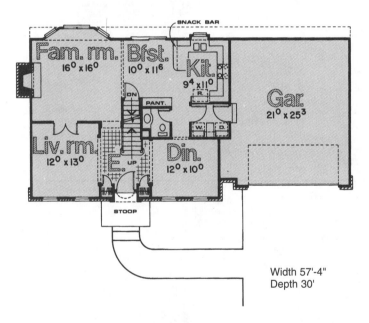

SNACK BAR

Fam. rm.
16⁰ x 16⁰

Bfst.
10⁰ x 11⁶

Kit.
9⁴ x 11⁰

Gar.
21⁰ x 25³

PANT.

Liv. rm.
12⁰ x 13⁰

UP

Din.
12⁰ x 10⁰

W. D.

STOOP

Width 57'-4"
Depth 30'

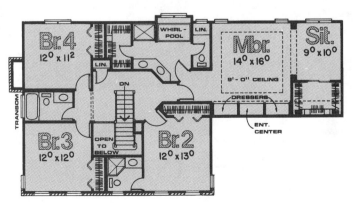

Br. 4
12⁰ x 11²

WHIRL-POOL

LIN.

Mbr.
14⁰ x 16⁰

Sit.
9⁰ x 10⁰

LIN.

9'- 0" CEILING

DRESSERS

Br. 3
12⁰ x 12⁰

OPEN TO BELOW

Br. 2
12⁰ x 13⁰

ENT. CENTER

TRANSOM

Design 9344

First Floor: 1,000 square feet
Second Floor: 1,345 square feet
Total: 2,345 square feet

An arched entry, shutters and a brick facade highlight the exterior of this modern, two-story Colonial home. Living and dining rooms at the front of the plan accomodate formal occasions. The rear of the plan is designed for informal gatherings, with a generous family room with warming fireplace and bayed conversation area, a bright breakfast area and a well-equipped U-shaped kitchen with snack bar. Bright windows and French doors add appeal to the living room. Upstairs, a U-shaped balcony hall overlooks the entry below and connects four bedrooms, including a master suite. This retreat features a private sitting room, two walk-in closets, compartmented bath, separate vanities and a window-brightened whirlpool tub.

DESIGN BY

Design Basics, Inc.

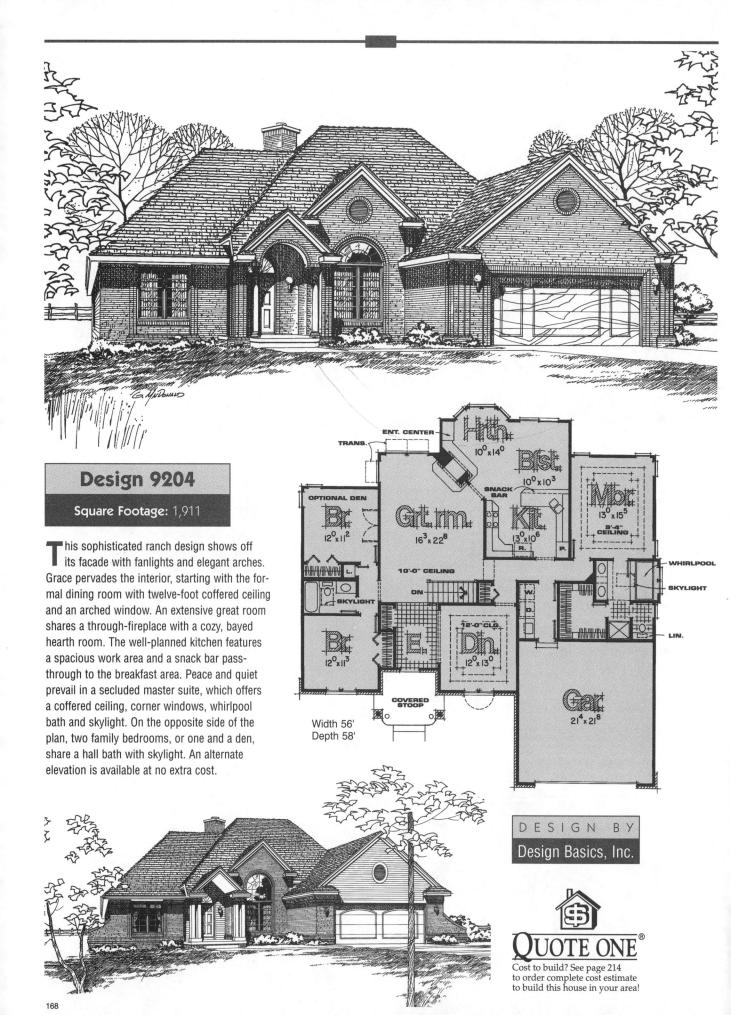

Design 9204

Square Footage: 1,911

This sophisticated ranch design shows off its facade with fanlights and elegant arches. Grace pervades the interior, starting with the formal dining room with twelve-foot coffered ceiling and an arched window. An extensive great room shares a through-fireplace with a cozy, bayed hearth room. The well-planned kitchen features a spacious work area and a snack bar pass-through to the breakfast area. Peace and quiet prevail in a secluded master suite, which offers a coffered ceiling, corner windows, whirlpool bath and skylight. On the opposite side of the plan, two family bedrooms, or one and a den, share a hall bath with skylight. An alternate elevation is available at no extra cost.

Width 56'
Depth 58'

DESIGN BY
Design Basics, Inc.

QUOTE ONE®

Cost to build? See page 214
to order complete cost estimate
to build this house in your area!

Design 9362

Square Footage: 2,172

QUOTE ONE®

Cost to build? See page 214
to order complete cost estimate
to build this house in your area!

Beautiful arches and grand rooflines announce an interior that is both spectacular and convenient. The entry leads to a magnificent great room with centered fireplace and views to the rear grounds—a perfect complement to a front-facing formal living room. The dining room with tray ceiling and double arched windows opens from the entry and is just steps away from the kitchen—which features a food preparation island, pantry, and access to a rear patio through the breakfast area. Bedroom 3 offers the possibility of a guest room at this end of the plan, with a nearby full bath. To the right of the plan, a glorious master suite, with raised ceiling and triple transoms, offers a relaxing bath with windowed whirlpool tub, twin lavatories and walk-in closet. A nearby family bedroom has access to a hall bath. The three-car garage offers extra storage space.

DESIGN BY

Design Basics, Inc.

Width 76'
Depth 46'

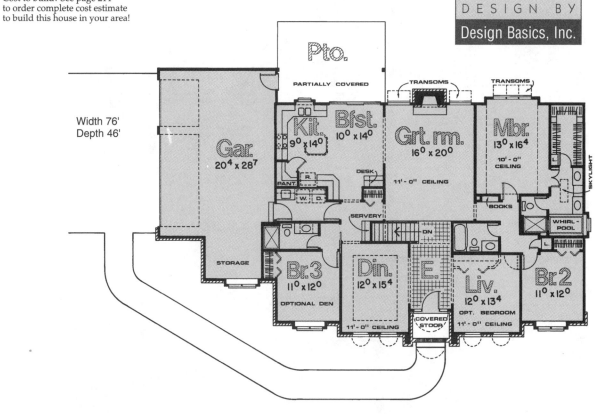

A two-level entry, varying rooflines and multipane windows add to the spectacular appeal of this three-bedroom home. To the right of the foyer, the formal dining room offers elegant columns and archways that open to the main living areas. A generous family room offers space for an optional fireplace and an abundance of light through triple windows. An angled peninsular counter in the tiled kitchen opens that area to natural light from the bayed breakfast nook and the glass doors to the covered patio. A gracious master suite is carefully placed to the rear of the plan for privacy, offering views of the rear grounds as well as a roomy tiled bath with garden tub, separate shower and walk-in closet. Two additional bedrooms share a full bath.

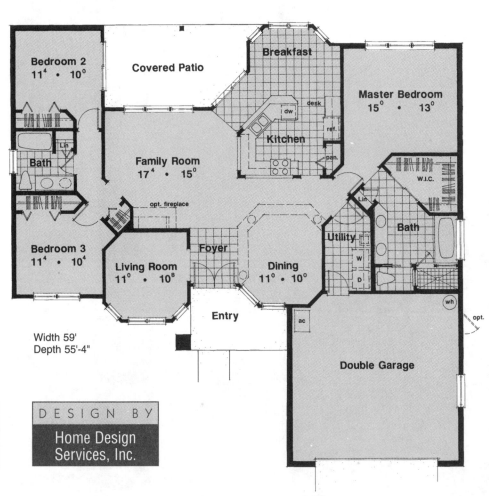

Width 59'
Depth 55'-4"

Design 8644

Square Footage: 1,831

DESIGN BY
Home Design
Services, Inc.

Design HPT440042

First Floor: 1,104 square feet
Second Floor: 1,144 square feet
Total: 2,248 square feet
Bonus Room: 242 square feet

DESIGN BY
Stephen Fuller, Inc.

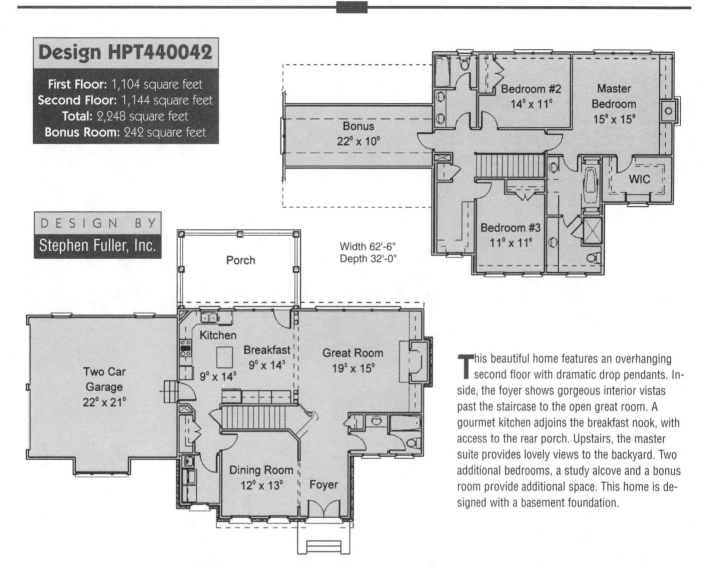

Bonus
22⁰ x 10⁰

Bedroom #2
14⁰ x 11⁰

Master
Bedroom
15⁹ x 15⁹

WIC

Bedroom #3
11⁰ x 11⁶

Width 62'-6"
Depth 32'-0"

Porch

Kitchen
9⁰ x 14³

Breakfast
9⁰ x 14³

Great Room
19³ x 15⁰

Two Car
Garage
22⁰ x 21⁰

Dining Room
12⁰ x 13⁰

Foyer

This beautiful home features an overhanging second floor with dramatic drop pendants. Inside, the foyer shows gorgeous interior vistas past the staircase to the open great room. A gourmet kitchen adjoins the breakfast nook, with access to the rear porch. Upstairs, the master suite provides lovely views to the backyard. Two additional bedrooms, a study alcove and a bonus room provide additional space. This home is designed with a basement foundation.

Design 6629

Square Footage: 2,214

Make yourself at home in this delightful one-story design. An arched entry greets family and visitors and announces a comfortable and stylish interior design. Volume ceilings highlight the main living areas, including a formal dining room and a great room with access to a rear veranda. The convenient kitchen opens to a skylit breakfast nook and offers dual access to a split veranda. The homeowner will find repose in the cozy, turreted study, offering privacy through double doors. Off to one side of the plan, a spacious master suite offers a vaulted ceiling, a bumped-out whirlpool tub, a split walk-in closet and corner windows. Secondary bedrooms on the opposite side of the plan share a full bath and a gallery hall that leads to a rear veranda.

DESIGN BY

The Sater Design Collection

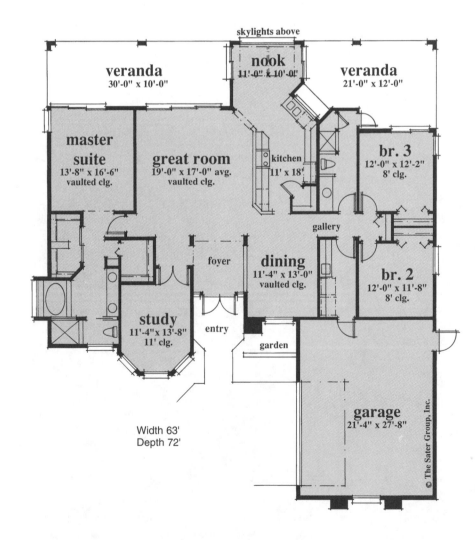

skylights above

veranda
30'-0" x 10'-0"

nook
11'-0" x 10'-0"

veranda
21'-0" x 12'-0"

master suite
13'-8" x 16'-6"
vaulted clg.

great room
19'-0" x 17'-0" avg.
vaulted clg.

kitchen
11' x 18'

br. 3
12'-0" x 12'-2"
8' clg.

gallery

foyer

dining
11'-4" x 13'-0"
vaulted clg.

br. 2
12'-0" x 11'-8"
8' clg.

study
11'-4" x 13'-8"
11' clg.

entry

garden

garage
21'-4" x 27'-8"

© The Sater Group, Inc.

Width 63'
Depth 72'

SCREEN PORCH
20-8 x 9-6
(cathedral ceiling)

DECK

PORCH

GARAGE
21-0 x 20-8

walk-in closet

MASTER BED RM.
12-8 x 17-2

fireplace

GREAT RM.
15-4 x 19-4
(cathedral ceiling)

BRKFST.
10-8 x 9-8

UTIL.
7-6 x 7-10

w   d

storage

balcony above

KIT.
13-0 x 13-6

up

master bath

bath

lin.

lin.

up

BED RM./ STUDY
12-8 x 11-4

cl

cl

cl

FOYER
13-0 x 8-10
(vaulted ceiling)

DINING
12-8 x 12-8

PORCH

© 1997 Donald A Gardner Architects, Inc.

D E S I G N   B Y
Donald A. Gardner Architects, Inc.

Width 77'-11"
Depth 53'-2"

attic storage

great room below

attic storage

railing

balcony

BED RM.
12-8 x 12-0

down

BED RM.
12-8 x 12-0

cl

cl

bath

cl

cl

attic storage

foyer below

attic storage

BONUS RM.
12-0 x 20-8

down

A lovely arch-top window and a wraparound porch set off this country exterior. Inside, formal rooms open off the foyer, which leads to a spacious great room. This living area has a fireplace and access to a screened porch with a cathedral ceiling. Bay windows allow natural light into the breakfast area and formal dining room. The master bedroom provides a spacious bath and access to a private area of the rear porch. Two second-floor bedrooms share a bath and a balcony overlook to the great room.

Design HPT440043

First Floor: 1,743 square feet
Second Floor: 555 square feet
Total: 2,298 square feet
Bonus Room: 350 square feet

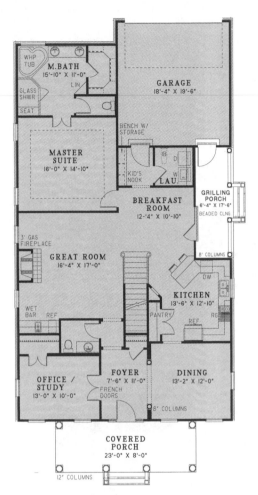

WHP TUB
M.BATH
15'-10" X 11'-0"
GLASS SHWR
SEAT
LIN

GARAGE
18'-4" X 19'-6"

BENCH W/ STORAGE

MASTER SUITE
16'-0" X 14'-10"

KID'S NOOK

LAU

GRILLING PORCH
6'-4" X 17'-6"
BEADED CLNG.

BREAKFAST ROOM
12'-4" X 10'-10"

3' GAS FIREPLACE

GREAT ROOM
16'-4" X 17'-0"

8" COLUMNS

WET BAR   **REF**

KITCHEN
13'-6" X 12'-10"

PANTRY

DW

REF

OFFICE / STUDY
13'-0" X 10'-0"

FOYER
7'-6" X 11'-0"
FRENCH DOORS

DINING
13'-2" X 12'-0"

8" COLUMNS

COVERED PORCH
23'-0" X 8'-0"

12" COLUMNS

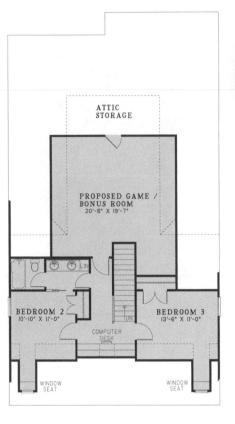

ATTIC STORAGE

PROPOSED GAME / BONUS ROOM
20'-8" X 19'-7"

LIN

BEDROOM 2
10'-10" X 11'-0"

BEDROOM 3
13'-6" X 11'-0"

COMPUTER DESK

WINDOW SEAT   **WINDOW SEAT**

Width 35'-4"
Depth 71'-6"

Design HPT440044

First Floor: 1,698 square feet
Second Floor: 533 square feet
Total: 2,231 square feet
Bonus Room: 394 square feet

For the homeowner who wants luxury on a narrow lot, this design is the way to go. Walk into the formal spaces—a study with French doors and a dining room with shapely columns. From there, step into the voluminous kitchen with a hefty pantry and angled snack bar. The great room and breakfast room flow from this point into the rear master suite and garage. The secondary bedrooms are tucked away upstairs. Please specify crawlspace or slab foundation when ordering.

DESIGN BY
Michael E. Nelson, Nelson Design Group, LLC

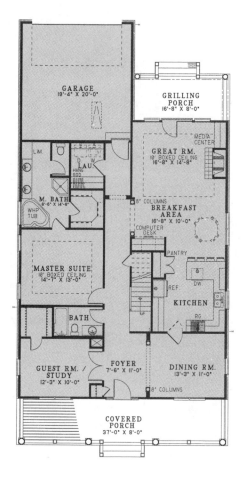

GARAGE
19'-4" X 20'-0"

GRILLING PORCH
16'-8" X 8'-0"

MEDIA CENTER

LIN

LAU
HANG ROD

D. W.

M. BATH
8'-6" X 14'-8"

WHP TUB

8" COLUMNS

GREAT RM.
10' BOXED CEILING
16'-8" X 14'-8"

BREAKFAST AREA
16'-8" X 10'-0"

COMPUTER DESK

MASTER SUITE
10' BOXED CEILING
14'-7" X 13'-0"

PANTRY

REF

DW

BATH

KITCHEN

RG

FOYER
7'-6" X 11'-0"

DINING RM.
13'-3" X 11'-0"

GUEST RM. / STUDY
12'-3" X 10'-0"

8" COLUMNS

COVERED PORCH
37'-0" X 8'-0"

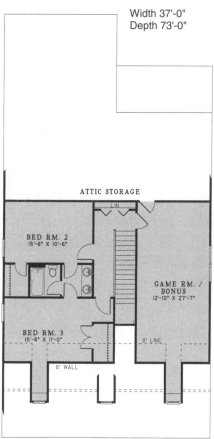

Width 37'-0"
Depth 73'-0"

ATTIC STORAGE

BED RM. 2
15'-6" X 10'-6"

LIN

BED RM. 3
15'-6" X 11'-0"

GAME RM. / BONUS
12'-10" X 27'-7"

8' LINE

6' WALL

Design HPT440045

First Floor: 1,713 square feet
Second Floor: 610 square feet
Total: 2,323 square feet
Bonus Room: 384 square feet

This well-balanced design includes three dormers, a columned porch and a charming brick-and-siding exterior. The foyer ushers guests into the formal dining room or through the French doors of the study/guest room. The master suite provides a walk-in closet, whirlpool tub, separate shower and twin vanities. The great room is enhanced by a focal-point fireplace and built-in media center. Upstairs, two family bedrooms share a walk-through bath. Please specify basement, crawlspace or slab foundation when ordering.

DESIGN BY
Michael E. Nelson, Nelson Design Group, LLC

Design HPT440046

Square Footage: 2,053

Shutters, multi-pane glass windows and cross-hatched railing on the front porch make this a beautiful country cottage. To the left of the foyer is a roomy great room and a warming fireplace, framed by windows. To the right of the foyer, two family bedrooms feature walk-in closets and share a fully appointed bath. The efficient kitchen centers around a long island workstation and opens to the large dining/sitting room. The rear porch adds living space. French doors, a fireplace and columns complete this three-bedroom design. Please specify basement, crawlspace or slab foundation when ordering.

DESIGN BY
Larry James & Associates, Inc.

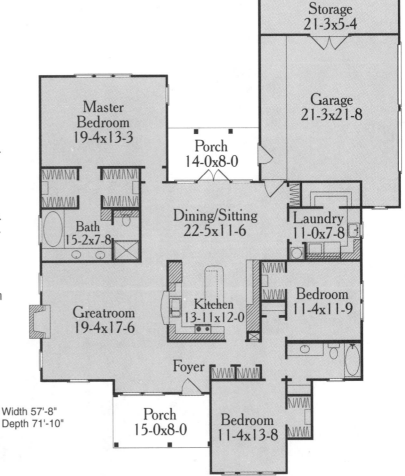

Storage
21-3x5-4

Garage
21-3x21-8

Master
Bedroom
19-4x13-3

Porch
14-0x8-0

Bath
15-2x7-8

Dining/Sitting
22-5x11-6

Laundry
11-0x7-8

Greatroom
19-4x17-6

Kitchen
13-11x12-0

Bedroom
11-4x11-9

Foyer

Width 57'-8"
Depth 71'-10"

Porch
15-0x8-0

Bedroom
11-4x13-8

A TOUCH OF CLASS

Affordable Dream Homes

World-class luxury homes aren't better because they're bigger—the most sensational plans build real homes that ground us, steady us and help us take root in a region. Design integrity, architectural balance and proportion, and attention to detail are part of a quality home, no matter what its size. And some of the best dream homes are the most affordable.

Lavish exteriors loaded with charm make an alluring statement but it's the quality and comfort within that really make a house step out in style. Open, bright interiors that transcend fads of the day are the true heart of a home. This selection of plans shows off some of our new ideas for interior spaces: wide kitchens, secluded dining rooms, grand great rooms, extraordinary master suites, and even a one-golf-cart garage.

Plans that may seem sprawling and untamed on paper build to cozy sanctuaries when braced with simple themes and subtle divisions of space. Design 3664 (page 179) affords private places to nestle as well as wide, open places that soar and sparkle—all with a casual elegance. And Design 3433 (page 191) combines a classic Southwestern look, earthy and spirited, with fresh ideas for indoor/outdoor relationships—from sunny sitting areas to cool breakfast *portales*.

Our plans capture the spirit and diversity of many regions. And whether the backdrop for your home is the big city or the wide open spaces, we'll help you create a home that redefines luxury. What kind of homes do innovative design, plucky creativity and timeless craftsmanship build? The possibilities could be endless.

iagonals used wisely in this Contemporary design make it a versatile choice for a variety of lot arrangements. Open planning inside creates visual appeal—the entry offers interior vistas through decorative columns and graceful arches. A fabulous great room offers a corner fireplace framed by walls of windows, which allow stunning views to outdoor areas. An exquisite formal dining room with a coffered ceiling shares the natural light of the great room. An island kitchen with a snack bar, a planning desk, and a walk-in pantry opens to a breakfast area with bayed nook. Homeowners will retreat to the restful master suite, which offers a coffered ceiling, corner whirlpool bath, a glass-enclosed shower, twin lavatories and a walk-in closet. Two family bedrooms share a nearby full bath. The three-car garage holds extra storage space and allows access to the house through the mud/laundry room.

Design 9250

Square Footage: 2,133

DESIGN BY
Design Basics, Inc.

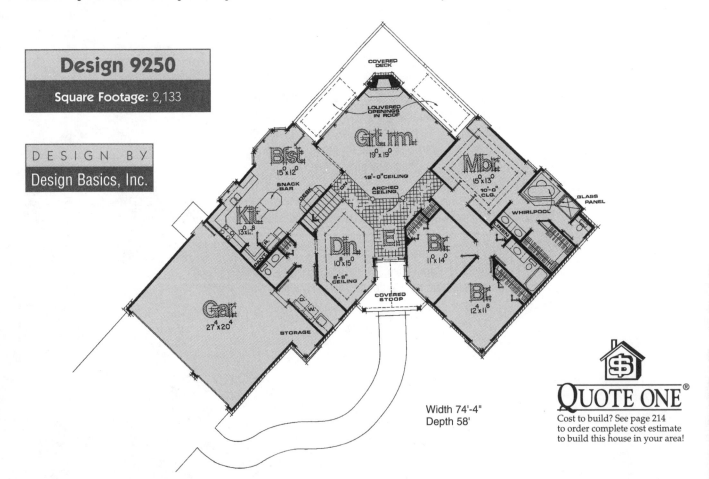

Width 74'-4"
Depth 58'

Classic keystones, quoins and stately arches create an elegant exterior and complement a grand, vaulted entry. Guests may linger in the tiled gallery off the foyer, but they'll certainly want to enjoy some of the uncommon amenities this plan has to offer. A sizable great room makes leisure and casual entertaining a pleasure, and features a handsome fireplace with extended hearth, framed by decorative niches. Plant shelves decorate this area, above triple doors to the patio retreat. The kitchen features a cooktop/utility island and built-in desk and opens to a windowed breakfast bay which allows an abundance of natural light. An eating counter accomodates quick snacks and invites family conversations. For formal occasions, this plan has a great dining room—off to one side to permit private, unhurried evening meals. Rest and relaxation await the homeowners in a sensational master suite—and for true peace and quiet, retire to an inner retreat with access to a private patio. Two family bedrooms share a private bath, and one room opens to a covered patio. A small garage designed for a one-car golf cart adjoins a roomy two-car garage.

DESIGN BY
Home Planners

Design 3664

Square Footage: 2,471

Width 86'-4"
Depth 80'-2"

QUOTE ONE®

Cost to build? See page 214
to order complete cost estimate
to build this house in your area!

Design 9089

Square Footage: 1,849

DESIGN BY
Larry W. Garnett & Associates, Inc.

QUOTE ONE®

Cost to build? See page 214
to order complete cost estimate
to build this house in your area!

This cozy one-story design offers luxury in a compact size. A raised foyer opens to a rambling living room with centered fireplace flanked by double French doors. To the right, a formal dining room with high ceiling opens to the galley kitchen which offers a huge pantry and sunny breakfast area. The master suite with walk-in closet features a luxurious bath with garden tub and double lavatories. To the left of the plan, two family bedrooms share a hall bath.

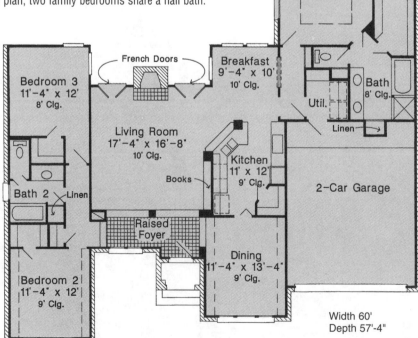

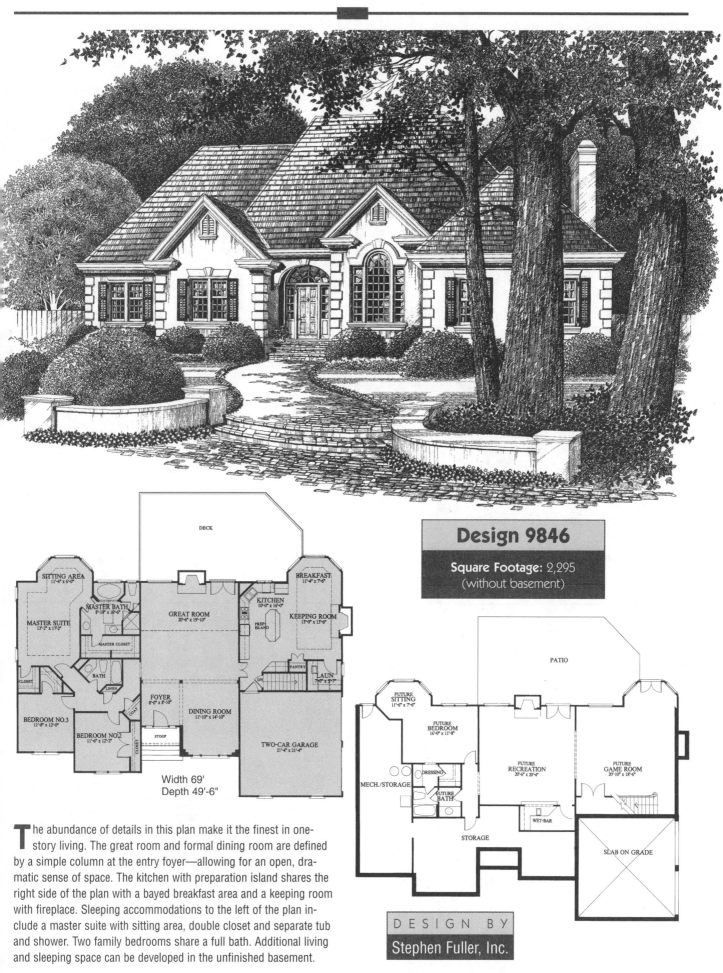

Design 9846

Square Footage: 2,295
(without basement)

DECK

SITTING AREA
11'-4" x 6'-0"

MASTER BATH
8'-10" x 10'-6"

MASTER SUITE
13'-2" x 17'-2"

MASTER CLOSET

CLOSET

BATH

LINEN

BEDROOM NO.3
11'-6" x 12'-0"

BEDROOM NO.2
11'-6" x 12'-2"

CLOSET

COAT

STOOP

GREAT ROOM
20'-6" x 19'-10"

KITCHEN
10'-0" x 16'-0"

BREAKFAST
11'-4" x 7'-6"

KEEPING ROOM
13'-0" x 13'-6"

PREP ISLAND

PANTRY

DN

LAUN
7'-6" x 9'-7"

FOYER
8'-0" x 8'-10"

DINING ROOM
11'-10" x 14'-10"

TWO-CAR GARAGE
21'-4" x 21'-4"

Width 69'
Depth 49'-6"

FUTURE
SITTING
11'-6" x 7'-6"

FUTURE
BEDROOM
16'-0" x 11'-8"

MECH./STORAGE

DRESSING

FUTURE
BATH

STORAGE

WET-BAR

PATIO

FUTURE
RECREATION
20'-6" x 20'-4"

FUTURE
GAME ROOM
20'-10" x 18'-6"

SLAB ON GRADE

The abundance of details in this plan make it the finest in one-story living. The great room and formal dining room are defined by a simple column at the entry foyer—allowing for an open, dramatic sense of space. The kitchen with preparation island shares the right side of the plan with a bayed breakfast area and a keeping room with fireplace. Sleeping accommodations to the left of the plan include a master suite with sitting area, double closet and separate tub and shower. Two family bedrooms share a full bath. Additional living and sleeping space can be developed in the unfinished basement.

DESIGN BY
Stephen Fuller, Inc.

181

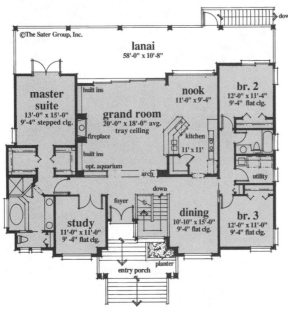

©The Sater Group, Inc.

lanai
58'-0" x 10'-8"

master suite
13'-0" x 15'-0"
9'-4" stepped clg.

built ins

grand room
20'-0" x 18'-0" avg.
tray ceiling

fireplace

built ins

opt. aquarium

arch

nook
11'-0" x 9'-4"

kitchen
11' x 11'

br. 2
12'-0" x 11'-4"
9'-4" flat clg.

utility

foyer

down

dining
10'-10" x 15'-0"
9'-4" flat clg.

br. 3
12'-0" x 11'-0"
9'-4" flat clg.

study
11'-0" x 11'-0"
9'-4" flat clg.

planter

entry porch

down

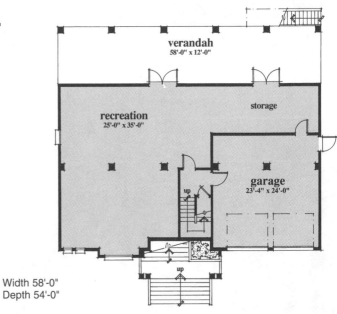

verandah
58'-0" x 12'-0"

recreation
25'-0" x 35'-0"

storage

garage
23'-4" x 24'-0"

up

up

Width 58'-0"
Depth 54'-0"

A dramatic set of stairs leads to the entry of this home. The foyer opens to an expansive grand room with a fireplace and built-in bookshelves. For formal meals, a front-facing dining room offers plenty of space and a bumped-out bay. The kitchen serves this area easily as well as the breakfast room. A study and three bedrooms make up the rest of the floor plan. Two secondary bedrooms share a full bath. The master suite contains two walk-in closets and a full bath.

QUOTE ONE®

Cost to build? See page 214
to order complete cost estimate
to build this house in your area!

See page 214 to order complete cost estimate to build this house in your area!

Design HPT440047

Square Footage: 2,190

DESIGN BY
The Sater Design Collection

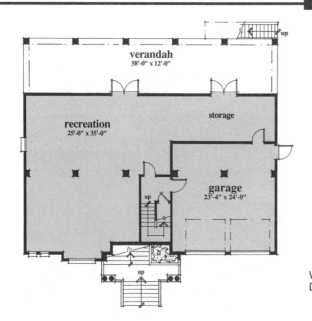

verandah
58'-0" x 12'-0"

recreation
25'-0" x 35'-0"

storage

garage
23'-4" x 24'-0"

up

up

up

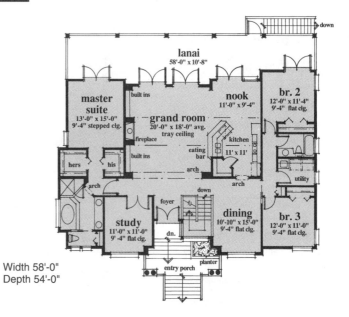

lanai
58'-0" x 10'-8"

master suite
13'-0" x 15'-0"
9'-4" stepped clg.

built ins

nook
11'-0" x 9'-4"

br. 2
12'-0" x 11'-4"
9'-4" flat clg.

grand room
20'-0" x 18'-0" avg.
tray ceiling

fireplace

built ins

kitchen
11' x 11'

eating bar

hers

his

arch

arch

utility

arch

study
11'-0" x 11'-0"
9'-4" flat clg.

foyer

down

dining
10'-10" x 15'-0"
9'-4" flat clg.

br. 3
12'-0" x 11'-0"
9'-4" flat clg.

dn.

planter

entry porch

Width 58'-0"
Depth 54'-0"

The dramatic arched entry of this Southampton-style cottage borrows freely from its Southern coastal past. The foyer and central hall open to the grand room. The kitchen is flanked by the dining room and morning nook, which opens to the lanai. On the left side of the plan, the master suite also accesses the lanai. Two walk-in closets, a compartmented bath with separate tub and shower and a double-bowl vanity complete the opulent master retreat. The right side of the plan includes two secondary bedrooms and a full bath.

Design HPT440048

Square Footage: 2,190

DESIGN BY
The Sater Design Collection

Design 8601

Square Footage: 2,125

A luxurious master suite is just one of the highlights offered with this lovely plan—an alternate plan for this suite features a sitting room, wet bar and fireplace. Two family bedrooms to the right of the plan share a full bath with twin lavatories, and a gallery hall which leads to a covered patio. Tile adds interest to the living areas and surrounds a spacious great room, which offers a fireplace and access to the rear patio. A formal dining room and secluded den or study are to the front.

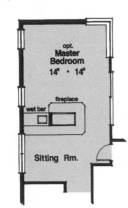

opt.
Master Bedroom
14⁰ · 14⁰

wet bar · fireplace

Sitting Rm.

Master Bedroom
16⁰ · 14⁰

Covered Patio

Breakfast

w.l.c.

Bedroom 3
12⁴ · 12⁰

w.l.c.

Great Room
22⁰ · 17⁰

fireplace

dw

Kitchen

ref

pantry

Bath

Bedroom 2
12⁴ · 12⁰

Dress

up

Den/Study
12⁰ · 11⁰

Bath

opt.

Foyer

Dining
13¹⁰ · 11⁸

Utility

lin

w

d

ac

wh

ac

Entry

Double Garage

DESIGN BY
Home Design Services, Inc.

Width 65'
Depth 56'-8"

J.H. HANSEN P.T.L.

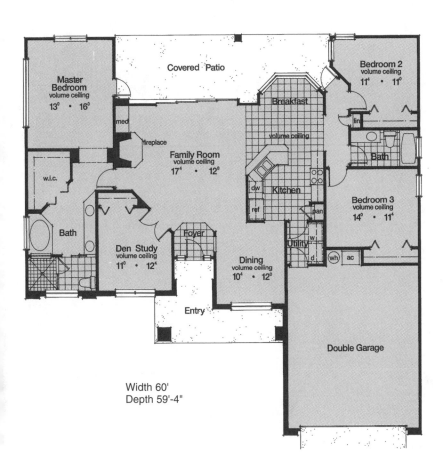

Covered Patio

Master Bedroom
volume ceiling
13⁰ · 16⁰

med

fireplace

w.i.c.

Bath

Den Study
volume ceiling
11⁰ · 12⁴

Foyer

Family Room
volume ceiling
17⁴ · 12⁸

Breakfast

volume ceiling

dw

ref

Kitchen

Dining
volume ceiling
10⁴ · 12⁰

Utility

w
d

wh ac

pan

Bedroom 2
volume ceiling
11⁴ · 11⁰

lin

Bath

Bedroom 3
volume ceiling
14⁰ · 11⁴

Entry

Double Garage

Width 60'
Depth 59'-4"

Design 8684

Square Footage: 1,898

Family living is at the core of this brick one-story home inspired by the design of Frank Lloyd Wright. To the left of the foyer, double doors open onto a den/study which could easily be converted to a nursery. The nearby master suite features a spacious bedroom and a pampering bath with a large walk-in closet, a separate shower and a relaxing tub. Centrally located, the family room with a cozy fireplace opens to a bayed breakfast nook and a well-appointed kitchen—a perfect arrangement for casual gatherings. The family sleeping wing offers two bedrooms and a full bath, plus patio access via a "kids" door.

DESIGN BY

Home Design
Services, Inc.

This elegant exterior houses a very livable plan. Every bit of space has been put to good use. The front country kitchen is a good place to begin.

Design 2668

First Floor: 1,206 square feet
Second Floor: 1,254 square feet
Total: 2,460 square feet

L

It is efficiently planned with its island cooktop, built-ins and pass-through to the dining room. The large great room will be the center of all family activities. Quiet times can be enjoyed in the front library. The second floor contains the sleeping zone made up of three family bedrooms and a grand master suite.

Width 52'
Depth 42'

Quote One®
Cost to build? See page 214
to order complete cost estimate
to build this house in your area!

DESIGN BY
Home Planners

© Design Traditions

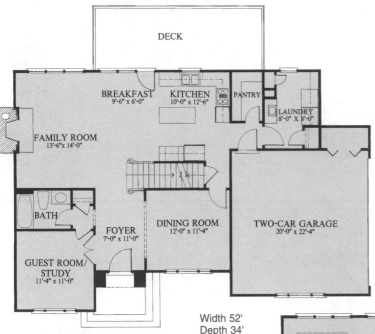

DECK

BREAKFAST
9'-6" x 6'-0"

KITCHEN
10'-0" x 12'-6"

PANTRY

LAUNDRY
8'-0" X 8'-0"

FAMILY ROOM
13'-6" x 14'-0"

BATH

FOYER
7'-0" x 11'-0"

DINING ROOM
12'-0" x 11'-4"

TWO-CAR GARAGE
20'-0" x 22'-4"

GUEST ROOM/
STUDY
11'-4" x 11'-0"

Width 52'
Depth 34'

Design 9900

First Floor: 1,103 square feet
Second Floor: 1,103 square feet
Total: 2,206 square feet
Bonus Room: 212 square feet

Decorative keystones and muntin windows complement a stucco exterior, creating European appeal with this design. An open living area, including a family room with fireplace, a breakfast area with rear deck access and an island kitchen, invites casual gatherings. A dining room to the front of the plan offers more private space for formal occasions. Upstairs, a master suite with coffered ceiling offers a sitting area and a bath with dual vanity, whirlpool tub, separate shower and walk-in closet. Two family bedrooms share a full bath with dual vanity. The bonus room would make a great home office. This home is designed with a basement foundation.

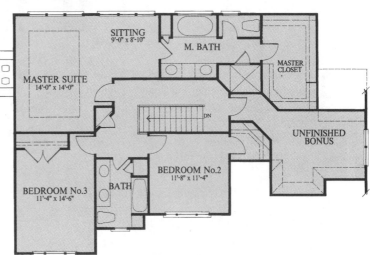

SITTING
9'-0" x 8'-10"

M. BATH

MASTER
CLOSET

MASTER SUITE
14'-0" x 14'-0"

UNFINISHED
BONUS

DN

BEDROOM No.2
11'-8" x 11'-4"

BEDROOM No.3
11'-4" x 14'-6"

BATH

D E S I G N   B Y

Stephen Fuller, Inc.

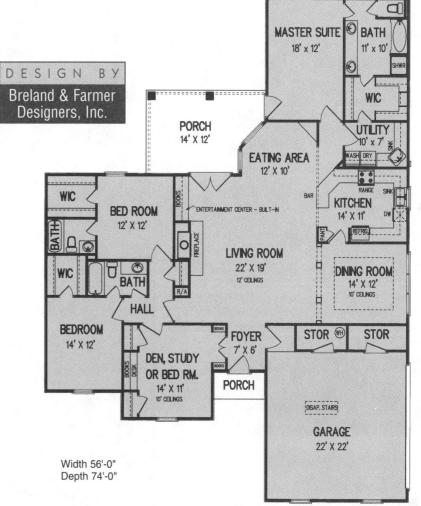

Design HPT440049

Square Footage: 2,200

DESIGN BY
Breland & Farmer Designers, Inc.

A versatile swing room is a highlight of this compact and charming French-style home. Using the optional door opening to the entry, the swing room makes a perfect office, or it can be used as a bedroom or study. The king-size master suite is isolated for privacy and has a spacious bath and walk-in closet with passage to the utility room. The open and spacious living room features twelve-foot ceilings. Two secondary bedrooms offer walk-in closets and private baths. Please specify crawlspace or slab foundation when ordering.

MASTER SUITE
18' x 12'

BATH
11' x 10'

SHWR

WIC

PORCH
14' X 12'

UTILITY
10' x 7'

WASH DRY   SINK

EATING AREA
12' X 10'

BAR

RANGE   SINK

KITCHEN
14' x 11'

DW

ENTERTAINMENT CENTER – BUILT-IN

PANT   REFRIG.

WIC

BED ROOM
12' X 12'

BOOKS

BATH

FIREPLACE

LIVING ROOM
22' X 19'
12' CEILINGS

DINING ROOM
14' X 12'
10' CEILINGS

WIC

BATH

R/A

HALL

BEDROOM
14' X 12'

BOOKS
DESK

DEN, STUDY
OR BED RM.
14' X 11'
10' CEILINGS

BOOKS

BOOKS

FOYER
7' X 6'

STOR   WH   STOR

PORCH

DISAP. STAIRS

GARAGE
22' X 22'

Width 56'-0"
Depth 74'-0"

Floor Plan Labels

Bedroom 2
11⁰ · 10⁰

Bath

lin

Covered Patio

Master Bedroom
16¹⁰ · 13⁰

w.i.c.

Nook

Bedroom 3
12⁰ · 11⁰

fireplace

Family Room
19⁰ · 15¹⁰

desk

Bath

linen

Bath

lin

Kitchen

dw

Utility

w

d

Living Room
12⁸ · 10¹⁰

ref

pan

ac

wh

ac

Bedroom 4
12⁰ · 11⁰

Foyer

Dining
12⁸ · 10¹⁰

Double Garage

Entry

Width 61'-8"
Depth 50'-4"

DESIGN BY
Home Design
Services, Inc.

Design 8637

Square Footage: 2,089

This four-bedroom, three-bath home offers the finest in modern amenities. The formal living spaces have a classic split design, perfect for quiet time and conversation. The unique design of the bedroom wing affords flexibility and offers a livable environment for the family. Bedrooms 3 and 4 share their own bath while Bedroom 2 has a private bath with pool access, making it the perfect guest room. The huge family room, which opens up to the patio with twelve-foot, pocket sliding doors, has space for a fireplace and media equipment. The master suite, located just off the kitchen and nook, offers a private retreat and features a double door entry and a bed wall with glass above. The angled entry to the bath allows a dressing area near the walk-in closet. The step-down shower, private toilet room, and knee-space vanity make this a super bath!

J. N. HANSEN P.L.

Design 3644

Square Footage: 2,015

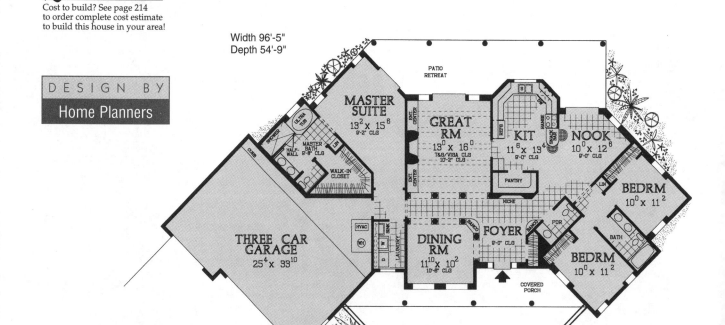

Quote One®

Cost to build? See page 214
to order complete cost estimate
to build this house in your area!

DESIGN BY
Home Planners

This Santa Fe-style home is as warm as a desert breeze and just as comfortable. Outside details are reminiscent of old-style adobe homes, while the interior caters to convenient living. The front covered porch leads to an open foyer. Columns define the formal dining room and the giant great room. The kitchen has an enormous pantry, a snack bar and is connected to a breakfast nook with rear patio access. Two family bedrooms are found on the right side of the plan. They share a full bathroom with twin vanities. The master suite is on the left side of the plan and has a monstrous walk-in closet and a bath with spa tub and separate shower. The home is completed with a three-car garage.

Width 96'-5"
Depth 54'-9"

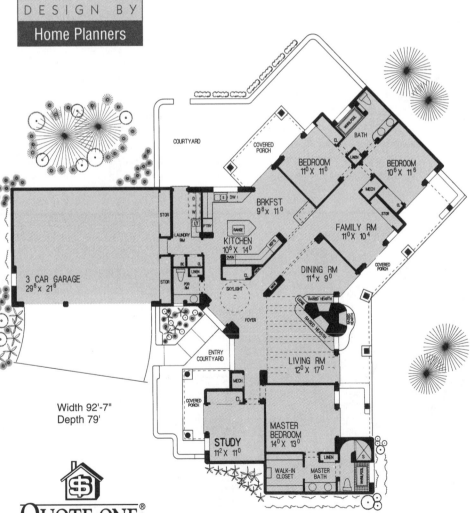

COURTYARD

COVERED PORCH

BEDROOM
11⁰ X 11⁰

BATH

BEDROOM
10⁶ X 11⁶

LINEN

MECH

STOR

BRKFST
9⁸ X 11⁰

FAMILY RM
11⁰ X 10⁴

KITCHEN
10⁶ X 14⁰

RANGE

STOR

W

PNTRY

DW

3 CAR GARAGE
29⁸ x 21⁶

LAUNDRY RM

STOR

CL
LINEN

PDR RM

DINING RM
11⁴ X 9⁰

COVERED PORCH

SKYLIGHT

RAISED HEARTH

FOYER

LIVING RM
12⁰ X 17⁰

ENTRY COURTYARD

COVERED PORCH

MECH

CL

MASTER BEDROOM
14⁰ X 13⁰

STUDY
11² X 11⁰

WALK-IN CLOSET

MASTER BATH

LINEN

Width 92'-7"
Depth 79'

Design 3433

Square Footage: 2,350

L

Santa Fe styling creates interesting angles in this one-story home. A grand entrance leads through a skylit courtyard, and opens through the foyer to a magnificent living room with a triple fireplace—shared by the dining room and an outdoor entertainment area. A gourmet kitchen with island range is designed for easy entertaining, both formal and informal. The family will enjoy gathering in the spacious breakfast room nearby, which offers access to one of the covered porches. A master suite with superior amenities offers privacy and repose to the home-owner, and a study with access to a private covered porch is nearby—perfect for enjoying the view or quiet contemplation. Two family bedrooms to the rear of the plan share a full bath and offer access to outdoor areas.

Design 3660

Square Footage: 2,086

L

Quote One®

Cost to build? See page 214
to order complete cost estimate
to build this house in your area!

This home exhibits wonderful dual-use space in the sunken living room and media area. Anchoring each end of this spacious living zone is the raised-hearth fireplace and the entertainment center. The outstanding kitchen has an informal breakfast bay and looks over the snack bar to the family area. To the rear of the plan, a few steps from the kitchen and functioning with the upper patio, is the formal dining room. Through the archway are two children's bedrooms and a bath with twin vanities. At the far end of the plan is the master suite. It has a sitting area with fine, natural light. A few steps away, French doors open to the covered master patio.

DESIGN BY
Home Planners

Width 82'
Depth 58'-4"

Photo by Oscar Thompson Photography

This home, as shown in the photograph, may differ from the actual blueprints. For more detailed information, please check the floor plans carefully.

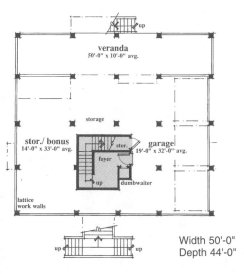

veranda
50'-0" x 10'-0" avg.

storage

stor./ bonus
14'-0" x 33'-0" avg.

stor.

garage
19'-0" x 32'-0" avg.

foyer

up

dumbwaiter

lattice work walls

up   up

Width 50'-0"
Depth 44'-0"

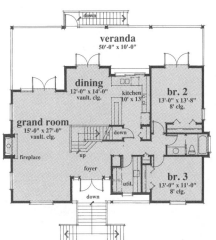

down

veranda
50'-0" x 10'-0"

dining
12'-0" x 14'-0"
vault. clg.

kitchen
10' x 13'

br. 2
13'-0" x 13'-8"
8' clg.

grand room
15'-0" x 27'-0"
vault. clg.

down

fireplace

up

br. 3
13'-0" x 11'-0"
8' clg.

foyer

util.

down

Design HPT440050

First Floor: 1,586 square feet
Second Floor: 601 square feet
Total: 2,187 square feet

DESIGN BY
The Sater Design Collection

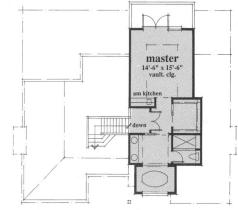

master
14'-6" x 15'-6"
vault. clg.

am kitchen

down

Lattice walls, pickets and horizontal siding complement a relaxed Key West design that's perfect for waterfront properties. The grand room, with a fireplace, the dining room and Bedroom 2 open through French doors to the veranda. The master suite occupies the second floor. Bedrooms 2 and 3 reside on the first floor, where they share a full bath. Enclosed storage plus bonus space is on the lower level. This home is designed with a pier foundation.

Design 3657

Square Footage: 2,319

QUOTE ONE®

Cost to build? See page 214
to order complete cost estimate
to build this house in your area!

A magnificent arched entry announces splendid planning with this Floridian design. The tiled foyer invites guests toward a gracious gathering room with fireplace and views to the rear grounds—although they may want to linger on the front covered patio. Decorative half-walls define the formal dining area which offers rear patio access. The nearby kitchen is equipped to serve formal and informal occasions, and even features a snack counter for mini-meals. An office or guest room in this area, with a nearby powder room, accomodates visitors. An archway off the foyer leads to sleeping quarters, which include an outstanding master suite with His and Hers walk-in closets, step-down shower, knee-space vanity, and whirlpool tub. Two family bedrooms off a gallery hall share a full bath.

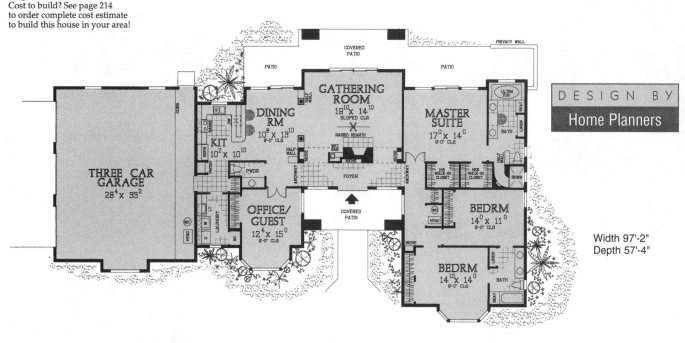

DESIGN BY
Home Planners

Width 97'-2"
Depth 57'-4"

A classic pediment and low-pitched roof are topped by a cupola on this gorgeous coastal design. Savory style blended with a contemporary seaside spirit invites entertaining as well as year-round living—plus room to grow. The beauty and warmth of natural light splash the spacious living area with a sense of the outdoors and a touch of joie de vivre. The great room features a wall of built-ins designed for even the most technology-savvy entertainment buff. Dazzling views through walls of glass are enlivened by the presence of a breezy portico. The master suite features a luxurious bath, a dressing area and two walk-in closets. Glass doors open to the portico and provide generous views of the seascape, while a nearby study offers an indoor retreat. Please specify pier or block foundation when ordering.

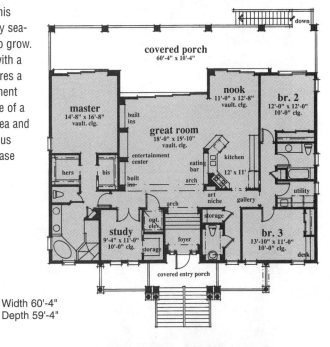

Width 60'-4"
Depth 59'-4"

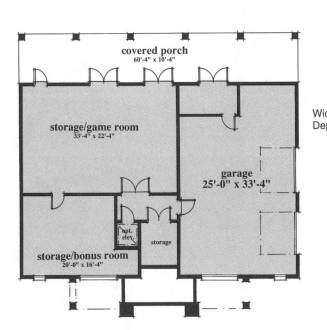

Design HPT440051

Main Level: 2,385 square feet
Lower Level : 80 square feet
Total: 2,465 square feet

DESIGN BY
The Sater Design Collection

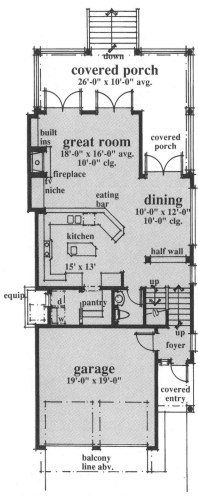

covered porch
26'-0" x 10'-0" avg.

down

built ins

great room
18'-0" x 16'-0" avg.
10'-0" clg.

covered porch

fireplace

tv

niche

eating bar

dining
10'-0" x 12'-0"
10'-0" clg.

kitchen
15' x 13'

half wall

equip

d

w

pantry

up

up

foyer

garage
19'-0" x 19'-0"

covered entry

balcony line abv.

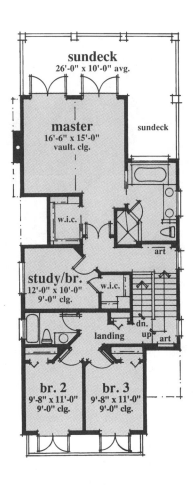

sundeck
26'-0" x 10'-0" avg.

master
16'-6" x 15'-0"
vault. clg.

sundeck

w.i.c.

art

study/br.
12'-0" x 10'-0"
9'-0" clg.

w.i.c.

dn. up

landing

art

br. 2
9'-8" x 11'-0"
9'-0" clg.

br. 3
9'-8" x 11'-0"
9'-0" clg.

Design HPT440052

First Floor: 878 square feet
Second Floor: 1,245 square feet
Total: 2,121 square feet

A captivating front balcony draws attention to this picturesque design. Inside, French doors open from the great room to views from the back covered porch. The kitchen features a large pantry and shares an eating bar with the dining room and great room. Upstairs, the master suite opens to a sun deck, while two secondary bedrooms access the front balcony. The study could be used as a fourth bedroom.

DESIGN BY

The Sater Design Collection

Width 27'-6"
Depth 64'-0"

COMPLETE RETREATS

Hardworking Vacation Homes

W ho hasn't dreamed of a getaway cabin in the woods, on a lakeshore or perched on a secluded hilltop? Rustic retreats surrounded by wilderness beckon with promises of regeneration and a respite from commutes and cubicles—and a taste of the American dream. Frank Lloyd Wright said that living deep in nature called our democratic spirit out of the confusion of the city and planted it in *terra firma.*

Vacation-home builders today may be seeking solace, or simply a second home—a change of atmosphere and view. Perhaps a gathering place for family and friends for holidays and vacations. One Home Planners customer wanted a fishing lodge for business guests; others just want a place to escape the beeps and bumps of city life. Some hardworking couples build their dream home as a vacation spot then eventually retire there.

Imagine Design 2488 (page 198) on Walden Pond— of course, we've offered a few improvements to the great American classic cabin. Ours has personality, all right, and all the charm it takes to transport its inhabitants to simpler times. But we've thrown in some additional square footage, a few 21st-Century amenities and a splash of pizazz for good measure.

So linger in the shade of a cool front porch, light a fire in the fireplace, sit and read a good book (we offer lots of them—please see pages 222-223). But, most importantly, lead a better life nestled in a Home Planners vacation home you'd be sad to leave.

Photo by Lazlo Regos

This home, as shown in the photograph, may differ from the actual blueprints. For more detailed information, please check the floor plans carefully.

Design 2488

First Floor: 1,113 square feet
Second Floor: 543 square feet
Total: 1,656 square feet

D

A cozy cottage tailor-made for a country lifestyle! This winsome design performs equally well serving active families as a leisure-time retreat or a retirement cottage that provides a quiet haven. As a year-round home, the upstairs with its two sizable bedrooms, full bath and lounge area overlooking the gathering room comfortably holds family and guests. The second floor may also be used to accommodate a home office, a study, a sewing room, a music area or a hobby room. No matter what the lifestyle, this design functions well.

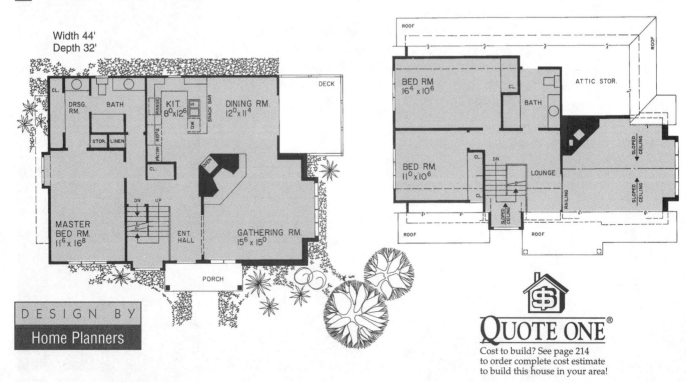

Width 44'
Depth 32'

DESIGN BY
Home Planners

QUOTE ONE®
Cost to build? See page 214
to order complete cost estimate
to build this house in your area!

This compact design is an ideal vacation retreat—with three spacious bedrooms and two full baths, it's actually bigger than it looks! Living areas include a two-story gathering room with warming fireplace and sloped ceiling, a formal dining room and a deck for outdoor eating and entertaining. The well-equipped kitchen is ready for any occasion. A main floor master bedroom offers a large bath with twin lavatories, while upstairs, two family bedrooms share a full bath. An upstairs lounge offers a private balcony.

DESIGN BY
Home Planners

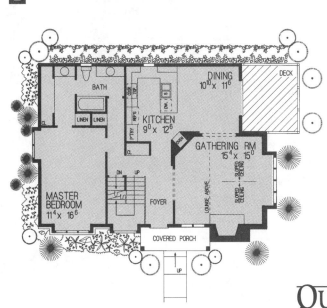

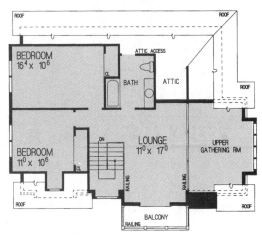

Width 43'
Depth 32'

QUOTE ONE®

Cost to build? See page 214
to order complete cost estimate
to build this house in your area!

This home, as shown in the photograph, may differ from the actual blueprints. For more detailed information, please check the floor plans carefully.

Photo by Bob Greenspan

Design 3680

First Floor: 1,093 square feet
Second Floor: 580 square feet
Total: 1,673 square feet

L **D**

Cost to build? See page 214
to order complete cost estimate
to build this house in your area!

D E S I G N B Y
Home Planners

Brackets and balustrades on front and rear covered porches spell old-fashioned country charm on this rustic retreat. Warm evenings will invite family and guests outdoors for watching sunsets and stars. In cooler weather, the raised-hearth fireplace will make the great room a cozy place to gather. The nearby well-appointed kitchen serves both snack bar and breakfast nook. Two family bedrooms and a full bath complete the main level. Upstairs, a master bedroom with sloped ceiling offers a secluded window seat and a complete bath with garden tub, separate shower and twin lavatories. The adjacent loft/study overlooks the great room and shares the glow of the fireplace.

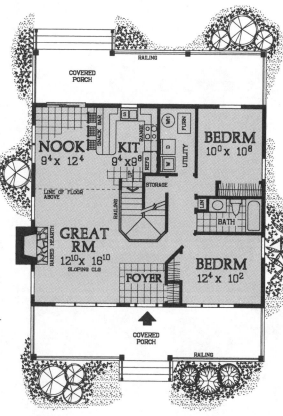

Width 36'
Depth 52'

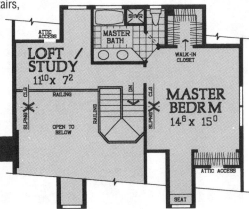

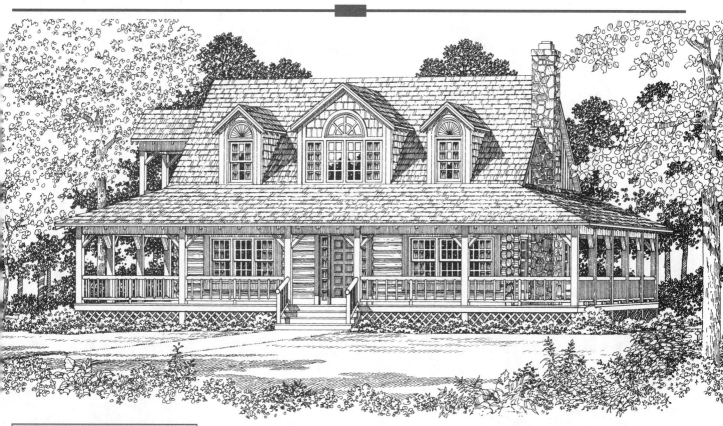

Design 3683

First Floor: 1,139 square feet
Second Floor: 576 square feet
Total: 1,715 square feet

L **D**

DESIGN BY
Home Planners

A be Lincoln most likely would have looked upon this log home as a palace. And he would have been correct! A rustically royal welcome extends from the wraparound porch, inviting one and all into a comfortable interior. To the right of the foyer, a two-story great room enhanced by a raised-hearth fireplace sets a spirited country mood. Nearby, a snack bar joins the living area with an efficient, U-shaped kitchen and an attached nook. Two family bedrooms, a full bath and a utility room with space for a washer and dryer complete the first floor. The second-floor master suite features amenities that create a private, restful getaway. Curl up in the window seat with a good book or enjoy fresh air from your own private balcony. A walk-in closet, a soothing master bath and a loft/study for quiet contemplation complete this special retreat.

Width 52'
Depth 46'

Design 1499

Main Level: 896 square feet
Upper Level: 298 square feet
Lower Level: 896 square feet
Total: 2,090 square feet

Three living levels accomodate family needs with a delightful informality. A dormitory balcony overlooks the main level living room which offers deck access. Hours fly by in this relaxing retreat—you'll be tempted to live here! A well-equipped kitchen will easily accomodate meals. The plan offers sleeping quarters on each of the three levels—two bedrooms and a dormitory—plus extra space for games and recreation. Two full baths, a laundry room and extra storage space complete the plan.

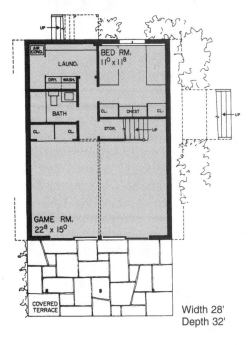

Width 28'
Depth 32'

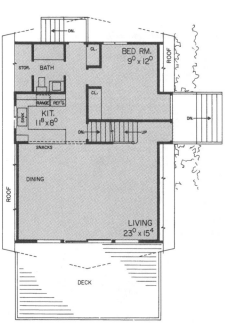

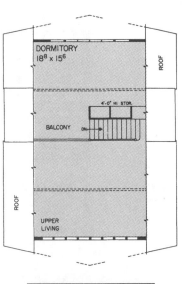

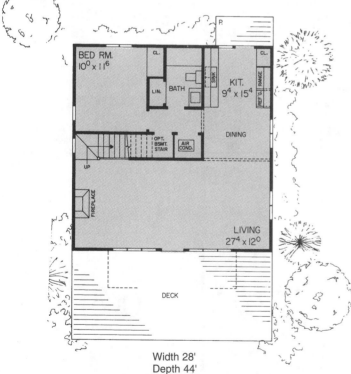

Width 28'
Depth 44'

Good things come in small packages! The size and shape of this design will help hold down construction costs without sacrificing livability. A spacious living room accomodates leisurely gatherings and offers a fireplace and access to a front deck. The kitchen serves a dining area and offers convenient amenities as well as a back porch. Perhaps the most carefree characteristic is the balcony, off the master bedroom on the second level. Also on the second floor is the three-bunk dormitory. Panels through the knee walls give access to an abundant storage area.

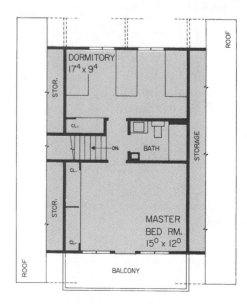

Design 2427

First Floor: 784 square feet
Second Floor: 504 square feet
Total: 1,288 square feet

DESIGN BY
Home Planners

Perfect as a second home or a vacation getaway, this home offers many amenities. A wall of windows graces the living room, presenting wonderful views of the surrounding countryside and access to the wraparound terrace. A kitchen area is located at one end of the living room for ease in serving meals. Two bedrooms and a full bath complete the first floor. Upstairs, a large dormitory with plenty of closet space is available for children or guests.

Design 3658

First Floor: 784 square feet
Second Floor: 275 square feet
Total: 1,059 square feet

L D

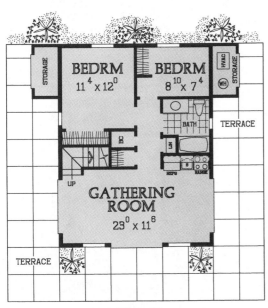

STORAGE

BEDRM
11⁴ x 12⁰

BEDRM
8¹⁰ x 7⁴

HVAC

WH

STORAGE

BATH

TERRACE

UP

GATHERING ROOM
23⁰ x 11⁶

TERRACE

Width 32'
Depth 30'

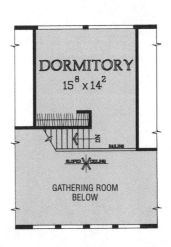

DORMITORY
15⁸ x 14²

DN

RAILING

SLOPED CEILING

GATHERING ROOM
BELOW

QUOTE ONE®

Cost to build? See page 214
to order complete cost estimate
to build this house in your area!

DESIGN BY
Home Planners

B. NATHAN.

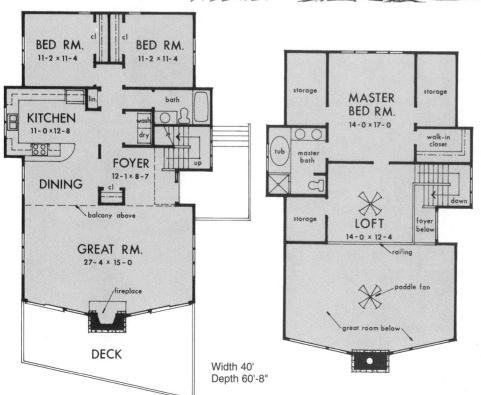

BED RM.
11-2 × 11-4

cl cl

BED RM.
11-2 × 11-4

lin.

KITCHEN
11-0 × 12-8

bath

wash

dry

DINING

FOYER
12-1 × 8-7

cl

up

balcony above

GREAT RM.
27-4 × 15-0

fireplace

DECK

storage

MASTER
BED RM.
14-0 × 17-0

storage

tub

master
bath

walk-in
closet

storage

LOFT
14-0 × 12-4

down

foyer
below

railing

paddle fan

great room below

Width 40'
Depth 60'-8"

Design 9630

First Floor: 1,374 square feet
Second Floor: 608 square feet
Total: 1,982 square feet

This rustic three-bedroom vacation home allows for casual living both inside and out. The two-level great room offers dramatic space for entertaining, with windows to the sloped roof maximizing the outdoor views. A natural rock fireplace dominates this room. Bedrooms on the first floor share a full bath. The second floor holds the master bedroom with spacious master bath and walk-in closet. A large loft area overlooks the great room and entrance foyer.

DESIGN BY
Donald A. Gardner, Architects, Inc.

B·NATHAN·

Design 9697

First Floor: 1,039 square feet
Second Floor: 583 square feet
Total: 1,622 square feet

Charming and compact, this delightful two-story plan fits primary and secondary living needs. For the small family or empty-nester, it has all the room necessary for day-to-day activities. For the vacation home builder, it functions as a cozy retreat with fireplace and outdoor living spaces. Note that the master suite is on the first floor, away from two secondary bedrooms. The kitchen area has an island and attached dining area with boxed window. A two-story great room allows plenty of room for entertaining and relaxing.

DESIGN BY

Donald A. Gardner, Architects, Inc.

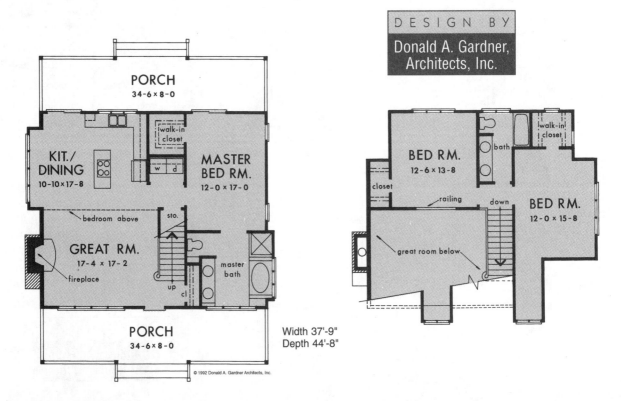

PORCH
34-6 × 8-0

walk-in closet

KIT./DINING
10-10 × 17-8

MASTER BED RM.
12-0 × 17-0

w   d

bedroom above

sto.

GREAT RM.
17-4 × 17-2

fireplace

up   cl

master bath

PORCH
34-6 × 8-0

Width 37'-9"
Depth 44'-8"

BED RM.
12-6 × 13-8

bath

walk-in closet

closet

railing

down

great room below

BED RM.
12-0 × 15-8

LOFT/
STUDY
12-0 x 13-9

railing

great room
below

MASTER
BED RM.
12-0 x 14-0

master
bath

walk-in
closet

down

attic
storage

Width 36'-8"
Depth 45'-0"

UTILITY
8-4 x 7-8

w d cl

PORCH

KIT.
8-0 x 11-4

DINING
10-4 x 11-2

bath

BED RM.
12-0 x 10-0

cl

lin.

cl

cl

balcony above

cl

GREAT RM.
17-4 x 17-0

fireplace

© 1994 DAGA
All rights reserved

up

BED RM.
12-0 x 13-4

PORCH

This rustic three-bedroom home conveys a relaxing country image with its front and rear covered porches. Open planning extends to the great room, the dining room and the efficient kitchen. A shared cathedral ceiling creates an impressive space. Completing the first floor are two family bedrooms, a full bath and a handy utility area. The second floor contains the master suite featuring a spacious walk-in closet and a master bath with a whirlpool tub and a separate corner shower. A generous loft/study overlooks the great room below.

Design HPT440053

First Floor: 1,100 square feet
Second Floor: 584 square feet
Total: 1,684 square feet

QUOTE ONE®
Cost to build? See page 214
to order complete cost estimate
to build this house in your area!

© 1991 Donald A. Gardner Architects, Inc.

B·NATHAN·

Design 9663

First Floor: 1,002 square feet
Second Floor: 336 square feet
Total: 1,338 square feet

A mountain retreat, this rustic home features covered porches front and rear. Open living is enjoyed in a great room and kitchen/dining room combination. Here, a fireplace provides the focal point and a warm welcome that continues into the L-shaped island kitchen. The cathedral ceiling that graces the great room gives an open, inviting sense of space. Two bedrooms—one with a walk-in closet—and a full bath on the first level are complemented by a master suite on the second level which includes a walk-in closet and deluxe bath. There is also attic storage on the second level. Please specify basement or crawlspace foundation when ordering.

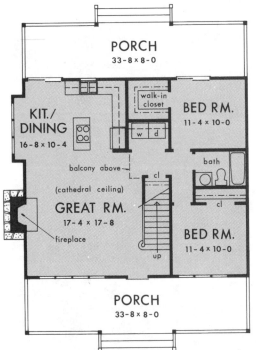

PORCH
33-8 × 8-0

walk-in closet

BED RM.
11-4 × 10-0

KIT./DINING
16-8 × 10-4

w   d

balcony above

bath

(cathedral ceiling)

cl

GREAT RM.
17-4 × 17-8

fireplace

cl

up

BED RM.
11-4 × 10-0

PORCH
33-8 × 8-0

DESIGN BY
Donald A. Gardner, Architects, Inc.

Width 36'-8"
Depth 44'-8"

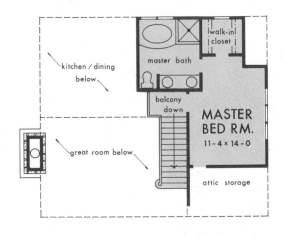

kitchen / dining below

master bath

walk-in closet

balcony down

great room below

MASTER BED RM.
11-4 × 14-0

attic storage

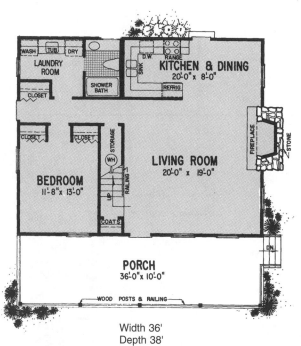

Width 36'
Depth 38'

QUOTE ONE®

Cost to build? See page 214
to order complete cost estimate
to build this house in your area!

DESIGN BY
Home Planners

T his charming farmhouse
design will be economical
to build and a pleasure to
occupy. Like most vacation
homes, this design features an
open plan. The large living area
includes a living room, a din-
ing room and a massive stone fireplace. A partition separates the kitchen
from the living room. The first floor also holds a bedroom, a full bath
and a laundry room. Upstairs is a spacious sleeping loft overlooking the
living room. Don't miss the large front porch—this will be a favorite spot
for relaxing.

Design 4061

First Floor: 1,008 square feet
Second Floor: 323 square feet
Total: 1,331 square feet

D

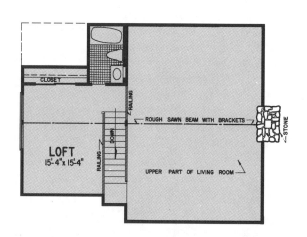

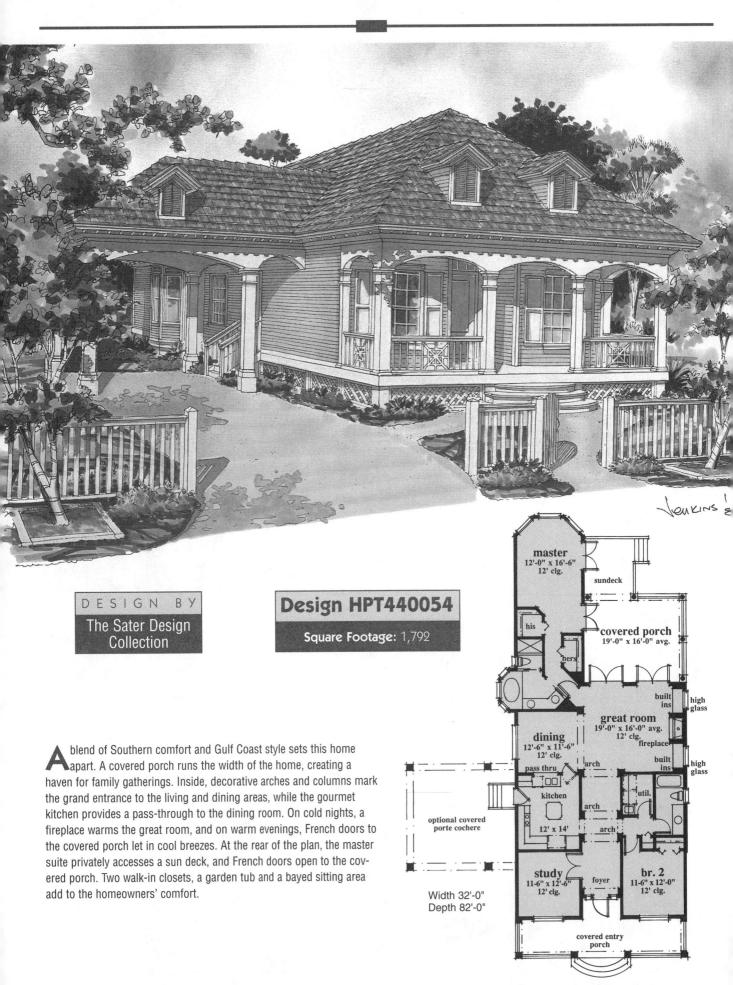

Design HPT440054

Square Footage: 1,792

A blend of Southern comfort and Gulf Coast style sets this home apart. A covered porch runs the width of the home, creating a haven for family gatherings. Inside, decorative arches and columns mark the grand entrance to the living and dining areas, while the gourmet kitchen provides a pass-through to the dining room. On cold nights, a fireplace warms the great room, and on warm evenings, French doors to the covered porch let in cool breezes. At the rear of the plan, the master suite privately accesses a sun deck, and French doors open to the covered porch. Two walk-in closets, a garden tub and a bayed sitting area add to the homeowners' comfort.

master
12'-0" x 16'-6"
12' clg.

sundeck

his

hers

covered porch
19'-0" x 16'-0" avg.

built ins

high glass

great room
19'-0" x 16'-0" avg.
12' clg.

fireplace

dining
12'-6" x 11'-6"
12' clg.

arch

built ins

high glass

pass thru

kitchen

util.

optional covered porte cochere

arch

arch

12' x 14'

arch

study
11'-6" x 12'-6"
12' clg.

foyer

br. 2
11'-6" x 12'-0"
12' clg.

Width 32'-0"
Depth 82'-0"

covered entry porch

This home, as shown in the photograph, may differ from the actual blueprints. For more detailed information, please check the floor plans carefully.

Photos by Andrew D. Lautman

Width 50'-7"
Depth 38'-0"

Design 3699

First Floor: 1,356 square feet
Second Floor: 490 square feet
Total: 1,846 square feet

Split-log siding and a rustic balustrade create country charm with this farmhouse-style retreat. An open living area features a natural stone fireplace and a cathedral ceiling with exposed rough-sawn beam and brackets. A generous kitchen and dining area complement the living area and share the warmth of the fireplace. A master bedroom with complete bath, and a nearby family bedroom with hall bath complete the main floor. Upstairs, a spacious loft affords extra sleeping space—or provides a hobby/recreation area—and offers a full bath.

WHEN YOU'RE READY TO ORDER...

LET US SHOW YOU OUR HOME BLUEPRINT PACKAGE.

Building a home? Planning a home? Our Blueprint Package has nearly everything you need to get the job done right, whether you're working on your own or with help from an architect, designer, builder or subcontractors. Each Blueprint Package is the result of many hours of work by licensed architects or professional designers.

QUALITY

Hundreds of hours of painstaking effort have gone into the development of your blueprint set. Each home has been quality-checked by professionals to insure accuracy and buildability.

VALUE

Because we sell in volume, you can buy professional quality blueprints at a fraction of their development cost. With our plans, your dream home design costs only a few hundred dollars, not the thousands of dollars that architects charge.

SERVICE

Once you've chosen your favorite home plan, you'll receive fast, efficient service whether you choose to mail or fax your order to us or call us toll free at 1-800-521-6797. For customer service, call toll free 1-888-690-1116.

SATISFACTION

Over 50 years of service to satisfied home plan buyers provide us unparalleled experience and knowledge in producing quality blueprints.

ORDER TOLL FREE 1-800-521-6797

After you've looked over our Blueprint Package and Important Extras on the following pages, simply mail the order form on page 221 or call toll free on our Blueprint Hotline: 1-800-521-6797. We're ready and eager to serve you. For customer service, call toll free 1-888-690-1116.

Each set of blueprints is an interrelated collection of detail sheets which includes components such as floor plans, interior and exterior elevations, dimensions, cross-sections, diagrams and notations. These sheets show exactly how your house is to be built.

AMONG THE SHEETS INCLUDED MAY BE:

FRONTAL SHEET

This artist's sketch of the exterior of the house gives you an idea of how the house will look when built and landscaped. Large floor plans show all levels of the house and provide an overview of your new home's livability, as well as a handy reference for deciding on furniture placement.

FOUNDATION PLANS

This sheet shows the foundation layout including support walls, excavated and unexcavated areas, if any, and foundation notes. If slab construction rather than basement, the plan shows footings and details for a monolithic slab. This page, or another in the set, may include a sample plot plan for locating your house on a building site.

DETAILED FLOOR PLANS

These plans show the layout of each floor of the house. Rooms and interior spaces are carefully dimensioned and keys are given for cross-section details provided later in the plans. The positions of electrical outlets and switches are shown.

HOUSE CROSS-SECTIONS

Large-scale views show sections or cut-aways of the foundation, interior walls, exterior walls, floors, stairways and roof details. Additional cross-sections may show important changes in floor, ceiling or roof heights or the relationship of one level to another. Extremely valuable for construction, these sections show exactly how the various parts of the house fit together.

INTERIOR ELEVATIONS

Many of our drawings show the design and placement of kitchen and bathroom cabinets, laundry areas, fireplaces, bookcases and other built-ins. Little "extras," such as mantelpiece and wainscoting drawings, plus molding sections, provide details that give your home that custom touch.

EXTERIOR ELEVATIONS

These drawings show the front, rear and sides of your house and give necessary notes on exterior materials and finishes. Particular attention is given to cornice detail, brick and stone accents or other finish items that make your home unique.

SAMPLE PACKAGE

FRONTAL SHEET

FOUNDATION PLANS

DETAILED FLOOR PLANS

EXTERIOR ELEVATIONS

INTERIOR ELEVATIONS

HOUSE CROSS-SECTIONS

IMPORTANT EXTRAS TO DO THE JOB RIGHT!

INTRODUCING
EIGHT IMPORTANT
PLANNING AND
CONSTRUCTION AIDS
DEVELOPED BY OUR
PROFESSIONALS TO
HELP YOU SUCCEED
IN YOUR HOME-
BUILDING PROJECT

MATERIALS LIST

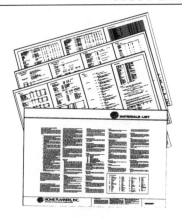

(Note: Because of the diversity of local building codes, our Materials List does not include mechanical materials.)

For many of the designs in our portfolio, we offer a customized materials take-off that is invaluable in planning and estimating the cost of your new home. This Materials List outlines the quantity, type and size of materials needed to build your house (with the exception of mechanical system items). Included are framing lumber, windows and doors, kitchen and bath cabinetry, rough and finish hardware, and much more. This handy list helps you or your builder cost out materials and serves as a reference sheet when you're compiling bids. A Materials List cannot be ordered before blueprints are ordered.

SPECIFICATION OUTLINE

This valuable 16-page document is critical to building your house correctly. Designed to be filled in by you or your builder, this book lists 166 stages or items crucial to the building process. It provides a comprehensive review of the construction process and helps in choosing materials. When combined with the blueprints, a signed contract, and a schedule, it becomes a legal document and record for the building of your home.

QUOTE ONE®

SUMMARY COST REPORT / MATERIALS COST REPORT

A new service for estimating the cost of building select designs, the Quote One® system is available in two separate stages: The Summary Cost Report and the Materials Cost Report.

The **Summary Cost Report** is the first stage in the package and shows the total cost per square foot for your chosen home in your zip-code area and then breaks that cost down into various categories showing the costs for building materials, labor and installation. The report includes three grades: Budget, Standard and Custom. These reports allow you to evaluate your building budget and compare the costs of building a variety of homes in your area.

Make even more informed decisions about your home-building project with the second phase of our package, our **Materials Cost Report.** This tool is invaluable in planning and estimating the cost of your new home. The material and installation (labor and equipment) cost is shown for each of over 1,000 line items provided in the Materials List (Standard grade), which is included when you purchase this estimating tool. It allows you to determine building costs for your specific zip-code area and for your chosen home design. Space is allowed for additional estimates from contractors and subcontractors, such as for mechanical materials, which are not included in our packages. This invaluable tool includes a Materials List. For most plans, a Materials Cost Report cannot be ordered before blueprints are ordered. Call for details. In addition, ask about our Home Planners Estimating Package.

The Quote One® program is continually updated with new plans. If you are interested in a plan that is not indicated as Quote One, please call and ask our sales reps. They will be happy to verify the status for you. To order these invaluable reports, use the order form on page 221 or call 1-800-521-6797.

CONSTRUCTION INFORMATION

If you want to know more about techniques—and deal more confidently with subcontractors—we offer these useful sheets. Each set is an excellent tool that will add to your understanding of these technical subjects. These helpful details provide general construction information and are not specific to any single plan.

PLUMBING

The Blueprint Package includes locations for all the plumbing fixtures, including sinks, lavatories, tubs, showers, toilets, laundry trays and water heaters. However, if you want to know more about the complete plumbing system, these Plumbing Details will prove very useful. Prepared to meet requirements of the National Plumbing Code, these fact-filled sheets give general information on pipe schedules, fittings, sump-pump details, water-softener hookups, septic system details and much more. Sheets also include a glossary of terms.

ELECTRICAL

The locations for every electrical switch, plug and outlet are shown in your Blueprint Package. However, these Electrical Details go further to take the mystery out of household electrical systems. Prepared to meet requirements of the National Electrical Code, these comprehensive drawings come packed with helpful information, including wire sizing, switch-installation schematics, cable-routing details, appliance wattage, doorbell hookups, typical service panel circuitry and much more. A glossary of terms is also included.

CONSTRUCTION

The Blueprint Package contains everything an experienced builder needs to construct a particular house. However, it doesn't show all the ways that houses can be built, nor does it explain alternate construction methods. To help you understand how your house will be built—and offer additional techniques—this set of Construction Details depicts the materials and methods used to build foundations, fireplaces, walls, floors and roofs. Where appropriate, the drawings show acceptable alternatives.

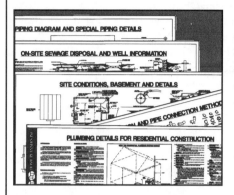

MECHANICAL

These Mechanical Details contain fundamental principles and useful data that will help you make informed decisions and communicate with subcontractors about heating and cooling systems. Drawings contain instructions and samples that allow you to make simple load calculations, and preliminary sizing and costing analysis. Covered are today's most commonly used systems from heat pumps to solar fuel systems. The package is filled with illustrations and diagrams to help you visualize components and how they relate to one another.

PLAN-A-HOME®

PLAN-A-HOME® is an easy-to-use tool that helps you design a new home, arrange furniture in a new or existing home, or plan a remodeling project. Each package contains:

✓ MORE THAN 700 REUSABLE PEEL-OFF PLANNING SYMBOLS on a self-stick vinyl sheet, including walls, windows, doors, all types of furniture, kitchen components, bath fixtures and many more.

✓ A REUSABLE, TRANSPARENT, ¼" SCALE PLANNING GRID that matches the scale of actual working drawings (¼" equals one foot). This grid provides the basis for house layouts of up to 140'x92'.

✓ TRACING PAPER and a protective sheet for copying or transferring your completed plan.

✓ A FELT-TIP PEN, with water-soluble ink that wipes away quickly.

Plan-A-Home® lets you lay out areas as large as a 7,500 square foot, six-bedroom, seven-bath house.

To Order, Call Toll Free 1-800-521-6797

To add these important extras to your Blueprint Package, simply indicate your choices on the order form on page 221. Or call us toll free 1-800-521-6797 and we'll tell you more about these exciting products. For customer service, call toll free 1-888-690-1116.

THE FINISHING TOUCHES...

THE DECK BLUEPRINT PACKAGE

Many of the homes in this book can be enhanced with a professionally designed Home Planners Deck Plan. Those home plans highlighted with a **D** have a matching Deck Plan, sold separately, which includes a Deck Plan Frontal Sheet, Deck Framing and Floor Plans, Deck Elevations and a Deck Materials List. A Standard Deck Details Package, also available, provides all the how-to information necessary for building *any* deck. Our Complete Deck Building Package contains one set of Custom Deck Plans of your choice, plus one set of Standard Deck Building Details, all for one low price. Our plans and details are carefully prepared in an easy-to-understand format that will guide you through every stage of your deck-building project. This page contains a sampling of six different Deck layouts (and a front-yard landscape) to match your favorite house. See page 218 for prices and ordering information.

EUROPEAN-FLAIR HOME
Landscape OLA088

WEEKEND-ENTERTAINER DECK
Deck ODA013

CENTER-VIEW DECK
Deck ODA015

KITCHEN-EXTENDER DECK
Deck ODA016

SPLIT-LEVEL ACTIVITY DECK
Deck ODA018

TRI-LEVEL DECK WITH GRILL
Deck ODA020

CONTEMPORARY LEISURE DECK
Deck ODA021

THE LANDSCAPE BLUEPRINT PACKAGE

For the homes marked with an **L** in this book, Home Planners has created a front-yard Landscape Plan that matches or is complementary in design to the house plan. These comprehensive blueprint packages include a Frontal Sheet, Plan View, Regionalized Plant & Materials List, a sheet on Planting and Maintaining Your Landscape, Zone Maps and Plant Size and Description Guide. These plans will help you achieve professional results, adding value and enjoyment to your property for years to come. Each set of blueprints is a full 18" x 24" in size with clear, complete instructions and easy-to-read type. Six of the forty front-yard Landscape Plans to match your favorite house are shown below.

Regional Order Map

Most of the Landscape Plans shown on these pages are available with a Plant & Materials List adapted by horticultural experts to 8 different regions of the country. Please specify the Geographic Region when ordering your plan. See pages 218-219 for prices, ordering information and regional availability.

Region	1	Northeast
Region	2	Mid-Atlantic
Region	3	Deep South
Region	4	Florida & Gulf Coast
Region	5	Midwest
Region	6	Rocky Mountains
Region	7	Southern California & Desert Southwest
Region	8	Northern California & Pacific Northwest

CAPE COD COTTAGE
Landscape OLA003

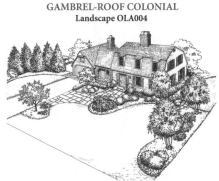

GAMBREL-ROOF COLONIAL
Landscape OLA004

CENTER-HALL COLONIAL
Landscape OLA005

CLASSIC NEW ENGLAND COLONIAL
Landscape OLA006

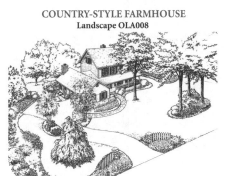

COUNTRY-STYLE FARMHOUSE
Landscape OLA008

TRADITIONAL SPLIT-LEVEL
Landscape OLA029

PRICE SCHEDULE & PLANS INDEX

HOUSE BLUEPRINT PRICE SCHEDULE

Prices guaranteed through December 31, 2001

TIERS	1-SET STUDY PACKAGE	4-SET BUILDING PACKAGE	8-SET BUILDING PACKAGE	1-SET REPRODUCIBLE	HOME CUSTOMIZER® PACKAGE
P1	$20	$50	$90	$140	N/A
P2	$40	$70	$110	$160	N/A
P3	$60	$90	$130	$180	N/A
P4	$80	$110	$150	$200	N/A
P5	$100	$130	$170	$230	N/A
P6	$120	$150	$190	$250	N/A
A1	$420	$460	$520	$625	$680
A2	$460	$500	$560	$685	$740
A3	$500	$540	$600	$745	$800
A4	$540	$580	$640	$805	$860
C1	$585	$625	$685	$870	$925
C2	$625	$665	$725	$930	$985
C3	$675	$715	$775	$980	$1035
C4	$725	$765	$825	$1030	$1085
L1	$785	$825	$885	$1090	$1145
L2	$835	$875	$935	$1140	$1195
L3	$935	$975	$1035	$1240	$1295
L4	$1035	$1075	$1135	$1340	$1395

OPTIONS FOR PLANS IN TIERS A1–L4

Additional Identical Blueprints in same order for "A1–L4" price plans ....$50 per set

Reverse Blueprints (mirror image) with 4- or 8-set order
for "A1–L4" price plans ....$50 fee per order

Specification Outlines ....$10 each

Materials Lists for "A1–C3" price plans ....$60 each

Materials Lists for "C4–L4" price plans ....$70 each

OPTIONS FOR PLANS IN TIERS P1–P6

Additional Identical Blueprints in same order for "P1–P6" price plans ....$10 per set

Reverse Blueprints (mirror image) for "P1–P6" price plans ....$10 per set

1 Set of Deck Construction Details ....$14.95 each

Deck Construction Package ....add $10 to Building Package price
(includes 1 set of "P1–P6" price plans, plus
1 set Standard Deck Construction Details)

1 Set of Gazebo Construction Details ....$14.95 each

Gazebo Construction Package ....add $10 to Building Package price
(includes 1 set of "P1–P6" price plans, plus
1 set Standard Gazebo Construction Details)

IMPORTANT NOTES

The 1-set study package is marked "not for construction."
Prices for 4- or 8-set Building Packages honored only at time of original order. Some basement foundations carry a $225 surcharge. Right-reading reverse blueprints, if available, will incur a $165 surcharge.

INDEX

To use the Index below, refer to the design number listed in numerical order (a helpful page reference is also given). Note the price index letter and refer to the House Blueprint Price Schedule above for the cost of one, four or eight sets of blueprints or the cost of a reproducible drawing. Additional prices are shown for identical and reverse blueprint sets, as well as a very useful Materials List for some of the plans. Also note in the Index below those plans that have matching or complementary Deck Plans or Landscape Plans. Refer to the schedules above for prices of these plans. All plans in this publication are customizable. However, only Home Planners

plans can be customized with the Home Planners Home Customizer® Package. These plans are indicated below with the letter "Y." See page 221 for more information. The letter "Y" also identifies plans that are part of our Quote One® estimating service and those that offer Materials Lists. See page 214 for more information.

To Order: Fill in and send the order form on page 221—or call toll free 1-800-521-6797 or 520-297-8200. FAX: 1-800-224-6699 or 520-544-3086

DESIGN	PRICE	PAGE	MATERIALS LIST	CUSTOMIZABLE®	QUOTE ONE®	DECK	DECK PRICE	LANDSCAPE	LANDSCAPE PRICE	REGIONS
1499	C1	202	Y		Y					
2427	A3	203	Y		Y					
2488	A4	198	Y	Y	Y	ODA003	P2			
2490	C2	63	Y	Y	Y					
2563	C1	38	Y	Y	Y	ODA015	P2	OLA002	P3	123568
2622	A3	33	Y	Y	Y	ODA004	P2	OLA001	P3	123568
2661	A4	36	Y	Y	Y	ODA014	P2	OLA003	P3	123568
2668	C1	186	Y	Y	Y			OLA015	P4	123568
2682	A4	34	Y	Y	Y	ODA016	P2	OLA001	P3	123568
2774	C1	147	Y	Y	Y	ODA001	P2	OLA001	P3	123568
2776	A4	81	Y	Y	Y	ODA014	P2	OLA008	P4	1234568
2822	A3	116	Y	Y	Y			OLA030	P3	12345678
2826	A4	117	Y	Y	Y	ODA017	P2			
2864	A3	9	Y	Y	Y	ODA001	P2	OLA026	P3	123568
2871	A4	10	Y	Y	Y	ODA018	P3			
2875	A4	121	Y	Y	Y	ODA014	P2	OLA037	P4	347
2878	A4	8	Y	Y	Y	ODA013	P2	OLA001	P3	123568
2905	A4	32	Y	Y	Y	ODA022	P3	OLA030	P3	12345678
2913	A4	11	Y	Y	Y	ODA025	P3			
2927	C1	115	Y	Y	Y	ODA001	P2			
2947	A4	12	Y	Y	Y	ODA013	P2	OLA001	P3	123568
2948	A4	120	Y	Y	Y					
2964	A4	60	Y	Y	Y					
2973	A4	126	Y	Y	Y			OLA024	P4	123568
2974	A4	67	Y	Y	Y			OLA024	P4	123568
3309	C1	127	Y	Y	Y			OLA010	P3	1234568
3316	A3	76	Y	Y	Y			OLA003	P3	123568
3331	A3	199	Y	Y	Y			OLA004	P3	123568
3332	C1	13	Y	Y	Y			OLA001	P3	123568
3340	A4	90	Y	Y				OLA025	P3	123568
3376	A3	124	Y	Y	Y	ODA015	P2	OLA006	P3	123568
3385	A3	61	Y	Y	Y	ODA001	P2	OLA008	P4	1234568
3431	A4	122	Y	Y	Y					
3433	C1	191	Y	Y	Y			OLA014	P4	12345678
3458	C1	57	Y	Y	Y	ODA006	P2	OLA023	P3	123568
3460	A3	15	Y	Y	Y			OLA001	P3	123568
3461	C1	80	Y	Y	Y			OLA005	P3	123568
3466	A3	44	Y	Y	Y	ODA011	P2	OLA008	P4	1234568
3487	A4	41	Y	Y	Y			OLA010	P3	1234568
3491	A4	43	Y	Y	Y	ODA012	P3	OLA016	P4	1234568
3569	A3	118	Y	Y	Y	ODA006	P2	OLA039	P3	3478
3609	A4	143	Y	Y	Y	ODA001	P2	OLA025	P3	123568
3619	A4	83	Y	Y	Y	ODA012	P3	OLA008	P4	1234568
3620	A4	70	Y	Y	Y					
3644	C1	190	Y	Y	Y					
3652	C1	45	Y	Y	Y	ODA006	P2	OLA021	P3	123568
3654	C1	129	Y	Y	Y			OLA093	P3	12345678
3655	A3	6	Y	Y	Y			OLA006	P3	123568

DESIGN	PRICE	PAGE	MATERIALS LIST	CUSTOMIZABLE	QUOTE ONE	DECK	DECK PRICE	LANDSCAPE	LANDSCAPE PRICE	REGIONS
3657	C1	194	Y	Y	Y					
3658	A3	204	Y	Y	Y	ODA003	P2	OLA003	P3	123568
3659	A3	7	Y	Y	Y			OLA091	P3	12345678
3660	C1	192	Y	Y	Y			OLA037	P4	347
3662	A4	152	Y	Y	Y			OLA088	P4	12345678
3664	A4	179	Y	Y	Y			OLA088	P4	12345678
3677	C1	142	Y	Y	Y	ODA011	P2	OLA023	P3	123568
3680	A4	200	Y	Y	Y	ODA012	P3	OLA083	P3	12345678
3681	A4	71	Y	Y	Y	ODA012	P3	OLA083	P3	12345678
3682	A4	50	Y	Y	Y	ODA012	P3	OLA083	P3	12345678
3683	A4	201	Y	Y	Y	ODA012	P3	OLA093	P3	12345678
3687	A4	66	Y	Y	Y	ODA011	P2	OLA083	P3	12345678
3699	A4	211	Y	Y	Y	ODA016	P2	OLA093	P3	12345678
4061	A3	209	Y	Y	Y	ODA016	P2			
6629	C1	172						OLA012	P3	12345678
7236	A4	135	Y							
7601	A3	16	Y							
7611	A3	55	Y							
8064	A3	138						OLA004	P3	123568
8126	A4	154								
8176	A3	99								
8180	A4	23								
8181	A3	24								
8183	A4	27								
8229	A4	22								
8601	C1	184								
8633	A4	119								
8637	C1	189								
8644	A4	170								
8684	A4	185								
8923	A4	101	Y		Y					
8997	A4	78								
8998	A3	79								
9012	A4	130	Y		Y					
9028	A3	25	Y		Y					
9055	A4	128	Y		Y					
9060	A4	68	Y							
9063	A4	69	Y		Y					
9088	C1	94	Y		Y					
9089	A3	180	Y		Y					
9201	A4	102	Y		Y					
9202	A4	103	Y							
9204	A4	168	Y							
9206	A4	134	Y		Y					
9235	A4	19	Y							
9238	A4	46	Y		Y					
9250	C1	178	Y		Y					
9251	C1	133	Y		Y					
9252	C1	132	Y							
9282	A4	31	Y							
9310	C1	136	Y		Y					
9344	C1	167	Y							
9362	C1	169	Y		Y					
9459	A3	47	Y					OLA001	P3	123568
9509	A3	18	Y					OLA004	P3	123568
9557	A4	85	Y		Y					
9585	A4	131	Y							
9606	A3	49	Y		Y					
9619	A4	91	Y							
9621	A3	74	Y		Y					
9630	A3	205	Y							
9645	A3	75	Y		Y					
9661	A3	114	Y		Y					
9662	A3	84	Y		Y					
9663	A2	208	Y							
9697	A3	206	Y							
9712	A4	145	Y		Y					
9734	A3	153	Y		Y					
9742	A3	140	Y		Y					
9747	A3	53	Y		Y					
9749	A3	73	Y		Y					
9764	A3	17	Y		Y					
9771	A3	72	Y							
9773	A4	141	Y		Y					
9779	A3	52	Y		Y					
9780	A3	48	Y		Y					

DESIGN	PRICE	PAGE	MATERIALS LIST	CUSTOMIZABLE	QUOTE ONE	DECK	DECK PRICE	LANDSCAPE	LANDSCAPE PRICE	REGIONS
9799	A4	151	Y							
9812	C2	106	Y		Y					
9813	C2	58	Y							
9831	C2	157	Y		Y					
9840	C1	98	Y		Y					
9842	C2	107	Y		Y					
9846	C2	181	Y		Y					
9849	C1	28	Y		Y					
9853	C2	93	Y		Y					
9862	C2	159	Y		Y					
9874	C2	105	Y		Y					
9877	C2	108	Y		Y					
9884	C2	104	Y		Y					
9885	C2	158	Y		Y					
9886	C2	166	Y							
9892	C2	111	Y		Y					
9893	C2	109	Y		Y					
9894	C1	96	Y		Y					
9900	C2	187								
9902	C1	29								
9907	C2	110								
9914	C1	59	Y		Y					
HPT440001	A3	14								
HPT440002	C1	20								
HPT440003	C1	21								
HPT440004	C2	26								
HPT440005	C1	30								
HPT440006	A4	62	Y	Y	Y	ODA006	P2	OLA030	P3	12345678
HPT440014	A3	77	Y							
HPT440015	A4	82	Y							
HPT440016	A4	86	Y							
HPT440017	A4	87	Y							
HPT440018	A4	88	Y							
HPT440019	C1	89	Y							
HPT440020	A4	92	Y		Y					
HPT440021	C1	95	Y		Y					
HPT440022	A4	97	Y							
HPT440023	A4	100	Y							
HPT440024	A4	112	Y							
HPT440025	C1	113	Y							
HPT440026	A4	123	Y							
HPT440027	A4	137								
HPT440028	A4	139	Y							
HPT440029	A4	144			Y					
HPT440030	A4	146			Y					
HPT440031	C2	148	Y							
HPT440032	A4	149	Y							
HPT440033	A4	150	Y		Y					
HPT440034	A4	155	Y							
HPT440035	C2	156								
HPT440036	C2	160								
HPT440037	C1	161								
HPT440038	A3	162								
HPT440039	C1	163								
HPT440040	A4	164								
HPT440041	A4	165								
HPT440042	C1	171								
HPT440043	A4	173	Y							
HPT440044	A4	174								
HPT440045	A4	175								
HPT440046	A4	176	Y							
HPT440047	C1	182	Y		Y					
HPT440048	A4	183								
HPT440049	A4	188	Y							
HPT440050	A4	193								
HPT440051	C1	195								
HPT440052	A4	196								
HPT440053	A3	207	Y		Y					
HPT440054	A4	210								
HPT440055	A4	39	Y							
HPT440056	A4	40	Y							
HPT440057	A3	42	Y							
HPT440058	A3	51	Y							
HPT440059	C2	64	Y							
HPT440060	C2	54	Y							
HPT440061	C2	56								

BEFORE YOU ORDER...

BEFORE FILLING OUT THE COUPON AT RIGHT OR CALLING US ON OUR TOLL-FREE BLUEPRINT HOTLINE, YOU MAY WANT TO LEARN MORE ABOUT OUR SERVICES AND PRODUCTS. HERE'S SOME INFORMATION YOU WILL FIND HELPFUL.

OUR EXCHANGE POLICY

Since blueprints are printed in response to your order, we cannot honor requests for refunds. However, we will exchange your entire first order for an equal or greater number of blueprints within our plan collection within 90 days of the original order. The entire content of your original order must be returned to our offices before an exchange will be processed. If the returned blueprints look used, redlined or copied, we will not honor your exchange. Fees for exchanging your blueprints are as follows: 20% of the amount of the original order...*plus* the difference in cost if exchanging for a design in a higher price bracket or *less* the difference in cost if exchanging for a design in lower price bracket. **(Reproducible blueprints are not exchangeable.)** Please add $25 for postage and handling via Regular Service; $35 via Priority Service; $45 via Express Service. Shipping and handling charges are not refundable.

ABOUT REVERSE BLUEPRINTS

If you want to build in reverse of the plan as shown, we will include any number of reverse blueprints (mirror image) from a 4- or 8-set package for an additional fee of $50. Although lettering and dimensions will appear backward, reverses will be a useful aid if you decide to flop the plan.

REVISING, MODIFYING AND CUSTOMIZING PLANS

The wide variety of designs available in this publication allows you to select ideas and concepts for a home to fit your building site and match your family's needs, wants and budget. Like many homeowners who buy these plans, you and your builder, architect or engineer may want to make changes to them. Some changes may be made by your builder, but we recommend that most changes be made by a licensed architect or engineer. If you need to make alterations to a design that is customizable, you need only order our Home Customizer® Package to get you started. As set forth below, we cannot assume any responsibility for blueprints which have been changed, whether by you, your builder or by professionals selected by you or referred to you by us, because such individuals are outside our supervision and control.

ARCHITECTURAL AND ENGINEERING SEALS

Some cities and states are now requiring that a licensed architect or engineer review and "seal" a blueprint, or officially approve it, prior to construction due to concerns over energy costs, safety and other factors. Prior to application for a building permit or the start of actual construction, we strongly advise that you consult your local building official who can tell you if such a review is required.

ABOUT THE DESIGNS

The architects and designers whose work appears in this publication are among America's leading residential designers. Each plan was designed to meet the requirements of a nationally recognized model building code in effect at the time and place the plan was drawn. Because national building codes change from time to time, plans may not comply with any such code at the time they are sold to a customer. In addition, building officials may not accept these plans as final construction documents of record as the plans may need to be modified and additional drawings and details added to suit local conditions and requirements. We strongly advise that purchasers consult a licensed architect or engineer, and their local building official, before starting any construction related to these plans.

LOCAL BUILDING CODES AND ZONING REQUIREMENTS

At the time of creation, our plans are drawn to specifications published by the Building Officials and Code Administrators (BOCA) International, Inc.; the Southern Building Code Congress (SBCCI) International, Inc.; the International Conference of Building Officials (ICBO); or the Council of American Building Officials (CABO). Our plans are designed to meet or exceed na-tional building standards. Because of the great differences in geography and climate throughout the United States and Canada, each state, county and municipality has its own building codes, zone requirements, ordinances and building regulations. Your plan may need to be modified to comply with local requirements regarding snow loads, energy codes, soil and seismic conditions and a wide range of other matters. In addition, you may need to obtain permits or inspections from local governments before and in the course of construction. Prior to using blueprints ordered from us, we strongly advise that you consult a licensed architect or engineer—and speak with your local building official—before applying for any permit or beginning construction. We authorize the use of our blueprints on the express condition that you strictly comply with all local building codes, zoning requirements and other applicable laws, regulations, ordinances and requirements. **Notice: Plans for homes to be built in Nevada must be re-drawn by a Nevada-registered professional. Consult your building official for more information on this subject.**

FOUNDATION AND EXTERIOR WALL CHANGES

Depending on your specific climate or regional building practices, you may wish to change a full basement to a slab or crawlspace foundation. Most professional contractors and builders can easily adapt your plans to alternate foundation types. Likewise, most can easily change 2x4 wall construction to 2x6, or vice versa.

DISCLAIMER

We and the designers we work with have put substantial care and effort into the creation of our blueprints. However, because we cannot provide on-site consultation, supervision and control over actual construction, and because of the great variance in local building requirements, building practices and soil, seismic, weather and other conditions, WE CANNOT MAKE ANY WARRANTY, EXPRESS OR IMPLIED, WITH RESPECT TO THE CONTENT OR USE OF OUR BLUEPRINTS, INCLUDING BUT NOT LIMITED TO ANY WARRANTY OF MERCHANTABILITY OR OF FITNESS FOR A PARTICULAR PURPOSE.

TERMS AND CONDITIONS

These designs are protected under the terms of United States Copyright Law and may not be copied or reproduced in any way, by any means, unless you have purchased Sepias or Reproducibles which clearly indicate your right to copy or reproduce. We authorize the use of your chosen design as an aid in the construction of one single family home only. You may not use this design to build a second or multiple dwellings without purchasing another blueprint or blueprints or paying additional design fees.

HOW MANY BLUEPRINTS DO YOU NEED?

A single set of blueprints is sufficient to study a home in greater detail. However, if you are planning to obtain cost estimates from a contractor or subcontractors—or if you are planning to build immediately—you will need more sets. Because additional sets are cheaper when ordered in quantity with the original order, make sure you order enough blueprints to satisfy all requirements. The following checklist will help you determine how many you need:

___ Owner

___ Builder (generally requires at least three sets; one as a legal document, one to use during inspections, and at least one to give to subcontractors)

___ Local Building Department (often requires two sets)

___ Mortgage Lender (usually one set for a conventional loan; three sets for FHA or VA loans)

___ TOTAL NUMBER OF SETS

Have You Seen Our Newest Designs?

At least 50 of our latest creations are featured in each edition of our New Design Portfolio. You may have received a copy with your latest purchase by mail. If not, or if you purchased this book from a local retailer, just return the coupon below for your FREE copy. Make sure you consider the very latest of what Home Planners has to offer.

Yes! Please send my FREE copy of your latest New Design Portfolio.

Offer good to U.S. shipping address only.

Name _____

Address_____

City_____State _____Zip _____

HOME PLANNERS, LLC
Wholly owned by Hanley-Wood, LLC
3275 WEST INA ROAD, SUITE 110
TUCSON, ARIZONA 85741

Order Form Key

HPT44

 TOLL FREE 1-800-521-6797

REGULAR OFFICE HOURS:
8:00 a.m.-12:00 a.m. EST, Monday-Friday, 10:00 a.m.-7:00 p.m. EST Sat & Sun.

If we receive your order by 3:00 p.m. EST, Monday-Friday, we'll process it and ship within **two business days.** When ordering by phone, please have your credit card ready. We'll also ask you for the Order Form Key Number at the bottom of the coupon.

By FAX: Copy the Order Form on the next page and send it on our FAX line:
1-800-224-6699 or 520-544-3086.

Canadian Customers — Order Toll Free 1-877-223-6389

For faster service, Canadian customers may now call in orders directly to our Canadian supplier of plans and charge the purchase to a credit card. Or, you may complete the order form at right, adding the current exchange rate to all prices and mail in Canadian funds to:

Home Planners Canada, c/o Select Home Designs
301-611 Alexander Street • Vancouver, BC, Canada • V6A 1E1

OR: Copy the Order Form and send it via our FAX line: 1-800-224-6699.

 **The Home Customizer**®

HOME PLANNERS, LLC wholly owned by Hanley-Wood, LLC
3275 WEST INA ROAD, SUITE 110 • TUCSON, ARIZONA • 85741

"This house is perfect...if only the family room were two feet wider." Sound familiar? In response to the numerous requests for this type of modification, Home Planners has developed **The Home Customizer® Package**. This exclusive package offers our top-of-the-line materials to make it easy for anyone, anywhere to customize any Home Planners design to fit their needs. Check the index on page 218-219 for those plans which are customizable.

Some of the changes you can make to any of our plans include:

- exterior elevation changes
- kitchen and bath modifications
- roof, wall and foundation changes
- room additions and more!

The Home Customizer® Package includes everything you'll need to make the necessary changes to your favorite Home Planners design. The package includes:

- instruction book with examples
- architectural scale and clear work film
- erasable red marker and removable correction tape
- ¼"-scale furniture cutouts
- 1 set reproducible drawings
- 1 set study blueprints for communicating changes to your design professional
- a copyright release letter so you can make copies as you need them
- referral letter with the name, address and telephone number of the professional in your region who is trained in modifying Home Planners designs efficiently and inexpensively.

The Home Customizer® Package will not only save you 25% to 75% of the cost of drawing the plans from scratch with an architect or engineer, it will also give you the flexibility to have your changes and modifications made by our referral network or by the professional of your choice. Now it's even easier and more affordable to have the custom home you've always wanted.

THE BASIC BLUEPRINT PACKAGE
Rush me the following (please refer to the Plans Index and Price Schedule in this section):
___Set(s) of blueprints for plan number(s) _____. $_____
___Set(s) of reproducibles for plan number(s) _____. $_____
___Home Customizer® Package for plan(s)_____. $_____
___Additional identical blueprints (standard or reverse) in same order @ $50 per set. $_____
___Reverse blueprints @ $50 fee per order. Right-reading reverse @ $165 surcharge $_____

IMPORTANT EXTRAS
Rush me the following:
___Materials List: $60 (Must be purchased with Blueprint set.) Add $10 for Schedule C4–L4 plans. $_____
___**Quote One**® Summary Cost Report @ $29.95 for one, $14.95 for each additional, for plans _____ $_____
  Building location: City _____ Zip Code _____
___**Quote One**® Materials Cost Report @ $120 Schedules P1–C3; $130 Schedules C4–L4, for plan_____(Must be purchased with Blueprints set.) $_____
  Building location: City _____ Zip Code _____
___Specification Outlines @ $10 each. $_____
___Detail Sets @ $14.95 each; any two $22.95; any three $29.95; all four for $39.95 (save $19.85). $_____
___❑ Plumbing ❑ Electrical ❑ Construction ❑ Mechanical
___Plan-A-Home® @ $29.95 each. $_____

DECK BLUEPRINTS
(Please refer to the Plans Index and Price Schedule in this section)
___Set(s) of Deck Plan _____. $_____
___Additional identical blueprints in same order @ $10 per set. $_____
___Reverse blueprints @ $10 per set. $_____
___Set of Standard Deck Details @ $14.95 per set. $_____
___Set of Complete Deck Construction Package (Best Buy!) Add $10 to Building Package
  Includes Custom Deck Plan _____ Plus Standard Deck Details

LANDSCAPE BLUEPRINTS
(Please refer to the Plans Index and Price Schedule in this section)
___Set(s) of Landscape Plan _____. $_____
___Additional identical blueprints in same order @ $10 per set. $_____
___Reverse blueprints @ $10 per set. $_____
Please indicate the appropriate region of the country for Plant & Material List.
(See map on page 217): Region _____

POSTAGE AND HANDLING	1–3 sets	4+ sets
Signature is required for all deliveries. **DELIVERY** No CODs (Requires street address—No P.O. Boxes)		
•Regular Service (Allow 7–10 business days delivery)	❑ $20.00	❑ $25.00
•Priority (Allow 4–5 business days delivery)	❑ $25.00	❑ $35.00
•Express (Allow 3 business days delivery)	❑ $35.00	❑ $45.00
OVERSEAS DELIVERY	fax, phone or mail for quote	

Note: All delivery times are from date Blueprint Package is shipped.

POSTAGE **(From box above)** $_____
SUBTOTAL $_____
SALES TAX (AZ & MI residents, please add appropriate state and local sales tax.) $_____
TOTAL **(Subtotal and tax)** $_____

YOUR ADDRESS **(please print)**

Name _____

Street_____

City _____State_____Zip _____

Daytime telephone number (_____) _____

FOR CREDIT CARD ORDERS ONLY

Credit card number _____ Exp. Date: (M/Y) _____
Check one ❑ Visa ❑ MasterCard ❑ Discover Card ❑ American Express

Signature_____

Please check appropriate box: ❑ Licensed Builder-Contractor ❑ Homeowner

ORDER TOLL FREE!
FOR INFORMATION ABOUT ANY OF OUR SERVICES OR TO ORDER CALL

1-800-521-6797 OR 520-297-8200
Browse our website:
www.eplans.com

BLUEPRINTS ARE NOT REFUNDABLE EXCHANGES ONLY

FOR CUSTOMER SERVICE,
CALL TOLL FREE **1-888-690-1116.**

 **ORDER TOLL FREE!**
1-800-521-6797 or 520-297-8200

Order Form Key

HPT44

HOME PLANNERS WANTS YOUR BUILDING EXPERIENCE TO BE AS PLEASANT AND TROUBLE-FREE AS POSSIBLE.

That's why we've expanded our library of Do-It-Yourself titles to help you along. In addition to our beautiful plans books, we've added books to guide you through specific projects as well as the construction process. In fact, these are titles that will be as useful after your dream home is built as they are right now.

BIGGEST & BEST	ONE-STORY	MORE ONE-STORY	TWO-STORY	VACATION	HILLSIDE	FARMHOUSE	COUNTRY HOUSES

1001 of our best-selling plans in one volume. 1,074 to 7,275 square feet. 704 pgs $12.95 1K1	450 designs for all lifestyles. 800 to 4,900 square feet. 384 pgs $9.95 OS	475 superb one-level plans from 800 to 5,000 square feet. 448 pgs $9.95 MOS	443 designs for one-and-a-half and two stories. 1,500 to 6,000 square feet. 448 pgs $9.95 TS	465 designs for recreation, retirement and leisure. 448 pgs $9.95 VSH	208 designs for split-levels, bi-levels, multi-levels and walkouts. 224 pgs $9.95 HH	200 country designs from classic to contemporary by 7 winning designers. 224 pgs $8.95 FH	208 unique home plans that combine traditional style and modern livability. 224 pgs $9.95 CN

BUDGET-SMART	BARRIER FREE	ENCYCLOPEDIA	ENCYCLOPEDIA II	AFFORDABLE	VICTORIAN	ESTATE	LUXURY

200 efficient plans from 7 top designers, that you can really afford to build! 224 pgs $8.95 BS	Over 1,700 products and 51 plans for accessible living. 128 pgs $15.95 UH	500 exceptional plans for all styles and budgets—the best book of its kind! 528 pgs $9.95 ENC	500 completely new plans. Spacious and stylish designs for every budget and taste. 352 pgs $9.95 E2	Completely revised and updated, featuring 300 designs for modest budgets. 256 pgs $9.95 AF	NEW! 210 striking Victorian and Farmhouse designs from today's top designers. 224 pgs $15.95 VDH2	Dream big! Twenty-one designers showcase their biggest and best plans. 208 pgs $15.95 EDH	154 fine luxury plans—loaded with luscious amenities! 192 pgs $14.95 LD2

EUROPEAN STYLES	COUNTRY CLASSICS	WILLIAM POOLE	TRADITIONAL	COTTAGES	CLASSIC	CONTEMPORARY	EASY-LIVING

200 homes with a unique flair of the Old World. 224 pgs $15.95 EURO	Donald Gardner's 101 best Country and Traditional home plans. 192 pgs $17.95 DAG	70 romantic house plans that capture the classic tradition of home design. 160 pgs $17.95 WEP	85 timeless designs from the Design Traditions Library. 160 pgs $17.95 TRA	25 fresh new designs that are as warm as a tropical breeze. A blend of the best aspects of many coastal styles. 64 pgs $19.95 CTG	Timeless, elegant designs that always feel like home. Gorgeous plans that are as flexible and up-to-date as their occupants. 240 pgs $9.95 CS	The most complete and imaginative collection of contemporary designs available anywhere. 240 pgs. $9.95 CM	200 efficient and so-phisticated plans that are small in size, but big on livability. 224 pgs $8.95 EL

SOUTHERN	SOUTHWESTERN	WESTERN	NEIGHBORHOOD	CRAFTSMAN	COLONIAL HOUSES	DUPLEX & TOWNHOMES	WATERFRONT

207 homes rich in Southern styling and comfort. 240 pgs $8.95 SH	138 designs that capture the spirit of the Southwest. 144 pgs $10.95 SW	215 designs that capture the spirit and diversity of the Western lifestyle. 208 pgs $9.95 WH	170 designs with the feel of main street America. 192 pgs $12.95 TND	170 Home plans in the Craftsman and Bungalow style. 192 pgs $12.95 CC	181 Classic early American designs. 208 pgs $9.95 COL	Over 50 designs for multi-family living. 64 pgs $9.95 DTP	200 designs perfect for your waterside wonderland. 208 pgs $10.95 WF

PROJECT GUIDES

WINDOWS	STREET OF DREAMS	MOVE-UP	OUTDOOR	GARAGES	DECKS	HOME BUILDING	BOOK & CD-ROM

  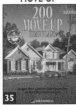     

33 Discover the power of windows with over 160 designs featuring Pella's best. 192 pgs $9.95 WIN

34 Over 300 photos showcase 54 prestigious homes. 256 pgs $19.95 SOD

35 200 stylish designs for today's growing families from 9 hot designers. 224 pgs $8.95 MU

36 42 unique outdoor projects—gazebos, strombellas, bridges, sheds, playsets and more! 96 pgs $7.95 YG

37 101 multi-use garages and outdoor structures to enhance any home. 96 pgs $7.95 GG

38 25 outstanding single-, double- and multi-level decks you can build. 112 pgs $7.95 DP

39 Everything you need to know to work with contractors and subcontractors. 212 pgs $14.95 HBP

40 Both the Home Planners Gold book and matching Windows™ CD-ROM with 3D floor-plans. $24.95 HPGC Book only $12.95 HPG

LANDSCAPE DESIGNS

SOFTWARE	EASY-CARE	FRONT & BACK	BACKYARDS	BUYER'S GUIDE	FRAMING	BASIC WIRING	TILE

41 Home design made easy! View designs in 3D, take a virtual reality tour, add decorating details and more. $59.95 PLANSUITE

42 41 special landscapes designed for beauty and low maintenance. 160 pgs $14.95 ECL

43 The first book of do-it-yourself landscapes. 40 front, 15 backyards. 208 pgs $14.95 HL

44 40 designs focused solely on creating your own specially themed backyard oasis. 160 pgs $14.95 BYL

45 A comprehensive look at 2700 products for all aspects of landscaping & gardening. 128 pgs $19.95 LPBG

46 For those who want to take a more hands-on approach to their dream. 319 pgs $21.95 SRF

47 A straightforward guide to one of the most misunderstood systems in the home. 160 pgs $12.95 CBW

48 Every kind of tile for every kind of application. Includes tips on use, installation and repair. 176 pgs $12.95 CWT

BATHROOMS	KITCHENS	HOUSE CONTRACTING	VISUAL HANDBOOK	ROOFING	WINDOWS & DOORS	PATIOS & WALKS	TRIM & MOLDING

49 An innovative guide to organizing, remodeling and decorating your bathroom. 96 pgs $10.95 CDB

50 An imaginative guide to designing the perfect kitchen. Chock full of bright ideas to make your job easier. 176 pgs $16.95 CKI

51 Everything you need to know to act as your own general contractor, and save up to 25% off building costs. 134 pgs $14.95 SBC

52 A plain-talk guide to the construction process; financing to final walk-through, this book covers it all. 498 pgs $19.95 RVH

53 Information on the latest tools, materials and techniques for roof installation or repair. 80 pgs $7.95 CGR

54 Installation techniques and tips that make your project easier and more professional looking. 80 pgs $7.95 CGD

55 Clear step-by-step instructions take you from the basic design stages to the finished project. 80 pgs $7.95 CGW

56 Step-by-step instructions for installing baseboards, window and door casings and more. 80 pgs $7.95 CGT

Additional Books Order Form

To order your books, just check the box of the book numbered below and complete the coupon. We will process your order and ship it from our office within two business days. Send coupon and check (in U.S. funds).

YES! Please send me the books I've indicated:

❑ 1:IKI $12.95	❑ 20:TRA $17.95	❑ 39:HBP $14.95
❑ 2:OS $9.95	❑ 21:CTG $19.95	❑ 40:HPG $12.95
❑ 3:MOS $9.95	❑ 22:CS $9.95	❑ 40:HPGC $24.95
❑ 4:TS $9.95	❑ 23:CM $9.95	❑ 41:PLANSUITE .. $59.95
❑ 5:VSH $9.95	❑ 24:EL $8.95	❑ 42:ECL $14.95
❑ 6:HH $9.95	❑ 25:SH $8.95	❑ 43:HL $14.95
❑ 7:FH $8.95	❑ 26:SW $10.95	❑ 44:BYL $14.95
❑ 8:CN $9.95	❑ 27:WH $9.95	❑ 45:LPBG $19.95
❑ 9:BS $8.95	❑ 28:TND $12.95	❑ 46:SRF $21.95
❑ 10:UH $15.95	❑ 29:CC $12.95	❑ 47:CBW $12.95
❑ 11:ENC $9.95	❑ 30:COL $9.95	❑ 48:CWT $12.95
❑ 12:E2 .... $9.95	❑ 31:DTP $9.95	❑ 49:CDB $10.95
❑ 13:AF $9.95	❑ 32:WF $10.95	❑ 50:CKI $16.95
❑ 14:VDH2 .... $15.95	❑ 33:WIN $9.95	❑ 51:SBC $14.95
❑ 15:EDH $15.95	❑ 34:SOD $19.95	❑ 52:RVH $19.95
❑ 16:LD2 .... $14.95	❑ 35:MU $8.95	❑ 53:CGR $7.95
❑ 17:EURO $15.95	❑ 36:YG $7.95	❑ 54:CGD $7.95
❑ 18:DAG $17.95	❑ 37:GG $7.95	❑ 55:CGW $7.95
❑ 19:WEP $17.95	❑ 38:DP $7.95	❑ 56:CGT $7.95

Additional Books Subtotal (Please print) $ _____
ADD Postage and Handling (allow 4–6 weeks for delivery) $ 4.00
Sales Tax: (AZ & MI residents, add state and local sales tax.) $ _____
YOUR TOTAL (Subtotal, Postage/Handling, Tax) $ _____

YOUR ADDRESS (PLEASE PRINT)

Name _____

Street _____

City _____ State _____ Zip _____

Phone (_____) _____ — _____

YOUR PAYMENT

Check one: ❑ Check ❑ Visa ❑ MasterCard ❑ Discover ❑ American Express
Required credit card information:

Credit Card Number _____

Expiration Date (Month/Year) _____ / _____

Signature Required _____

Home Planners, LLC
Wholly owned by Hanley-Wood, LLC
® 3275 W. Ina Road, Suite 110, Dept. BK, Tucson, AZ 85741

Canadian Customers Order Toll Free 1-877-223-6389

HPT44

Design 3662, page 152

OVER 3 MILLION BLUEPRINTS SOLD

"We instructed our builder to follow the plans including all of the many details which make this house so elegant…Our home is a fine example of the results one can achieve by purchasing and following the plans which you offer…Everyone who has seen it has assured us that it belongs in 'a picture book.' I truly mean it when I say that my home 'is a DREAM HOUSE.'"

S.P.
Anderson, SC

"We have had a steady stream of visitors, many of whom tell us this is the most beautiful home they've seen. Everyone is amazed at the layout and remarks on how unique it is. Our real estate attorney, who is a Chicago dweller and who deals with highly valued properties, told me this is the only suburban home he has seen that he would want to live in."

W. & P.S.
Flossmoor, IL

"Your blueprints saved us a great deal of money. I acted as the general contractor and we did a lot of the work ourselves. We probably built it for half the cost! We are thinking about more plans for another home. I purchased a competitor's book but my husband wants only your plans!"

K.M.
Grovetown, GA

"We are very happy with the product of our efforts. The neighbors and passersby appreciate what we have created. We have had many people stop by to discuss our house and kindly praise it as being the nicest house in our area of new construction. We have even had one person stop and make us an unsolicited offer to buy the house for much more than we have invested in it."

K. & L.S.
Bolingbrook, IL

"The traffic going past our house is unbelievable. On several occasions, we have heard that it is the 'prettiest house in Batvia.' Also, when meeting someone new and mentioning what street we live on, quite often we're told, 'Oh, you're the one in the yellow house with the wrap-around porch! I love it!'"

A.W.
Batvia, NY

"I have been involved in the building trades my entire life…Since building our home we have built two other homes for other families. Their plans from local professional architects were not nearly as good as yours. For that reason we are ordering additional plan books from you."

T.F.
Kingston, WA

"The blueprints we received from you were of excellent quality and provided us with exactly what we needed to get our successful home-building project underway. We appreciate your invaluable role in our home-building effort."

T.A.
Concord, TN